Race and Class
in American Society

Race and Class in American Society
Black, Latino, Anglo
Second Revised Edition

by H. Edward Ransford

Schenkman Books, Inc.
Rochester, Vermont

Copyright © 1977, 1994

Schenkman Books, Inc.
118 Main Street
Rochester, Vermont 05767

Library of Congress Cataloging in Publication Data:

Ransford, H. Edward.
    Race and Class in American society: Black, Latino, Anglo / by H.
Edward Ransford. — 2nd. rev. ed.
       p.   cm.
    Includes bibliographical references.
    ISBN 0-87047-068-X (cloth) : $29.95— ISBN 0-87047-069-8
(paper) : $16.95
       1. United States—Race relations. 2. Afro-Americans—Social
conditions—1975–3. Mexican Americans—Social conditions. 4. Los Angeles
Region (Calif.)—Race relations. 5. Afro-Americans—California—Los Angeles
Region—Social conditions. 6. Mexican Americans—California—Social
conditions. 7. Social Classes—California—Los Angeles Region. I. Title.
    E184.A1R34 1994
    305.8'00973—dc20   94-13489
                                          CIP

ISBN 0-87047-068-X cl
ISBN 0-87047-069-8 pbk

Printed in the United States of America

Contents

Acknowledgments ix

Introduction to the Second Edition xi

Summary of Reorganization and Additions

Introduction xiii

**Part I: Concepts, Theory, and Empirical
Trends in Mobility**

1   Origins and Development of Racial Stratification 3

From Origins to Stable Systems 5

Racial Stratification Under Competitive Systems 11

*Applications of Paternalistic-Competitive Model to Blacks,
Mexican Americans, and Native Americans 14*

2   The Interaction Between Race and Class in
Contemporary America 29

Two Hierarchies 30

Racial-Ethnic Stratification 32

Individual versus Institutional Racism 36

Dominant White Stratum or Power Elite 37

*Comparisons Between the Social Class and
Race-Ethnic Orders 39*

The Lack of Research on Race-Class Interaction 41

3   Three Models 45

Open Market Place of Status Configurations 45

Minority Subcommunity Perspective 54

Ethclass 59

The Three Models and Prediction 63

4   Social Mobility: The Rise of the Middle-class
    and Skilled Working Strata for Blacks and
    Mexican Americans 71

    *Mobility of Blacks: Income, Occupation, Education,
        Elected Officials, Sports* 71
    *Mobility of Mexican Americans: Income,
        Occupation, Education* 84
    Summary 90

Part II: Empirical Explorations and Reviews of Research
on Race, Class, and Gender Interactions

5   Black and Latino Perceptions of Inequality:
    Ghetto Rebellions and the Anger of
    the Black Middle Class 99

    *Minority Group Protest: Comparisons of
        the 1992 Los Angeles Civil Disorder and
        the 1965 Watts Riot* 99
    The Watts Riot 100
    Non-Change Since Watts 104
    Demographic Changes in Los Angeles 105
    *Minority Group Protest Rather than
        Black-White Confrontation* 106
    *Korean American Store Owners and
        Black and Latino Customers* 108
    Black Middle Class Perceptions of Inequality 111
    *Race, Class, and Discrimination:
        Comparisons Between Mexican Americans
        and Blacks* 118
    Mexican-American Farmworkers 122

6   Adding Gender to the Equation:
    Race, Class, and Gender 133

    *Individual and Institutional Sexism and
        Sex Discrimination* 134
    Gender in Interaction with Race and Class 139
    Race, Sex, and Feminist Outlooks 141

7   Race and Class Interactions:
    Friendship Choice and Inequality in the Schools ... 167

    Race versus Class in Friendship Choice 167

    Race, Class, and Educational Inequality: Misuse of
    IQ Tests, Language Problems, Tracking,
    Effective Schools 176

8   The White Working Class 197

    Blue Collar Anger 200

    White Ethnicity and the Blue Collar Situation 208

    A Blue Collar Anger Update 210

Selected Bibliography 215

Acknowledgments

Various reviewers have contributed valuable comments and criticisms during the development and writing of this book. In particular I would like to thank Professor Tom Lasswell for his many contributions. Tom had envisioned a series of focused short texts on stratification's various aspects, and a number of these were published by Schenkman Publishing Company. Tom provided valuable editorial and conceptual criticism, and was a continual source of encouragement. Appreciation is also expressed to Jon Miller, F. James Davis, Wayne Villemez, and Lynn Ransford for conceptual criticisms of earlier drafts of the first edition. Al Schenkman was always a source of enthusiastic support in the writing of the first edition and I appreciate it.

Lynn Ransford made valuable contributions to the conceptual clarity and readability of the entire manuscript. I am also grateful for her continual understanding and support throughout both editions of the book. I would also like to thank Marjorie Shields, for careful editing and updates in the second edition. Any remaining errors or misinterpretations are solely my responsibility.

Introduction to the Second Edition

SUMMARY OF REORGANIZATION AND ADDITIONS

In the seventeen years that have elapsed since the first edition of this book, there has been a proliferation of studies on the interaction of race, class, and gender in American society. Increasingly, sociological analyses deal with multiple inequalities.

This book predated many of the debates and increased interest in multiple stratification hierarchies. Yet, even with recent developments, certain themes in the first edition have weathered rather well, and continue to have great significance for a race-class analysis in the 1990s. For example, the first edition noted the development of increased class stratification in both black and Mexican American groups. Class differentiation continues to be very apparent in both these groups. It was further argued that middle-class strata of these groups face very different strains and discrimination battles than do lower class strata. Race and class (as well as gender) must be considered conjointly to fully understand the life-chances, strains, and opportunities of these ethclass groups. Three ways of conceptualizing race-class interaction were presented in the first edition. These models continue to be useful for explaining the complexities of race-class interaction in the 1990s.

Given the continued relevance of the concepts in this book, how best might a new edition be updated? Certainly, some terminology needs to be changed. For example, the terms *Mexican American* or *Latino* is more commonly used now than *Chicano*. Old studies might all be replaced with new ones. However, some in the first edition are now regarded as classic, and so many of them are preserved in this edition, with new studies added. Though many of the themes, findings and concepts in the old chapters remain historically important or relevant to the present, five new thrusts seem strategically important for updating the book and will be noted most readily by the following organization.

First, one of the longest and most hotly argued debates—*The Declining Significance of Race*—is summarized in chapter 3. This is one of the most important debates on the interaction of race and class in American Society, and does not appear in the first edition which was printed just prior to the initial publications on the topic.

Second, chapter 4, dealing with the socioeconomic mobility of blacks and Mexican Americans, is completely rewritten and updated using 1987–1992 census data. This chapter emphasizes the dual mobility trends in both groups—one segment's striking gains moving into middle-class occupations and incomes, while other segments are trapped by poverty as ever.

Third, chapter 5 on black and Latin perceptions of inequality presents a completely new analysis on inner city tensions and ghetto rebellions. The 1992 Los Angeles civil disorder is compared with the Watts riot of 1965. The similarities in underlying conditions are noted (e.g., racial isolation, police tension, and lack of jobs). The differences are also noted (e.g., the much greater ethnic diversity in the ghetto today, and the loss of social services and job networking with the exodus of middle class blacks from the ghetto). Do inner city race/class discrimination barriers disappear or ease considerably with socioeconomic advancement? In other words, how are middle class blacks and Latinos faring? Current studies, summarized in this chapter, on the "hidden rage" of successful blacks, indicate that discrimination is often still present in the form of insults, rebuffs and avoidance.

Fourth, gender inequality is added to the equation of race and class inequalities in a new chapter 6. Gender (i.e., male and female inequality in accessing power, privilege and prestige) is increasingly conceptualized as another stratification order. Although the book deals primarily with race and class, I feel it is important to introduce gender as another dimension of inequality and to suggest interactions among race, class, and gender. An article by Ransford and Miller on the effects of gender, race, and class on feminist outlooks is reprinted here to illustrate interactions among the three hierarchies.

Fifth, chapter 7, presents a much more extended discussion of educational inequality. The first edition briefly covered culturally biased IQ tests and curriculum tracking. This edition extends the topic with discussions of language problems, bilingual education, student peer culture effects, and "effective schools."

Introduction

A major goal of this book is to explore the interrelationships in the United States between the social class hierarchy and a racial hierarchy of the white majority and the conquered minorities— African Americans, Mexican Americans, and American Indians. The motivation to write this book stemmed from what I perceived to be major shortcomings in the sociology of racial stratification:

1. Despite apparent continued poverty and oppression in the ghettos and barrios, in the last twenty years a fairly sizeable portion of African Americans have moved into skilled and white-collar positions. Even so, much of the social science literature continues to treat blacks and Mexican Americans as uniformly poor and unskilled. Little is known about the outlooks, values, and unique battles against discrimination fought by Chicanos and blacks in skilled and white-collar positions. Moreover, there are few models for exploring these mobile populations. Often the literature falls back on the old assumption that the middle class segment of any minority group detaches itself from ethnic identification and becomes an undifferentiated part of the white middle class. However, with the ethnic identity movements of the last decades (represented by such slogans as "Black is Beautiful," "Black Power," "La Raza," and "Brown Power") the acculturation-assimilation assumption seems totally unjustified. Many middle class African Americans and Mexican Americans express a strong sense of ethnic identification. Some evidence suggests that younger blacks and Chicanos recently graduated from or presently enrolled in colleges and universities have an extremely intense ethnic consciousness and a strong commitment to collective progress for their groups. Sociologists simply have

not developed an explanatory model to handle the simultaneous trends of upward mobility and increased ethnic identification among America's conquered racial minorities.

2. A second problem area to be addressed is the tendency to view the stratification of minority populations only in the contexts of encapsulated ghettos or barrios. Skilled and white-collar minority persons are seen as relatively high in position, but only within their own ethnic or racial categories. Thus, middle-class blacks are viewed as persons of relatively high class within a caste. The assumption seems to be that no matter how high the socioeconomic achievement of a black, his or her "blackness" is a more important factor in social differentiation than his or her occupation or income. Although this class-within-a-caste model was extremely important for explaining race relations in the rural South in the 1940s, it is not sufficient to explain contemporary race relations.

    This book will attempt to break out of the traditional caste perspective and to note the effects of upward mobility on the rising skilled black and Chicano populations in the larger society. Many of these persons are employed in the predominantly "Anglo" occupational structure as foremen, machinists, parole officers, and teachers, rather that in the separate ghetto structures. They are interacting in a more open status marketplace than a caste perspective would suggest.

    The existence of this new mobility raises important questions about the relationships of these minority groups with the white majority. To what extent does class achievement override racial restriction? If a black person moves into a professional position does his/her increased power erode racial barriers or do many restrictions remain? As blacks move into positions of authority and power in formal organizations, to what extent are traditional role relationships with whites affected? How do whites react to the upward mobility of blacks and Chicanos?

3. Many of the theories and generalizations in racial stratification are extremely out-of-date. For example, generalizations have been made in the past about the black middle class, theories which have not been reexamined in recent years. Classic accounts (some published as late as the mid-1960s) assume that this class is striving to be white and politically conservative,

strongly rejecting the lower-class blacks. It is time that we reviewed such generalizations with current data that take into account the civil rights movement, ghetto rebellions, the rise of Black Power, and ethnic pride ideologies. How have different class groups within the black community reacted to, participated in, or otherwise been affected by recent African American movements?

4. There is also a need for developing new concepts to explain social organization at the lower end of the race and class hierarchies. Too often there is a tendency to view oppression in ghettos and barrios through a single prism of race or class. We speak of the culture of poverty (a class explanation of social barriers) *or* racial discrimination (a racial explanation), but fail to search for the more complex barriers that may be caused by the interaction of race and class.

5. When minority and majority populations have been viewed hierarchically, there has been too much emphasis upon inequalities of social honor and status, and not enough emphasis on power inequality. There have been many racial stratification studies based on social distance schemes in which Anglos have been asked the degree of intimacy they would grant to various racial minorities (e.g., Would you find it distasteful to have a black move next door?. . . Marry your daughter?). This almost exclusive concern for social honor and social distance has reflected predominantly white concerns and has not dealt with the basic equation that is of primary concern to disprivileged minorities: which persons have control over their own lives and institutions and which persons are relatively powerless? Throughout this book there is an attempt to put power inequality "up front" as the prime mover of a racial stratification system.

One book cannot fully explore, correct, and develop new formulations to solve these five problems. But this book is a beginning toward a revised conceptualization, theory, and empirical exploration of race and class in interaction. A complete account of the interactions between race and class would involve the inclusion of a great many strata: the white poor in Appalachia, the white aged poor, and white ethnic groups as well as the black, Chicano, and Indian lower and middle classes. To cover all these populations would be an impossible task in a volume of this size. Instead, this book focuses on the growing class heterogeneity within the black and Mexican American populations. But this is not to say that class diversity within the white majority is completely ignored, since many of the empirical explorations and theoretical models presented involve the *joint* consideration of race and class—for example, comparisons between lower and middle-class whites, blacks, and Chicanos. Further, the effect of the rise of black and Chicano middle classes on the attitudes, behavior, and prejudices of the white majority will be examined. Additionally, gender can be considered as another dimension of inequality. Race, class, and gender interactions are explored in chapter 6.

Some brief comments on the overall organization and content of this book are in order. The first half of the book deals with concepts, theory, and (in the case of blacks and Latinos) demographic profiles. Chapter 1 presents origins of racial stratification and the application of van den Berghe's paternalistic-competitive model to the historical facts of African-American, Mexican-American, and Native-American subordination in the U.S. Chapters 2 and 3 pertain to current issues and models for the ways in which race and class interact in contemporary America. Chapter 4 reviews (1987–1992) census data in order to note the size and growth of the Chicano and black working and middle class strata.

The second half of the book deals with empirical explorations and reviews of research in race and class. Chapter 5 analyzes inner city tensions and ghetto rebellions. The Watts versus. 1992 disorders are contrasted. Tensions between Korean American store-owners and black and Latino customers are noted. Black and middle-class perceptions of inequality are also discussed. Using survey data, chapter 6 explores the relations of race, class, and gender. Chapter 7 includes a selective review of studies that deal with the pile-up of race-class barriers faced by minority students in educational institutions—IQ test scores, "tracking," and bilingual education. Chapter 8 deals with the reactions of white working class persons to student and black protests, using a Los Angeles survey to test some hypotheses.

PART I

CONCEPTS, THEORY, AND
EMPIRICAL TRENDS IN MOBILITY

Origins and Development of Racial Stratification

In most multiracial societies, racial groups are found in a hierarchy of power, wealth, and prestige. The most important of these three variables is differential power. In this case, power means the ability of one race to impose its will upon another.[1] The dominant stratum in the power hierarchy has the most immediate access to the means of force (such as monopoly on the use of weapons), to the technology, and to the control of economic institutions and the mass media. When we speak of racial stratification, it is important to note that we are referring to a *system* of power inequality. The hierarchy normally represents unequal power *institutionalized* in such a way that the mechanisms of domination and control of the most powerful stratum over minority communities survive over time. Like all stratification systems, racial inequality usually endures beyond the lifetimes of single individuals.

What are the origins of racial stratification systems? A number of recent works have attempted to ferret out the key variables in the development of racial hierarchies. Donald Noel argues that there are three crucial components of racial stratification: ethnocentrism, competition, and differential power.[2] When two distinct ethnic populations come into contact with each other, inequalities or stratified relations are only likely to occur when all three of these variables are operating simultaneously. Ethnocentrism, a term referring to a tendency for members of a social entity to view their values, institutions, and belief systems as more natural or superior to those of others, is a propensity factor, but ethnocentrism alone is not enough to set in motion a system of stratification. Thus, although Population One may regard the beliefs, accumulation of knowledge, and social institutions of Population Two as hopelessly backward, this fact in itself may not lead to a system of inequality. In addition, Noel argues there must be a strong desire for Population One to seize and exploit the resources of Population Two. Typically, this is land or other natural resources. In the conquest of the American Indians, for example, the white conquerors were strongly led by one goal: to seize the choice fertile land held by the Indians. A variant of economic competition is that Ethnic Group One may define a goal as desirable while Ethnic Group Two is indifferent to the same goal. In such a case, Group One may attempt to exploit the labor of Group Two to maximize goal attainment.

Yet, ethnic stratification will not be generated until Noel's third condition, that of differential power, occurs.

> Without differential power it would simply be impossible for one group to achieve dominance and impose subordination to its will and ideals upon the other(s).[3]

Superior organization, technology, and gun power were crucial facts in European colonization, American slavery, and the forcing of Indians onto barren reservations.

Diagrammatically the Noel thesis can be summarized thusly:

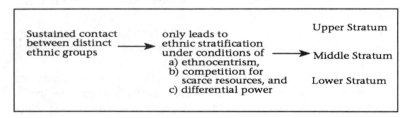

If one of these three conditions is missing then something other than racial or ethnic stratification develops. If ethnocentrism is absent, the two populations would be likely to merge (because of cultural similarity) with competition and stratification, developing along class rather than ethnic lines. Similarly, if ethnocentrism and competition are present, but a power differential is missing, a kind of structural pluralism may emerge with the two closed societies competing for scarce resources but unable to dominate each other.

We have stated that ethnic stratification refers to an enduring system of power inequality. Accordingly, the next question is: How are these three factors—belief in cultural superiority, desire for scarce resources, and superior power—translated into an enduring system?

FROM ORIGINS TO STABLE SYSTEMS OF STRATIFICATION

Systems can rarely be held together very long by force and coercion. Once having gained control, a more powerful stratum either strengthens and institutionalizes its position or it will be subject to the constant threat of rebellion. Racial strata are no exception to this rule. A system of mutually understood inequality legitimizes the gains of the dominant stratum. Most immediately, the natural resources and labor of the conquered stratum can be exploited on a regular and predictable basis. Most important, shared norms of interaction develop so that roles and statuses become complementary, members of each stratum having a clear definition of expected behavior. New generations of the less powerful stratum do not have to be conquered again, but are socialized into an ongoing system of superiority and deference.

Paternalistic Racial Stratification

Early systems of racial stratification (from roughly the mid-1500s to the mid-1800s) had an amazing similarity in form across different countries and in various instances of oppressor and oppressed. This similarity developed despite very different patterns of conquest. For example, in the case of European colonialism, a relatively small number of white (Dutch, Spanish, Portuguese, English) conquerors subjected large indigenous populations of another color (e.g., Africans or Aztec Indians). The result was a small white ruling class, representing European states, exerting control over a large indigenous population. In contrast, the subjugation of blacks in the United States (often called internal colonialism) resulted from a relatively powerless racial group being forced to enter a foreign society as slave labor, with a white ruling class having already established dominance over the majority of the population. Despite these differences in numerical ratio of white to non-whites and the ways in which the non-whites were brought under the control of the dominant society, the systems of inequality showed great consistency. Thus, van den Berghe speaks of a common paternalistic form to describe the early systems in South

Africa, the United States, Brazil, and Mexico.[4] Of the many characteristics of a paternalistic system, there are four that are most conspicuous.

1. Under paternalism, stratification approaches its most rigid, closed form—that of caste. The *caste line* (or *color bar*) results in a huge gap in power, wealth, health, status, and life-chances between the castes.

   The color bar is conceptualized as horizontal; there is no overlap in class achievement or statuses between races. Thus, even when individuals in the lower caste are respected for their wisdom or accomplishments, they are all still regarded as lower in social status than any member of the upper caste. Because caste is racially defined, there is no opportunity for members of the lower caste to rise into the upper caste or for members of the upper caste to fall into the lower caste. Crucial to the idea of caste is the total control that the powerful racial group exerts over the powerless.

   Unlike many modern systems of racial stratification in which the status and treatment of minority persons changes from situation to situation, a caste system implies that every part of the system observes the same rules. The subordinate racial population stays "in its place" because there is no other socially legitimate alternative. Protests and rising expectations of change become increasingly dimmer lights as the caste system takes firmer hold. To perpetuate the caste, three other characteristics are commonly found: endogamy (within-race marriage), rules of etiquette specifying appropriate deference when members of the subordinate race interact with members of the dominant race, and a supporting ideology justifying the subordination of the lower caste (e.g., on grounds that they are biologically inferior). In sum, a racial caste stratification system implies that there is one single dominant hierarchy and although obvious status differences within each caste do exist, they are always superseded by racial differences in affecting interaction.

   The visibility of racial characteristics adds to the ease of maintaining such a pattern on a racial basis; in fact, where it is lacking, casual observations suggest that some visible distinction will be supplied, ranging from brands to distinctive coiffures or clothing. Skin color is ideal for these purposes, since it is virtually impossible to conceal or change.

2. Important to the conceptions of paternalistic relations is the idea that racial stratification is naturally linked to the economic

system of its time. Van den Berghe notes that a pre-industrial, agricultural plantation economy is conducive to a particular kind of caste stratification—one in which large numbers of unskilled workers are completely controlled by their masters in face-to-face, intimate relations. So close is this interaction that van den Berghe labels it symbiotic.

3. The plantation system encourages another characteristic of paternalism: very little segregation or spatial separation between dominant and subordinate groups, unlike the American Indian reservations or the modern urban ghettos and barrios in which blacks and Latinos live. Contact on the plantation is intimate, but of unequal status. A classic example of this intimate but unequal relationship is the institutionalized concubinage between men of the ruling group and women of the subordinate racial group. In commenting on relations between white (Portuguese) masters and Negro slaves of the Brazilian *fazendas* (sugar cane plantations), van den Berghe notes, "when a white boy reached sexual maturity he was sexually initiated with one of his father's slaves and continued to engage in promiscuous concubinage with female slaves throughout his sexually active lifetime."[5]

Interracial concubinage with female slaves was completely accepted for white men. According to the dual standard of sexual morality, marriage was not considered an impediment to the maintenance of a slave harem in Brazil.

Similarly, Gilberto Freyre describes Brazilian planters:

> Slothful but filled to overflowing with sexual concerns, the life of the sugar planter tended to become a life that was lived in a hammock. A stationary hammock, with the master taking his ease, sleeping, dozing.
>
> Or a hammock on the move, with the master on a journey or a promenade between the heavy draperies or curtains. Or again, a squeaking hammock, with the master copulating in it.[6]

4. Finally, in paternalistic systems, there are highly developed stereotypes about the lower racial caste. "Child-like," "irresponsible," "intellectually inferior," and "lovable, when they stay in their places," are common descriptions. To explain the origin and persistence of such stereotypes, one must go beyond the tendency of the dominant Europeans to view the conquered people as backward, child-like heathens (i.e., simple ethnocentrism). Rather, a paternalistic system institutionalizes the parent-child relationship with many informal rules (caste

etiquette) requiring a lower caste person to take on a humble, inferior posture whenever in the presence of an upper caste person. Consider the following description of black-white relations in the Deep South:

> Negroes and whites must not shake hands when they meet; the white man must start the conversation (although the Negro can hint that he wants to talk); the Negro must address the white person as Mr., Mrs., or Miss, but he must never be addressed by these titles himself (Negroes are addressed by their first name, or called uncle, aunty, darky, nigger, or in some cases for politeness sake—may be called by their last name or by such titles as doctor, professor, or preacher). The topic of conversation must be limited to specific job matters or to personal niceties (e.g., inquiries after one's health); it must never stray over to bigger matters of politics or economics or to personal matters such as white husband-wife relationships. Negroes should never look into the eyes of white people when they talk to them but generally keep their eyes on the ground or shifting, and their physical posture in front of white people when they talk to them should be humble and self-demeaning.[7]

Classic examples of paternalistic roles can be seen in American movies of the 1920s and 1930s. In a typical example of these, a white child calls her black plantation servants by their first names and treats them as house pets. The blacks are always ready to sing and dance at her birthday parties or on other occasions.[8] Stereotypes are not only reinforced, but are created by system requirements.

In some paternalistic systems the role relationships are bolstered by racism, the belief that innate biological qualities of a racial group determine aptitudes or behavior patterns such as evilness, intelligence, or the capacity to produce a "high culture". Highly crystallized racism often develops late in the career of a paternalistic system to justify or rationalize the often brutal exploitation of a racial stratum by claiming that members of that stratum are something less than human beings. Early forms of paternalism may involve only ethnocentrism: devaluation of a peoples' culture without implying biological inferiority.[9]

From Paternalistic to Competitive Race Relations

As multiracial societies have changed from rural agricultural plantation economics to highly complex urban industrial systems, paternalistic race relations have given way to competitive relations. In a competitive society, one race is rarely completely superordinate, and another completely subordinate (though the wealth and power of a society are still concentrated in the hands of the original ruling group). Rather, the situation is more fluid, open, and, as a result, competitive. Criteria such as skill and performance become as important as race. As a result, racial roles are less clear and open competition develops as the subordinate racial group attempts to secure a larger share of wealth and power in the system. The stereotype of the subordinate race changes from a picture of happy, contented children to one of violent, aggressive, pushy persons. Van den Berghe notes:

> In . . . a dynamic industrial society with its great geographical mobility and its stress on impersonal market mechanisms and universalistic and achieved criteria of occupational selection, race relations are quite different from what they are under agrarian conditions. The master-servant model with its elaborate caste etiquette and its mechanisms of subservience and social distance breaks down to be replaced by acute competition between the subordinate caste and the working class within the dominant group.[10]

The exact causal sequence from paternalism to competitive relations varies from society to society according to unique historical events. However, certain patterns do stand out. Ideologies stressing liberty, equality, and fraternity were taking hold in Western European countries as well as in the United States during the early 1800s. The changes in political structure that occurred in many countries at this time tended to undermine paternalistic relations. Oligarchic, aristocratic, and colonial political structures shifted toward representative democracies with a much wider participation in the polity. Even so, blacks in the United States have until recently been excluded from this democratic participation.[11] Industrialization and urbanization no doubt contributed to the dissolution of paternalistic race relations, though these factors often may be given more casual significance than the facts warrant.

It is true that industrial economics tend to emphasize rationality, efficiency, and the use of achieved rather than ascribed criteria for assigning general status to persons. Industrial manufacturing systems require a free and mobile labor force, rather than a mass of unskilled workers tied to a plantation. The greater impersonality and diversity of norms in the urban setting mean that subordinate racial groups can escape some of the traditional patterns of etiquette and deference. In such a system it becomes inefficient and detrimental to production to make race the primary criterion for determining job position.

Herbert Blumer has argued that industrialization per se does not necessarily upset the existing racial order. It takes internal and external power pressures to bring about a total racial realignment. Drawing from data dealing with industrialization in the South, he concludes that, when industrialization is introduced into a racially ordered society, social organization conforms to the alignment and code of the existing racial order. Industrial slavery may substitute for agrarian slavery.[12]

Though Blumer is correct in pointing out that the process of industrialization does not automatically destroy a racial stratification system, it is also true that during periods of extreme need for production and skilled manpower, a subordinate race does make definite gains. Thus, during World Wars I and II, when factories were operating twenty-four hours a day and there was an extreme need for an increased labor force, the occupational structure "opened" sufficiently for many members of minorities to obtain semi-skilled, skilled, or white-collar jobs. In times of critical need for economic rationality, widespread changes do occur. However, when the paternalistic lid is lifted it does not follow that subordinate racial populations are fully liberated, or that a system of employment based solely on merit is fully realized. A major point in the van den Berghe typology is that a competitive system is not a completely open system. Rather, new means of coercion are instituted as a second line of defense to keep the dominant racial stratum in power. Instead of the intimate face-to-face control of the master-slave plantation, blacks, Chicanos, and Indians live in separate communities—ghettos, barrios, and reservations. Spatial separation and a duplicate set of inferior institutions replace the personal control of the plantation.

Internal Colonialism

Internal colonialism is the label often used today for separate and unequal minority communities.[13] Confinement of blacks to ghettos, Latinos to barrios, and Indians to reservations represent the new forms of coercion found in competitive race relations. The separate institutions found in the internal colony or ghetto are typically inferior to those found in the dominant system. Police harassment, schools of inferior quality, consumer exploitation, and overcrowded hospitals with perfunctory services are the trademarks of the barrio and the ghetto. The term *internal colonialism* focuses on one important fact: that ghettos and barrios are controlled and manipulated by dominant white outsiders. Viewed through the model of internal colonialism, policemen, social workers, teachers, and merchants are seen as custodians of the "colony." They enter the colony during the day to administer and return to suburbia in the evening. Unlike those of the white immigrant enclaves of the nineteenth century (e.g., Little Italy, etc.), the businesses of the ghetto or the reservation are not ordinarily controlled by blacks, Chicanos, or Indians.

Racial Stratification Under Competitive Systems

From the beginning of this synthesis, it has been stressed that racial stratification is based on power inequality. From the initial conquest of racial populations to plantation paternalism to the manipulation of internal colonies, a white power stratum has controlled the life chances and destinies of blacks, Latinos, and American Indians. However, a major theme of this book is that race relations in advanced competitive systems, such as present-day United States involve an increasingly complex interaction of race and class. Black and Latino populations are increasingly stratified with fairly sizeable upper-working and middle-class segments. This is occurring particularly where blacks and Latinos have turned from persuasion, faith, and legal reforms to direct exertions of counter power, from the demonstrations of the Civil Rights Movement, to the ghetto riot-rebellions, to the institutionalization of black power. A major characteristic of competitive systems is that the caste system declines and class systems gain in importance.

Class Within Caste

Nearly half a century ago, Lloyd Warner presented his classic conceptualization of class within caste.[14] It is one of the first statements that considers the idea of race and class in interaction, earlier works having assumed a unidimensional racial caste hierarchy. Warner and his colleagues studied a small city in the Deep South. Two black and two white social scientists lived in "Old City" for two years to study the class structure. Blacks and whites were separated by a definite caste line forbidding racial intermarriage, defining blacks as mentally inferior to whites, and reducing opportunities for black upward mobility. Even so, a socioeconomic structure existed within each caste; some blacks had achieved socioeconomic positions superior to some whites.

Figure 1.1 represents the caste-class model:

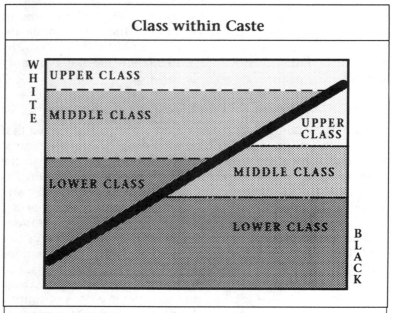

Adapted from *Deep South: A Social-Anthropological Study of Caste and Class*, by Allison Davis, Burleigh, B. Gardner and Mary R. Gardner. From an Introduction by W. Lloyd Warner, p.10, by permission of the University of Chicago Press, Copyright 1941 by the University of Chicago. See also the adaptation of this figure in Joseph A. Kahl, *The American Class Structure* (New York: Holt, Rinehart and Winston, 1957), p. 245.

Figure 1.1

Note that the caste line is not horizontal as it would be in paternalistic relations, but is slanted so that the highest class of blacks is higher in socioeconomic traits than the lowest class of white persons. Warner speculated that if trends continued, the caste line would swing further on its axis until it reached a vertical line; there then would be a complete class hierarchy within each caste, with proportional numbers of each race in each socioeconomic stratum. The present status of this trend is one that needs to be examined. However, Warner did not clearly spell out all the possible results of internal differentiation within the black caste, leaving significant questions unanswered;

- Does socioeconomic similarity produce a common value system, so that middle-class blacks and Latinos share more values, outlooks, and behavior patterns with middle-class whites than with lower-class people of their respective minority groups?

- To what extent does class similarity take precedence over two essential meanings of the caste line: differential power and social exclusion? For example, to what extent does class similarity between members of different castes break down social interaction barriers? To what extent is power socioeconomically achieved rather than caste ascribed?

- Do the middle-class segments of the subordinate racial group turn to militant protest to bring about full equality or do they turn toward identification with the white Anglo middle-class and rejection of the lower strata of their own race?

- What are the empirical possibilities of race and class in interaction? Under what conditions would race be expected to override class, class to override race, or the two to unite in producing special ethclass effects?

Application of Paternalistic-Competitive Model to Different Societies

Van den Berghe's account of paternalistic-competitive race relations is presented as a comparative model applicable to emerging race relations in many countries. He notes that black-white relations in the United States and Brazil have followed this trend toward competitive relations rather closely. In Mexico and South Africa, the model does not fit as well.

In Mexico, there has been a shift from caste-based paternalism to a class system. The conflicts and differences have shifted from racial stratification to economic stratification. Miscegenation among Spaniards, Indians, and Africans in Mexico and the extreme degree to which Spanish culture was forced on the indigenous population has resulted in a high degree of homogeneity in both skin color and culture.

In contemporary South Africa, one finds extreme contradictions in the racial stratification system. Because South Africa has evolved from an agricultural to a complex industrial economy, one would predict a more open society with competitive race relations. Instead, a very rigid racial caste system known as *apartheid* has existed until recently. Apartheid involved "pass laws" wherein blacks had to carry racial identification papers at all times. Blacks were segregated into separate colonies or ghettos and could only be in downtown or industrial areas during daytime hours. A police force upheld these laws. Van den Berghe notes that:

> Apartheid in my opinion ought to be interpreted as an endeavor to reestablish the old paternalistic master-servant relations that prevailed in the pastoral Boer Republics of the nineteenth century.
>
> It is only with great tension that an advanced industrial system (straining toward mobility, openness, and an efficient use of manpower) can practice a high degree of paternalism and keep blacks totally "in their places." To do so, the ruling class must resort to open coercion. It is no accident that police surveillance, job reservation, and other formal means of repressive control have been used and continue to some extent in South Africa.[15]

Presently, with the striking reforms under President Frederik W. de Klerk's rule (notably abolishing Pass Laws, freeing Nelson Mandela, establishing new laws to eliminate job segregation, and introducing models of increased political participation of blacks) South Africa is moving toward a more classic case of competitive race relations. At the time of this writing, power sharing talks between the government and black liberation groups are about to begin, the first ever in the history of South Africa. Black liberation groups are uniting and demanding a new constitution drawn up by a constituent assembly elected in a national one-person, one-vote election. These changes are classic examples of the political bargaining that take place in competitive systems.

APPLICATION OF PATERNALISTIC-COMPETITIVE MODEL TO BLACKS, MEXICAN AMERICANS, AND NATIVE AMERICANS

The paternalistic-competitive model has never been applied in a comparative way to summarize the treatment of minorities in the United States. A major purpose of this chapter is to superimpose the model on the experiences of three American minorities. Blacks, Mexican Americans, and American Indians are conquered minorities that have all gone through various forms of paternalism and are currently experiencing an awakening to the potentials of counter power in an industrial environment. There are some striking differences in the history of these three minorities. Our goal is not to rigidly force the experiences of blacks, Mexican Americans, and Indians into a common set of characteristics, but rather to note the patterns that fit and diverge from the paternalistic-competitive trend. The study of these three minorities within a paternalistic-competitive framework allows one to see the development of independent power bases within each minority as well as the emergence of patterns of social stratification within each.

Blacks in the United States

The early subordination of Black Americans follows rather closely the paternalistic-competitive conceptual scheme. Blacks were imported to the United States specifically for the exploitation of their labor on tobacco and cotton plantations. A pure case of paternalistic relations can be found in Southern plantation social organization. "Negroes were regarded as immature, irresponsible, unintelligent, physically strong, happy-go-lucky, musically gifted, grown up children."[16] American slavery was often brutal and harsh. A common explanation in the literature is that neither church nor state did anything to interfere with the arbitrary power of a plantation master.

Although the Civil War destroyed many of the paternalistic underpinnings, an extremely rigid substitute system of coercion and control developed after Reconstruction. With the threat of equalitarian relations between the races occasioned by the Confederacy's defeat in the Civil War, a substitute form of coercion evolved that had primarily paternalistic, but also some competitive, characteristics.

> In the economic sphere, slavery gave way to share-cropping and debt peonage. After an initial exodus to the towns, many freedmen had to return to the land to find a basis of subsistence. The plantation owners broke up their lands into small plots to be cultivated by individual tenants. The slave barracks near the big house gave way to a pattern of dispersed wooden shacks. Money lendings or rather the loan of food, seeds, tools, and other necessities to be charged at arbitrary prices against the value of the tenant's share of the crop, became an economic substitute for slavery. Through perpetual indebtedness, the tenant farmer was nearly as securely tied to the land and to his landlord as he was to his master under slavery. [17]

Perhaps the Jim Crow laws and caste etiquette were the most dramatic examples of the new coercion. These laws and customs enforced a systematic separation of the races in all potential situations of public intimacy such as restaurants, schools, drinking fountains, toilets, and public transportation. One of the most intensely felt caste rules was that black men must never have sexual relations with white women. Violations resulted in black men being lynched and compliant white women being exiled. On the other hand, many white men did have sexual relations with black women with impunity; under state laws the children of these unions were usually classified as Negro, but those who could "pass" for white often did. Equally repressive were the many informal rules of etiquette to demonstrate Negro inferiority to the white man. Blacks and whites did not shake hands when they met and did not eat in the same room (breaking bread together denotes equality) .

Arnold Rose notes that the black-white caste system was not fully formed until several decades after the end of slavery. It was legitimized by the famed Plessy vs. Ferguson decision of the U. S. Supreme Court some thirty years after the Civil War. It remained substantially unchallenged until the '40s.[18] Desegregation of the armed services in World War II, large scale migration from the South to more urban industrial environments, Civil Rights legislation, the mechanization of agriculture, and black protest all contributed to the disintegration of the caste system. Race relations more currently represent a classic example of competitive relations: there is opportunity within limits, some emphasis on skill and merit, and a rising black middle class, mixed with extreme spatial segregation, poverty, and white resentment of perceived preferential treatment for minorities. The open expressions of anger, pride, and militancy, and the fact that blacks can increasingly exert collective and individual power to move the white system aptly fits the competitive frame. The relatively high degree of socioeconomic differentiation that has developed recently among blacks is often ignored in studies of race relations. A major purpose of this book is to go beyond a black-white model and to develop a race-class interaction model.

American Indians

Unlike African Americans who were involuntarily forced into the United States as slaves, American Indians were conquered as indigenous people and forced from their fertile lands onto barren reservations. In many cases, initial relations between Indians and Europeans (English, Spanish, and French explorers) were friendly and involved the exchange of culture and resources. Nancy Lurie notes:

The establishment of permanent European settlements along the eastern seaboard and St. Laurence River in the early seventeenth century required the assistance of Indians in providing food, information, and skills to survive the first years in a new environment. As the fur trade took on importance . . . the Indian tribes enjoyed a good deal of bargaining power and learned to use it astutely in their own interests in regard to both commercial and military activities.[19]

Conflict and violence between white settlers and Indians was a result of the white European (and later American) effort to acquire choice land—fertile land for settlement, land teeming with timber and buffalo, and later in California, land containing the scarce yellow metal, gold. Thus, the conquest of American Indians represents an especially clear case of Noel's variable—competition for scarce resources. The expropriation of land involved a common pattern. Treaties were signed between the U.S. Government and Indian leaders. As the white settlers increased in number, they encroached further upon Indian Territory, continually breaking the conditions of their own treaties. For example, in 1829, Andrew Jackson, convinced that Indians and whites could not peacefully live together, proposed a separate Indian district west of the Mississippi as a *permanent* frontier. In 1834 Congress passed such a frontier act which stipulated that white persons would not be permitted to settle in the Indian country or to trade in that territory without a license. Moreover, the military forces of the United States would be employed to enforce provisions of the act.[20] The conditions of this act were not honored and the boundary of the "permanent frontier" was continually moved westward as white settlers negotiated new treaties and claimed new land. An extreme form of ethnocentrism (known as Manifest Destiny) was developed to justify the seizure of Indian land. Dee Brown, in *Bury My Heart at Wounded Knee*, notes:

To justify these breaches of the "permanent Indian frontier," the policy makers in Washington invented Manifest Destiny, a term which lifted land hunger to a lofty plane. The Europeans and their descendants were ordained by destiny to rule all of America. They were the dominant race and therefore responsible for the Indians— along with their lands, their forests, and their mineral wealth.[21]

Soldiers marched into the southwest area to fight Mexico; gold was discovered in California. With the realization that government treaties were meaningless, Indian nations often combined into coalitions to fight white settlers and soldiers. With the increase of

Indian raids and bloody fighting, the military force of the United States was employed. Indians were either slaughtered (as in the case of the Massacre of Sandcreek) or forced onto barren reserves.

The Reservation as a Form of Paternalism

In tracing the evolution of the relationship between Indians and the U.S. Government, Lurie notes that in an 1831 decision a Justice of the Supreme Court used the unfortunate term "ward" to describe the Indian, emphasizing the U.S. Government's obligation to protect Indians from hostile settlers and the U.S. Army. The term emphasized the federal government's acknowledgment of its responsibility to protect Indian tribes against "usurpation of their lands." Because the Indian Bureau sometimes became the uneasy and unhappy mediator between Indians and the U.S. Army, it was decided in 1862 to designate the members of Indian tribes as "wards" of the Indian Bureau rather than to let them be considered as sovereign or independent enemies. "Unfortunately and without ever really having legal sanction the term 'ward' took on administrative connotations by which the Bureau exercised incredible control over the lives and property of individuals much as a guardian would act for minors or helplessly retarded children."[22]

American Indians experienced a unique kind of paternalism as wards of the government, administered by their guardian, the Bureau of Indian Affairs (BIA). Much has been written about the paternalism of the Bureau. One of the more caustic accounts is found in Edgar S. Cahn's *Our Brother's Keeper*. Summarizing the conditions prior to 1970, he notes:

> From birth to death his home, his land, his reservation, his schools, his jobs, the stores where he shops, the tribal council that governs him, the opportunities available to him, the way in which he spends his money, disposes of his property, and even the way in which he provides for his heirs after death—are all determined by the Bureau of Indian Affairs acting as the agent of the United States Government.[23]

It may seem incorrect to cast the reservation Indian into a paternalistic framework since Indians are owners of land. However, Cahn notes that sales, exchanges, and transactions are all controlled by the Bureau.

> The Bureau prescribes the number of cattle which may graze on a parcel of land. It approves leases, controls prices, terms, and conditions. Often the leasing process is initiated not by the owner of the land but by the person desiring to lease it. Leases have been approved

without the owner's consent, and only the Bureau—not the tribe or individual owner—is empowered to cancel a lease.[24]

On the Indian's personal affairs he comments:

Mere supposition by a Bureau official that an Indian might prove indiscreet in handling money, might be exploited, or might at some future point be unable to provide for himself—any of these is considered reason enough to relieve the Indian of control over his possessions. Once the Indian is deemed incompetent he cannot even draw money from his own bank account without obtaining approval from a BIA guardian.[25]

Especially indefensible has been the separation of Indian children from their families to attend BIA boarding schools often located many miles from the reservation. In such schools there is often a forced denial of Indian culture, tradition, and values.

There are important similarities and differences between reservation paternalism and the plantation paternalism that van den Berghe describes. The overriding similarity is that in both cases the subordinate race is so completely dependent that it is impossible for identified members to build a collective power base or to acquire significant amounts of wealth, power, or prestige. The obstacles to upward mobility are virtually insurmountable. Thus, in both cases the development of a highly differentiated socioeconomic hierarchy within the subordinate race is not likely.

The differences between reservation and plantation paternalism are also noteworthy: the Indian reservation is a self-contained unit. The Indians' relationship to BIA officials is not the symbiotic, intimate, face-to-face relationship that one finds between master and slave on a plantation. As a result, Indians have not been forced to adapt to the rhythms and routines of a white labor system—a point that explains partially why they have been able to keep alive and intact some degree of cultural continuity. Another significant difference is that while the paternalism of southern plantations revolved around the exploitation of labor, this has not been a primary feature of reservation paternalism. In fact, it can be argued that Indians have been so disengaged from the production system that national changes from agriculture to industrial manufacturing have not affected them as they have other minority groups. In many ways, American Indians cannot be easily placed in an orthodox minority group conceptual framework. Their peculiar legal status with the BIA and their traditional insistence on preserving Indian identity and tribal affiliation and culture makes them unique.

So anxious are American Indians to protect their land and traditions that they have militantly opposed any action to do away with the BIA. Though the Bureau has taken advantage of the Indians again and again, the alternative—termination of this trusteeship and protective arrangement—is far less desirable. In those instances where termination has occurred, Indians have lost all their land, their special services and institutions and have become individual welfare cases. For example, with termination, Indian land comes under state and local property taxes. Indians are unable to pay the taxes and their land is absorbed or sold at public auctions.[26]

In spite of the historical control of Indian life on reservations, there has developed an increased degree of Indian self determination and militance in the last two decades.

Consistent with the competitive model, the activists tend to be young urban university students, rather than reservation dwellers. However, these Indian students have returned to their reservations to direct the action of others in protest. Commenting on the first "fish-ins" in the state of Washington, Robert C. Day noted:

> Protest efforts were initially blocked by the disunity, apathy, and traditional values of many tribal leaders (going to jail was perceived as undignified). Some questioned whether direct action was "the Indian way." Many worried about negative repercussions, but in the end there was no choice, the tribal leaders knew that if they lost their fishing rights they could not survive as a cultural unit.[27]

Tribal Nationalism is the name given to the reservation-based movement for change. In a meeting of young Indians the goals of the movement were defined. "Th(e) declaration stressing self government, sovereignty and nationalism made it clear that Indian people wanted complete autonomy to protect their land base from expropriation and to make their own plans and decisions in building an economic system to rid themselves of poverty while reasserting traditional cultural values."[28]

Although changes have been uneven from one reservation to the next, the dominant trend in recent years appears to be a greater independence from BIA supervision. Indian tribes have taken control, and tribal councils are making autonomous decisions. In many cases, Indian schools, controlled by the tribe, have been erected on reservation lands. In some tribes, new sources of economic self determination have materialized with the discovery of mineral wealth on the reservation, or with the development of legal gambling sites with winning stakes much higher than those set by the State.

American Indians appear to be moving from a peculiar form of Federal Paternalism to the development of an independent power base on the reservation. Internal stratification of the community has not occurred to any great degree, even though there are growing numbers of middle-class Indians in urban areas. Compared to blacks and Chicanos, class differentiation among Indians on reservations will be less likely to develop in the near future due to extreme poverty and strong communal ideologies that reject "political" climbing and internal differences.

Mexican Americans in the United States

Mexican Americans (Chicanos) constitute the nation's second largest minority population. As in the case of American Indians, Mexicans were not forced into America as slave labor, but rather conquered as an indigenous people. A unique fact about the conquest of the Mexicans is that paternalistic stratification systems were already intact and highly developed at the time white Anglos arrived. These were frontier extensions of Spanish colonialism in Mexico. They were caste systems based on "purity of blood," ranging from pure Spanish to Mestizo to Indian. The typical rancho consisted of a family of Spanish *gente de razon* and a legion of mestizo and Indian laborers.

The Americans often took advantage of the Mexican stratification system, identifying with the Spanish elite and thus acquiring a convenient supply of Indian and mestizo labor. As a result, Mexicans (Indians and mestizos) faced two systems of discrimination: internal Spanish colonial and external Anglo. It is interesting that the presence of aggressive American Indian tribes (that often attacked and raided Anglo and Spanish settlements) contributed to the view of the Mexican as inferior.

> The presence of Indians and their reputation for treachery and savagery probably had notable effects on the Anglo view of Mexicans. A conviction that Mexican immigrants in general were Indians in physique, temperament, character, and mentality is reflected in public documents spanning several decades in the nineteenth and twentieth centuries.[29]

The extreme conflict that developed between Mexico and the United States centered around competition for land. Through many border clashes and open warfare between the United States and Mexico, as well as by purchase of certain lands, the United States acquired what had become the states of Texas and New Mexico and parts of Colorado, Arizona, Utah, Nevada, and California.

Conquest of the Mexican Americans did not fall into a single pattern, but followed several patterns in different parts of the Southwest. For example, Joan Moore identifies three kinds of colonialism in the Southwest: "classic colonialism" as exemplified by New Mexico, "conflict colonialism" (Texas), and "economic colonialism" (California).[30]

In New Mexico, Spanish colonial (paternalistic) stratification was developed to a high degree. The American conquest of this system was a bloodless takeover and a merging of traditions, rather than a destruction of culture. Elite Spanish leadership was shared with Anglo domination to the extent that "sessions of the legislature were—by law—conducted in both languages."[31]

At the lower class level in the villages, Moore notes a patron (go between) system existed that allowed for some representation of the lower class. Thus in the case of New Mexico "an intact society rather than a structureless mass of individuals was taken into the territory of the United States with almost no violence."[32]

But in Texas, violent, open conflict was the rule. Many years after the annexation of Texas by the United States, armed clashes occurred between the guerilleros of Northern Mexico and the U.S. Army. Moore notes that the more violent clashes in Texas meant a termination of political participation by the Mexican elite. Any possibility of lower class political protest was ruthlessly suppressed by the Texas Rangers, a group of law enforcement officers organized in 1835 to protect the frontier. The Anglo political and economic dominance in Texas was at least in part attributable to the American conquest. Mexicans in New Mexico, on the other hand, retained the numerical majority for more than 100 years after being conquered. As a result of the pattern of conflict colonialism, it is not surprising that some of the most extreme versions of caste stratification developed in Texas.

Summarizing research done in Corpus Christi in the 1920s, Grebler, Morre, and Guzman note that

> Mexicans were "overwhelmingly" laborers in the cotton fields and definitely lower-class. Mexican clerks were hired only to attract the

Mexican trade and the few Mexican-American businessmen almost all served the ethnic populations. Mexican Americans went to segregated schools. Restrictive covenant clauses usually confined them to segregated neighborhoods. Discrimination in public accommodations was almost as stringent as it was against Negroes. Mexican Americans were allowed to sit at the drugstore fountain (though not at the tables) while Negroes would not be seated at all. Intermarriage was disparaged and the Anglo member of an intermarrying couple became socially a Mexican.[33]

California represents the extreme of economic exploitation. It was in here more than any other area of the Southwest that Mexican labor was manipulated to serve the interests of agricultural development. Attracted by the relatively high wages, hundreds of thousands of Mexicans entered the United States in the 1920s. During the Depression, a large fraction of these workers were forcibly deported ("repatriated") by California welfare agencies when their labor was not needed, and many were on the welfare rolls. This pattern contrasts sharply with that in Texas, where there were very few welfare provisions and, as a result, no need for forced deportation. With the tremendous economic expansion caused by World War II, there was a heightened need for Mexican labor. Normal immigration was supplemented by a contract labor arrangement known as the Bracero Program, under which large numbers of Mexicans could find employment as farm laborers for a season. But, as during the Depression, too many came to work in the United States, some without legal status. Again in 1954 massive sweeps of deportations eliminated Mexicans by the thousands in Operation Wetback—citizenship checks by the Border Patrol of the U.S. Immigration Service. "New Mexico was largely spared both waves of deportation; Texas was involved primarily, in Operation Wetback rather than in the welfare repatriations. California was deeply involved in both."[34] Thus it is especially in California that we find conscious economic manipulation of the large pool of Mexican labor.

How well does the sketch of Anglo-Mexican conquest fit the paternalistic-to-competitive model and the resulting forms of stratification? A system of dependent laborers working in dead-end agricultural jobs with poor wages and no union representation is certainly one version of paternalism. However, it differed considerably from the experience of Black Americans. Since the indigenous systems were often modified rather than destroyed, Mexican Americans have a more well-preserved culture than African

Americans. They retained their language, their Catholic religion, and their patterns of family organization. The proximity of the United States to Mexico, and the continuous back-and-forth immigration added to the persistence of their ethnic culture.

By definition, a paternalistic system necessitates a caste model of stratification. It is true that caste-like relations developed in certain areas (such as Corpus Christi, Texas) in the 1920s; but the Mexican Americans had more escape valves, more inconsistencies of status, and more opportunities for upward mobility than did the African Americans. As has been reported for the blacks, there was always a degree of sexual contact between castes. Upwardly mobile Mexican Americans who did not have extremely Indian-like appearances could claim all or predominantly Spanish blood in communities where the caste sanctions toward Mexicans were extreme. Further, Mexicans who had middle class occupations faced inconsistent caste status. San Antonio was seen as a relatively open place for the middle class—a very different milieu from Corpus Christi.[35]

In the last decades, the Mexican American population has changed drastically in a competitive direction. Fernando Penalosa notes that World War II was a major factor in the change. At that time there was a great flow of people out of the barrios.

> Young Mexican Americans took industrial jobs in increasing numbers, went off to war, traveled around the world, and were treated as individuals, some for the first time . . .Veterans especially returned to find themselves dissatisfied with the old ways and many went to college under the provisions of the G.I. Bill. Occupational skills were upgraded because of wartime industrial experience and because of the additional educational opportunities made available to young members of the group.[36]

There is an out-of-date stereotype of Mexicans as being highly concentrated in migratory farm labor. It is true that prior to World War II the Mexican-American population in the Southwest was largely rural, but it was two-thirds urban by 1950 and 90 percent urban by 1990.

Penalosa notes that the stratification system has changed dramatically in the last two or three decades. While formerly Mexican-Anglo relations leaned toward a caste system, Penalosa likens present-day Chicanos (in southern California) to "a European immigrant group of a generation ago such as, for example, the Italian-Americans in New York, Boston, or San Francisco."[37] The rigidity of caste barriers against intermarriage and equality of employment has diminished considerably. Consistent with a more competitive model, the Mexican-American population has developed a moderate degree of internal stratification. The modal occupation is semi-skilled or skilled blue-collar work.

CONCLUDING NOTE

The shift from paternalistic to competitive race relations for America's conquered minorities does not mean that all racial paternalism has disappeared from our institutions. Major pockets of paternalism continue to thrive in our advanced industrial society.

The welfare system in the United States has been strongly criticized as encouraging dependency and undermining self respect. In many states, Aid For Dependent Children benefits are available only when there is no male living in the house. The "man-in-the-house rule" has encouraged the break-up of many homes and perpetuated dependence on welfare. The relationship between welfare workers and the poor is often filled with tension and paternalism as a result of complicated eligibility requirements and, in some instances, "flagrant invasions of privacy."[38]

Migratory farm labor represents one of the most extreme survivals of paternalism in this country (see chapter 5). A great many Mexican American farm laborers are locked into a system that provides bare subsistence and totally controls their lives. Steiner captures well the paternalistic relations between grower and worker:

> When a grower says "my Mexicans" and "my boys" he means it affectionately. He is sentimental about the "old days," when it was "like a big happy family here"—men singing down by the camp at night. Women praying to their plaster saints . . . Like a good father, the grower feels he has to be stern at times . . . A father sometimes has to say no to his children for their own good and future well being.[39]

Although American Indians have entered a new period of militancy and self determination, illustrated by recent legal suits to recover land and fishing rights, there are still many Indian tribes living in abject poverty with most of their affairs controlled by the Bureau.

The shift from paternalism to competition is an important *macro*-societal trend, but within this society residues of paternalism remain.

NOTES

1. This definition comes from Max Weber's classic discussion of power. See Reinhard Bendix, *Max Weber: An Intellectual Portrait* (New York: Doubleday & Co., 1960), 294.

2. Donald Noel, "A Theory of the Origins of Ethnic Stratification," *Social Problems* 16 (Fall, 1968): 157–172

3. Ibid., 163.

4. Pierre L. van den Berghe, *Race and Racism* (New York: John Wiley & Sons, 1967).

5. Ibid., 65–66.

6. Gilberto Freyre, *The Masters and the Slaves* (New York: Alfred A. Knopf, 1964), 380.

7. See Arnold M. Rose, "Race and Ethnic Relations," Robert K. Merton and Robert A. Nisbet (eds.) *Contemporary Social Problems* (New York: Harcourt, Brace, 1961), 358.

8. One of the best films that I have seen on the portrayal of blacks in stereotypical roles in American movies is "Black History: Lost, Stolen or Strayed," narrated by Bill Cosby.

9. An interesting example of paternalistic roles without extreme racism is found in van den Berghe's discussion of Spanish-Indian relations in early Mexico. Indians were regarded as ''in need of enlightenment through exposure to the true faith, but they were basically human." That is, their culture was lacking but they were regarded as reasonably rational and intelligent members of the human race. In contrast, the attitudes of Spaniards toward Negroes constitutes a purer form of racism. They were regarded as intrinsically of unclean blood and low intelligence. Van den Berghe, *Race and Racism*, pp. 50–52.

10. Van den Berghe, *Race and Racism*, 29–30.

11. Rose notes that white Southerners at this time wanted to be modern and democratic and at the same time retain their vested interests in the institution of slavery. Racism became a convenient vehicle to resolve this conflict of interests. Since blacks were judged biologically inferior, they were not capable of intelligent participation in the polity or the economy. However, they could enjoy some of the benefits of democracy and Western culture by "serving the white race." Rose, "Race and Ethnic Relations," 355–357.

12. Herbert Blumer, *Industrialization and Race Relations, A Symposium* (London and New York: Oxford University Press, 1965), 245.

13. See Robert Blauner, "Internal Colonialism and Ghetto Revolt," *Social Problem* 16 (Spring, 1969): 393–408 and Robert L. Allen, *Black Awakening in Capitalist America* (New York: Doubleday & Co., 1969).

14. See W. Lloyd Warner's Introduction in Allison Davis, Burleigh R. Gardner and Mary R. Gardner, *Deep South* (Chicago: University of Chicago Press, 1941).

15. Van den Berghe, *Race and Racism*, 109.

16. Ibid., 82.

17. Ibid., 87–88.

18. Rose, "Race and Ethnic Relations," 359.

19. Nancy Oesteich Lurie, "The American Indian: Historical Background," in Norman R. Yetman and C. Hoy Steele (eds.) *Majority and Minority: The Dynamics of Race and Ethnicity in American Life* (Boston: Allyn and Bacon, 1971), 209.

20. Dee Brown, *Bury My Heart at Wounded Knee* (New York: Holt, Rinehart &Winston, Bantam Books, 1972), 6.

21. Ibid., 8

22. Lurie, "The American Indian: Historical Background," 221.

23. Edgar S. Cahn, *Our Brother's Keeper* (New York: World Publishing Co., 1969), 5.

24. Ibid., 9.

25. Ibid.

26. Ibid., 14–26.

27. Robert C. Day, "The Emergence of Activism as a Social Movement," in Howard M. Bahr, Bruce Chadwick and Rober C. Day (eds.) *Native Americans Today* (New York: Harper and Row, 1972), 508

28. Ibid., 511–512

29. Leo Grebler, Joan Moore, and Ralph Guzman, *The Mexican American People* (New York: Free Press, 1970), 44–45

30. Joan W. Moore, "Colonialism: The Case of the Mexican Americans," *Social Problems* 17 (Spring, 1970): 463–472

31. Ibid., 466.

32. Ibid.

33. Grebler, Moore, and Guzman, *The Mexican American People*, 323.

34. Moore, "Colonialism: The Case of the Mexican Americans," 469.

35. Grebler, Moore, and Guzman, *The Mexican American People*, 323–324.

36. Fernando Penalosa, "The Changing Mexican American in Southern California," in Norman R. Yetman and C. Hoy Steele (eds.) *Majority and Minority: The Dynamics of Race and Ethnicity in American Life* (Boston: Allyn and Bacon, 1971), 327.

37. Ibid., 332.

38. For a good summary of the welfare issue see Otto Kerner, *Report of the National Advisory Commission on Civil Disorders* (New York: Bantam Books, 1968), 457–466.

39. Stan Steiner, *La Raza: The Mexican Americans* (New York: Harper & Row Publisher, 1969), 260.

The Interaction Between Race and Class in Contemporary America

In viewing race relations in the United States as moving from paternalistic to competitive, one examines the foci of history on a time-scale of increased status differentiation *within* minorities and finds an increasing need for reconceptualizing social organization on a race-class perspective. The paternalistic-competitive model clarifies and illuminates the trend from rigid racial castes to a more fluid situation in which a) several economic-power strata form within each race, and b) there is increased competition and conflict between ethnic groups (as well as classes) for scarce resources. Marvin Olsen has summarized this trend well.

> This paternalistic pattern may give way to a more "competitive" type of race relations . . . as a society becomes more industrialized and urbanized, as slavery is declared illegal, and as members of the subordinate class become more physically mobile and slowly gain education, occupational skills, and wealth. In place of wholly superordinate and wholly subordinate racial populations, two parallel racial categories develop, each having its own organizational structure, division of labor, and socioeconomic status gradations. The formerly dominant population may continue to enjoy numerous advantages in power, privilege, and prestige for a long period of time, but it no longer totally controls the previously subordinate racial population. The old patterns of paternalism and voluntary subservience give way to competition and conflict between the two racial categories as the subordinate one struggles to increase its share of power, privilege, and prestige in society. Race relations are no longer static and "peaceful"; dynamic conflict and change now prevail.[1]

However, the specific ways in which ethnicity and class interact in such a competitive society appear to be an open frontier for exploration. Though there are excellent essays and empirical studies on the subject,[2] on the whole, "race and class in interaction" is a remarkably understudied conceptual area. Moreover, the ethnic power and ethnic identity movements of the last decades make the topic especially intriguing when the ethnic groups under study are Mexican Americans, blacks and American Indians.

Do upwardly mobile Mexican Americans or blacks reject or min-imize their ethnicity and become middle-class consumers as some accounts would suggest, or have the ethnic pride movements generated a whole new set of constraints encouraging middle-class black, Chicano, or urban Indian persons to retain their ethnic identifications at the same time that they enjoy a middle-class life-style? Further, it is quite possible that class differentiation has distinctly different meanings and consequences for each minority group. For example, upwardly mobile Mexican Americans (who have reached a skilled or white-collar stratum) may both resemble and differ from upwardly mobile blacks in such areas as perceived discrimination, assimilation options, and propensity toward militant action. The point is that many of the traditional concepts and theories in the study of class and ethnic relations are not adequate to explain the simultaneous emergence of an increased skilled and white-collar stratum coupled with heightened ethnic consciousness among American ethnic minorities.

TWO HIERARCHIES

Our basic perspective is that racial-ethnic qualities and socioeconomic characteristics result in two distinct but interacting hierarchies. Although there are significant differences between these two orders, they share a common basis—both determine access to power, economic privilege, and social honor. The basic assumption of ethnic stratification is that *physical* and/or *cultural* distinction from the dominant ethnic stratum results in power inequality and limited access to important rewards. Quite apart from one's wealth or education, membership in an ethnic group per se determines to some extent one's life chances. This is especially the case when the ethnic minority has gone through a long-standing paternalistic relationship in which beliefs of inherent inferiority have developed and in which unequal power has become highly institutionalized. In contrast, the socioeconomic hierarchy deals with the economic earnings, education, and occupational status of persons.

A given socioeconomic stratum (often used interchangeably with social class in our discussion) refers to a category of people with roughly comparable levels of occupational attainment, education, and income. One sometimes finds the term "achieved rank" used when referring to SES or socioeconomic status (as opposed to ascribed rank in the case of race). But SES is not always entirely "achieved," since initiative effort, and ability are not the only determinants.

Equally important are inherited wealth and privilege. Upper middle-class children typically inherit not only material wealth and possessions, but a high achievement motivation from their home environment. They also attend the best schools, and have parental connections with the most influence. Diagramatically, the two-hierarchy perspective would look like this:

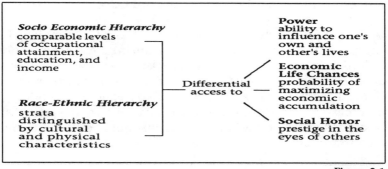

Figure 2.1

Until recently, the correlation between race (black, Chicano, Native Americans), and low socioeconomic position was so consistent that the two categories were rarely separated. That is, it was assumed that practically all blacks, Mexican Americans, and Indians were lower class. Though the poverty rate is still high for all three groups, increasingly large numbers of urban blacks and Mexican Americans have attained better socioeconomic positions in the last thirty years. The 1990 census indicates that somewhere between 30 percent and 40 percent of the employed black and Hispanic, populations (depending upon region of the country and the age and sex of the respondent) are either in skilled blue-collar positions (craftsmen or foremen), or white-collar occupations.[3] As one would expect, minority persons in white-collar positions tend to come from stable working-class or middle-class homes, rather than from poverty backgrounds. The child who faces the dual barrier of poverty and race has limited chances for substantial socioeconomic advancement, while minority children from stable working-class or middle-class homes do inherit some advantages.

The point is that in black, Chicano, and Indian populations the correlation between "race" and lower-class status is no longer .95 (as it would be under a paternalistic system) but has dropped to something like a moderate .50. This means that race and class increasingly interact in complex and interesting ways. A middle-class African American person may have very different outlooks and battles to fight than those of a lower-class black. The dual-hierarchy model allows for the possibility of a middle- or upper-class black person having greater power, wealth, and prestige than a lower-class white person. However, before examining these interaction possibilities, the ethnic race hierarchy needs to be more clearly defined.

There are many excellent discussions of social class ranking in the United States, but ethnic and racial ranking are less commonly viewed as hierarchical. In particular, blacks, Mexican Americans, and American Indians have not been commonly distinguished from other ethnic groups in hierarchical conceptions. Accordingly, a more extensive discussion of the ethnic-race hierarchy is presented below, followed by some important comparisons between race and class stratification.

RACIAL-ETHNIC STRATIFICATION

The term *race* is used to include groups distinguished primarily by visible physical criteria skin color (e.g., blacks and Asians). By contrast, *ethnic group* usually refers to cultural populations distinguished by language, heritage, or special traditions (e.g., American Jews). The three groups discussed most in this book—blacks, Mexican Americans, and American Indians—have either a high degree of visibility or a combination of physical and cultural characterisitics. To separate clearly the *conquered minorities* from white ethnic groups we will frequently use the term *race* when referring to blacks, Mexican Americans, and Native Americans.

Following the approaches of Lenski and Olsen, we view *power inequality* as the key variable for distinguishing strata in an ethnic-race hierarchy. That is, power inequality comes first, is the prime mover of the system, and determines the distribution of economic privileges and or prestige (social honor). From this viewpoint, improvements in economic privileges and or prestige for minority persons are only likely to occur when basic institutional arrangements are changed by the exertion of power. As Olsen puts it: "If racial inequality is in fact largely a consequence of power exertion by whites, it follows that *blacks seeking to change the situation so as to gain greater equality of privileges and prestige must in turn exercise power against the dominant whites.*"[4] Similarly, prejudice is viewed as the result or outcome of power inequality institutionalized (e.g., segregation). Olsen argues that racial prejudice is far more likely to be reduced by minority power action that affects these institutions (eliminates segregation), than by education or persuasion. In terms of power inequality and differential access to rewards, a racial-ethnic stratification order in the United States would look like this:

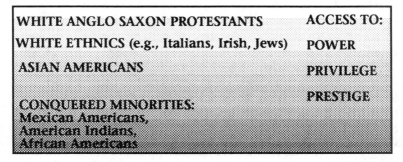

Figure 2.2

Descending the scale in figure 2.2, we find increasing degrees of political powerlessness, economic oppression, and social exclusion. Historically, White Anglo Saxon Protestants (WASPS) were the dominant group in the early American colonies. English language, law, and literature prevailed. Later arriving groups were judged according to their fit with this WASP model. White ethnics (e.g., Italians, Jews, Poles, Greeks) arrived in the U.S. during the later waves of immigration from 1880 to1920. The term white ethnic refers especially to immigrants from South Eastern Europe. These groups faced a moderate amount of prejudice and discrimination. White ethnics were often judged as backwards and boorish because of their lack of urban-industrial skills, their differences in religion, and their inability to speak English well.

Despite these handicaps, white ethnics had major advantages over racial minorities. First, they entered the United States voluntarily. They were not conquered groups. Secondly, white ethnics were able to set up enclaves or communities in which they could practice their traditions and religion. Thus, within the Italian, Greek, or Jewish areas of the city one finds separate support groups, newspapers, restaurants, churches and synagogues. These were communities of choice and they provided members with an alternative source of connection and self esteem.[5] Third, these groups were white and blended in physically with the majority group, allowing for more rapid accultration and assimilation.

Asian Americans represent an interesting intermediate stratum between the WASP and the most oppressed minorities. Though they are certainly physically visible—they are technically a racial minority—and currently face some degree of social exclusion,[6] their cultural stress on personal achievement, duty to the community, emphasis on long-range goals, etc., is highly compatible with that of the dominant culture. Further, Japanese and Chinese Americans did not enter this country as a conquered people. Compared with blacks, Chicanos, and Indians, Asian Americans have not remained in a highly dependent paternalistic relationship for long periods of time. Though legal controls against them have often been harsh ("Gentleman's Agreement," "Yellow Peril," and the Acts of Oriental Exclusion), and though relocation during World War II was one of the most extreme temporary forms of total control that the white majority has exerted on a racial minority, Asian Americans have not experienced the long-range powerlessness of the three "conquered minorities."

From the perspectives of unequal power and differential access, to scarce rewards, one finds blacks, Indians, and Chicanos at the lowest end of the ethnic hierarchy. As noted in chapter 1, not only were all three groups conquered but the unequal power relationship became institutionalized. All three groups experienced some version of a long-lasting paternalistic relationship with the white power structure (slavery, total control by the Bureau of Indian Affairs, the use of Mexicans as a commodity for farm labor). Such unequal power was not just an historical fact but continues to a large extent today, with the low degree of power and autonomy in many ghetto, barrio, and reservation communities (i.e., externally manipulated colonies). However, there are differences between blacks, Mexicans, and Indians on this dimension of differential access to scarce rewards. Mexican Americans and Native Americans face victimization due to cultural factors, blacks face discrimination mainly due to visibility and negative stereotypes attached to color.

Some segments of the Mexican-American and Indian populations have a distinctive culture that is at wide variance with the dominant culture. For example, Spanish language, greater emphasis on family cohesion, and less stress on individualistic achievement separates to some degree Anglo and Mexican-American outlooks. (However, the differences between Anglos and third generation urban Mexican Americans on these dimensions are probably very small). Moreover, these cultural differences are not neutral or without consequence.

Moore notes that there has typically been a gross and insensitive reaction to Mexican language and culture in most Anglo institutions.[7] In the schools, Mexican-American culture is often viewed as inferior in the sense that it causes bilingualism (assumed to be detrimental to education) and a lack of motivation. Federal financial assistance to schools in barrio communities is often based on the assumption that we must ". . . help Mexican-American children compensate for certain inadequacies they display compared to a 'standard' middle-class child."[8] Such efforts are aimed at changing the child rather than changing the system. Cultural differences in the case of Chicanos and American Indians have become further means of limiting opportunities and enacting oppression.

Blacks, in contrast to Chicanos and Indians, have fewer cultural differences in language and values but are more "locked in" by physical visibility, and by the ideologies attached to that color. Though the extreme racist ideologies that developed during slavery and the era of Jim Crow (blacks were defined as biologically inferior and were assessed as three-fifths of a man for determining the number of seats a state got in Congress) have subsided, many white Americans now embrace an ideology of differential effort. Current surveys show that many white Americans subscribe to an ideolgy of free will and lack of effort.[9] From this view, whites believe that blacks have a higher poverty rate and lower socioeconomic status because they have not extended the necessary effort. Such a view completely ignores patterns of racism in institutions and places all of the blame for black disadvantage on blacks themselves. Racial stratification that is tied to visibility and beliefs in differential effort is likely to be especially rigid, making upward mobility much more difficult. In contrast, skin color and physical features in the Mexican American group are more variable, and hence there is more inconsistency in status assignments based on visibility. Mexican Americans lighter in skin color, or with a more classical Spanish appearance may experience slightly less prejudice than darker skinned Latinos. However, visibility for Mexican Americans has not been as historically connected to ideologies of racial inferiority as it has been for blacks. In the sense of the permeability of a color line, upwardly mobile Mexican Americans and American Indians have more options for mobility than African Americans.

In sum, blacks, Mexican Americans, and Indians are lowest on the ethnic hierarchy (having the least access to scarce rewards) because of a combination of the following factors:

- Pronounced cultural differences (especially Mexican Americans and Indians);
- High visibility (especially blacks);
- Conquered status and long-lasting paternalistic relationship with the white majority;
- Relatively powerless communities controlled and manipulated by white society;
- Highly crystallized ideologies of inferiority or belief that the minority group has not invested necessary efforts for achievment.

INDIVIDUAL VERSUS INSTITUTIONAL RACISM

When speaking of a race-ethnic stratification order, it is important to distinguish between individual racism and discrimination. An employer who discriminates against a minority applicant because he/she believes that members of that group are inferior or lazy or non-productive is holding individual racist beliefs and engaging in individual discrimination. However, racism may be embedded in the system. Everyday, "business as usual" routines, procedures, and policies may appear neutral yet impact harmful consequences on minority persons.[10] Often there is no individual racist bigotry involved. That is, the policies appear to be benign, but in fact are discriminatory toward minority persons. Until very recently in

California, black elementary school age children were classified in mental ability according to standardized IQ test scores. Research in the 1970s uncovered the fact that many of these tests are intrinsically racist in that they are based on white middle class experiences (see Chapter 7). The test designers, and teachers and counselors who administer the test, are not racist in attitude; the problem is in the measuring instrument and in the system routine of using that instrument.

Not all forms of institutional racism and discrimination are so impersonal; in some cases there is a focus on racial characteristics. Experimental studies of discrimination in housing find that when black and white couples with identical economic profiles (education, work experience, salary, etc.) approach real estate agents, black couples are less likely to get to see a house, and are more likely to be "steered" toward areas of black concentration. Diana Pearce refers to this as institutional discrimination, because there is a consensus among real estate agents as to which areas are to remain all white that goes beyond individual instances of discrimination.[11] In this particular example, the motivation to steer black families away from exclusive white neighborhoods may be economic to provide ease of sales for incoming white buyers. Whatever the motivation, the discrimination involves organizational aggreements and patterned inequalities that go beyond individual actions of particular persons. African Americans, Mexican Americans, and American Indians have, in particular, experienced both individual and institutional racism and discrimination.

DOMINANT WHITE STRATUM OR POWER ELITE?

As we talk about power inequality being the essential fact of a racial stratification order, it is important to clarify several points dealing with the dispersal of power in the white population and in the minorities. Who has the power in this country? A widely held theory is that a small group of people (men primarily) at the top of major institutions make things move. C. Wright Mills argues that at the highest levels of the political, economic, and military hierarchies, a small group has an inordinate amount of control over the destinies of individual citizens of all *races*. "For they are in command of the major hierarchies and major organizations of modern society. They rule the big corporations. They run the machinery of the state and claim its prerogatives. they direct the military establishment."[12]

From this power elite model, it would seem inappropriate to use the terminology of "dominant white group" since some whites (the elite) have far more control over the racial stratification system than rank-and-file whites. One could even argue that the white and minority masses are equally dominated by a powerful few. However, from the perspective of this book, a group of whites much larger than a power elite have controlled the destinies of black, Chicano, and Indian peoples. Systems of racial inequality initiated by a small group of powerful whites (as in colonialism and Manifest Destiny) allowed for a wide dispersal of authority resulting in middle-class, working-class, and, to some degree, poor whites acting out the racial order. Consider C. Vann Woodward's statement about the wide dispersal of power occasioned by Jim Crow laws:

> The Jim Crow laws put the authority of the state or city in the voice of the street car conductor, the railway brakeman, the bus driver, the theater usher, and also into the voice of the hoodlums of the public parks and playgrounds. They gave free rein and the majesty of the law to mass agressions that might otherwise have been curbed, blunted, or deflected.[13]

Currently, many whites of modest status and economic attainment have prevented black encroachment in their trade unions and neighborhoods. Indeed, it is commonly noted that the white working class has most rigidly acted out the discrimination norms of the old caste order, since they face the greatest status threat and economic competition from an upwardly mobile black population. Sociologists having an internal colonization perspective also emphasize the fact that white agents (e.g., the white police) of powerful ruling groups enforce the system of inequality.[14] Thus, large numbers of whites far in excess of the power elite have been and continue to be involved in racial discrimination. But to refer to the white population as dominant in power, and the conquered minority populations as subordinate in power is only partially accurate. One exception worth noting is that some segments of the white majority have identified with the ethnic liberation movements and actively participated in them (one of the major support groups in Cesar Chavez's farm worker movement is white and middle class). The white majority group cannot be viewed as one homogeneous oppressor. Another very important fact is that increasingly some members of the minority populations have more personal influence and control over their environment than some whites. Not all whites are dominant over all blacks.

Two Kinds Of Power

If power is defined as control over major institutions and, in particular, control over the economy, then few minority persons have such top power compared with whites. Even at upper middle levels of institutional power (for example, mayors or senators) whites have far more representation and influence than blacks, Chicanos, and Indians. However, if power is thought of in more personal terms as the probability of exerting control over one's own life, then middle-class blacks often have more control than working- and lower-class whites. That is, middle-class blacks, in contrast to lower-class whites, typically have more money, influence in the context of their jobs, knowledge of redress channels when they face inequities, and general life chances. The terminology of dominant and subordinate racial strata completely misses this possibility.

COMPARISONS BETWEEN THE SOCIAL CLASS AND RACE-ETHNIC ORDERS

The Marxian Prediction

If both class and race hierarchies involve an unequal distribution of power, what, then, is the difference between them? Three important distinctions can be made: a) The clarity of the stratum boundary lines; b) the opportunities for mobility from one stratum to another; and c) the resulting potential for stratum solidarity and collective action to move the social structure in ways favorable to the lower class.

Social strata in the United States have been characterized by vague boundary lines, at least a moderate amount of social mobility from one stratum to another, and rather low degrees of shared fate, stratum solidarity, and collective action. For a hundred years, scholars have debated why a proletarian revolution has not occurred, i.e., why the working class has not been a more radical force for social change as Karl Marx predicted. The fluidity of the system and resulting mobility of individuals coupled with unlimited faith in the "American Dream" are possible explanations.

As Marvin Olsen notes, "to the extent that numerous opportunities for individual mobility do occur in a society, there is little impetus for the members of a subordinate class to organize for collective power exertion and class conflict . . ."[15] However, racial-ethnic stratification often comes much closer to a Marxian model. For the visible minorities, the stratum boundary lines are extremely clear and mobility to a higher ethnic stratum is virtually impossible in one lifetime. Moreover, power inequality is perceived as great by the minorities in the case of white-black, Anglo-Chicano, and white-Indian relations. The potential for collective action is further heightened by spatial segregation, that is, ghetto, barrio, and reservation communities in which frustrations and perceived wrongs can be easily shared and disseminated. Finally, blacks, Chicanos, and American Indians have faced severe economic oppression. In short, racial stratification in the United States has a much greater potential for producing stratum consciousness and stratum conflict than does socioeconomic stratification. But there are major differences between blacks and Mexican Americans on this dimension. There is tremendous diversity among Mexican Americans—by class, generation, and geographical area. This diversity tends to mute the potential for a sense of shared fate as a separate oppressed minority. Discrimination against Mexican Americans has been more inconsistent than it has been against blacks. To the extent that blacks are more visible, and more "locked in" to their racial stratum, the long-range potential for collective action will be greater for blacks than for Mexican Americans or American Indians.

Differences in the Concept of Social Honor

In Weber's classic discussion of the status hierarchy, a variety of criteria for social honor were mentioned: reputation of family, status attached to a particular occupation, manners, refinement and etiquette, and educational attainment.[16] High status groups with commonality on these characteristics tend to band together and exclude others without the proper qualifications. Race or ethnic status is another characteristic that may result in low social honor and social exclusion. However, a low racial status has been accompanied by more intense social exclusion in American society than a lack of refinement, or than a lower-class family origin. This is because race has been accompanied by beliefs in inherent differences and inferiority, while among Anglos social honor can be acquired (the nouveau riche can become accepted by the "right" friends and through donations to the "right" charities). To develop this point further, in both the class and ethnicity versions of social honor there is the element of exclusion. Prestigious upper-class persons tend to restrict entrance of lower-class persons into their elite clubs and associations; whites tend to exclude blacks (and, to a lesser extent, Chicanos[17]) from their peer groups. But social exclusion based on color is often more intense than that based on class; it frequently is accompanied by strong emotions, and violation of its unwritten rules involves more severe sanctions. No upper-class white person living in an exclusive residential area would consider burning a cross on the lawn of a newly entering white machinist. The same cannot be said with certainty in the case of a black machinist or even a black doctor.

Another consideration makes the assignment of social honor to minority persons far more complex than to majority persons. Social honor due to achieved merit may be constantly interacting with social honor due to race. Black doctors may receive high degrees of deference and esteem as a result of competence in their occupation, but when they leave their office and their insulated occupational role, they may be accorded the same low level of prestige in their social contacts as that accorded less successful blacks. Their social honor may be constantly shifting as they move from social situations that acknowledge their achieved rank to social situations where their racial status is most important.

THE LACK OF RESEARCH ON RACE CLASS INTERACTION

Sociologists have not adequately explored the ways in which ethnicity and class combine. The failure to consider race and class conjointly stems from two kinds of overemphasis: the stress on race to the exclusion of class and the stress on class to the exclusion of race.

Primacy of the Race-Ethnicity Dimension

Often the minority group is viewed as one homogeneous, impoverished, lower-class group. If the middle class of a minority is mentioned, it is usually depicted as a small peripheral segment, despite current census evidence that 30 to 40 percent of black and Latino persons hold skilled or white-collar occupations. It is as if being black in America is such an overriding factor that the class position of the person is unimportant or peripheral. For example, many use the analogy of internal colonialism when speaking of American Blacks, Chicanos and Indians. The model is important in that it clearly distinguishes between white ethnic communities of choice (e.g., Italian, Polish, and Irish enclaves) and ghettos, barrios, and reservations that are externally controlled and manipulated by white persons (white merchants, police, eligibility workers, etc.). Internal colonialism, however, does not stress social class differences. All members of the colonized group tend to be seen as facing the same degree of exploitation, racism, and reduced life chances. This approach misses—or at least de-emphasizes—some crucial points. The middle-class and upper working-class strata have far greater resources (money, connections, knowledge of redress channels, physical health) to challenge the system individually when facing personal discrimination, and collectively (for broad institutional reforms) than the lower-class stratum. Further, middle-class blacks have discrimination battles to fight that are very different from those of lower-class blacks. For example, Stanley Lieberson suggests that middle-class blacks especially face the problem of converting their incomes into the same economic privileges that middle-class whites automatically enjoy, (quality housing, good schools), whereas lower-class blacks may be far more concerned with the "gut" issues of steady employment and survival.[18]

Primacy of Class

Some theorists view social class as being such a powerful steam roller variable that it overrides all race-ethnic effects. Some have even asserted that racial discrimination is no longer a major problem; they suggest instead that poverty, lower-class apathy, and hopelessness create the actual barriers. Edwin C. Banfield comments that:

> If overnight Negroes turned white most of them would go on living under much the same handicaps for a long time to come. The great majority of New Whites would continue working at the same jobs, living in the same neighborhoods, and sending their children to the same schools. There would be no mass exodus from the blighted and slum neighborhoods where most Negroes now live. By and large New Whites would go on living in the same neighborhoods for the simple reason that they could not afford to move to better ones.[19]

Similarly, Wilson argues that there has been a declining significance of race, and that the life chances of blacks today have more to do with economic class factors, such as the shutdown of industrial plants and the resulting joblessness in the ghetto, than to racial discrimination.[20]

One interesting version of this line of reasoning is that there is a natural sequence from racial to class stratification. Initally, race-ethnicity is extremely important in determining differential power and privilege; however, once members of a race have been denied access to good jobs, education, and positions of power, the subordinate position of the race may continue because of class and poverty, rather than because of racial barriers.

> Once this has happened, once these discriminating lines of opportunities have been drawn, a process of impersonal but effective discrimination has been put into motion that endures often without much formal enforcement at all. For one generation of disadvantaged parents breeds a second generation of disadvantaged children, bereft of education, choices, and the capacity to raise their children in ways that might make it possible for them to move up the socioeconomic ladder. . .[21]

Although such an approach makes an important point (that poverty and powerlessness are automatically recycled without the repeated stimulus of the initial cause) the special joint effects or complex blends of race and class discrimination are ignored. At lower-class levels, ethnic and class discrimination often are combined to produce unique barriers that cannot be explained by either class or race discrimination alone. What is needed then is the development of models that explicitly take into account the joint effects of race and class. The following chapter attempts to do this.

NOTES

1. Marvin E. Olsen, "Power Perspectives on stratification and Race Relations," in Marvin E. Olsen (ed.) *Power in Societies* (New York: Macmillan Co., 1970), 301.

2. See, for example, Milton M. Gordon, *Assimilation in American Life* (New York: Oxford University Press, 1964), chs. 2–3; William Julius Wilson, *The Declining Significance of Race: Blacks and Changing American Institutions.* Chicago: University of Chicago Press, 1978; Joe R. Feagin, "The Continuing Significance of Race: Antiblack Discrimination in Public Places," *American Sociological Review* 56 (February, 1991): 101–116; Vincent Jeffries and H. Edward Ransford, *Social Stratification: A Multiple Hierarchy Approach,* Boston: Allyn and Bacon, 1980; Pitirim A. Sorokin, *Society, Culture, and Personality,* (New York; Harper & Brothers, 1947), ch. 15;

3. See chapter 4 of this book for a more specific discussion of the demographic characteristics of the black and Hispanic populations.

4. Olsen, "Power Perspectives on stratification and Race Relations," 302.

5. See Robert Blauner, Racial Oppression in America (New York: Harper & Row, 1972), chapter on Colonized and Immigrant Minorities.

6. See Harry L. Kitano, Japanese Americans: The *Evolution of a Subculture* (Englewood Cliffs, N.J.: Prentice-Hall, 1969), 50–51.

7. Joan W. Moore, *Mexican Americans* (Englewood Cliffs, N.J.: Prentice-Hall, 1970), 81.

8. Ibid., 81.

9. See James R. Kluegel, "Trends in Whites' Explanations of the Black-White Gap in Socioeconomic; Status, 1977–1989," *American Sociological Review* 55 (1990): 512–525; J.R. Kluegel and E. R. Smith, *Beliefs about Equality: American's Views of What is and What Ought to Be* (New York: Aldine de Gruyter, 1986); and Howard Schuman, "Free Will and Determinism in Beliefs about Race," in Norman R. Yetman and C. Hoy Steele (eds.), *Majority and Minority: the Dynamics of Racial and Ethnic Relations* (Boston: Allyn and Bacon, 1971).

10. See Norman R. Yetman and C. Hoy Steele, "Models of Discrimination in America," in Norman R. Yetman and C. Hoy Steele (eds.) *Majority and Minority: The Dynamics of Race and Ethnicity in American Life* (Boston: Allyn and Bacon, 1982).

11. Diana M. Pearce, "Gatekeepers and Homeseekers: Institutional Factors in Racial Steering," *Social Problems* 26 (1979): 325–42.

12. C. Wright Mills, "The Higher Circles," in *The Impact of Social Class,* ed. Paul Blumberg (New York: Thomas Y. Crowell Co., 1972), 278.

13. C. Vann Woodward, *The Strange Career of Jim Crow* (New York: Oxford University Press, 1957), 93.

14. Robert Blauner, *Racial Oppression in America,* 97–99.

15. Olsen, "Power Perspectives on Stratification and Race Relations," 300.

16. Max Weber, *From Max Weber: Essays in Sociology,* ed. and tr. Hans H. Gerth and C. Wright Mills (New York: Oxford University Press, 1946), 180–195.

17. Consistently, social distance research shows that Anglos are more willing to admit Chicanos into situations of social intimacy (same club, neighborhood, and marriage) than they are blacks. For example, in a survey in Texas, 50% of the Anglos were willing to admit a Mexican American into close kinship by marriage contrasted with only 10% of the Anglos willing to admit a Negro. See Chandler Davidson and Charles M. Gaitz, "Ethnic Attitudes as a Basis for Minority Cooperation in a Southwestern Metropolis," *Social Science Quarterly* 53 (March, 1973): 738–748.

18. Lieberson, *Social Stratification Research and Theory for the 1970s,* 180.

19. Edward C. Banfield, *The Unheavenly City* (Boston: Little, Brown & Co., 1968), 73.

20. William Julius Wilson, *The Declining Significance of Race: Blacks and Changing American Institutions* (Chicago: University of Chicago Press, 1978)

21. Melvin M. Tumin, *Comparative Perspectives on Race Relations* (Boston: Little, Brown & Co., 1969), 16.

3

Three Models

Three race-class perspectives are developed in this chapter. We refer to them as; *Open Marketplace of Status Configurations, Minority Subcommunity,* and *Ethclass.*

I. Open Marketplace of Status Configurations

According to this approach, individuals come into a marketplace of social interaction, each simultaneously asserting many different statuses. Most individuals will attempt to maximize rewards and "payoffs" and minimize barriers and stigma. (It is not only possible to consider ethnic and class stratification within such a model, but age and sex stratification as well. We are simply limiting this discussion to the two possibilities of race and class.)

The open marketplace model is designed to explain the interaction of minority persons in racially integrated settings. This model is therefore especially appropriate for the upper working-class and middle-class segments of the minority population, where a large part of each person's lifetime may be spent outside of the ghetto or barrio. Increasingly, the skilled and white-collar strata of the minority group are employed in the general societal occupational structure rather than in separate all-black or all-Chicano unions, schools, or other institutions.

In such an open marketplace of status claims, a number of important things can happen. A relatively high social class position can undermine or considerably offset (in terms of power, privilege, and prestige) a low ethnicity position. Many status audiences, both white and black, accord more deference and respect to a black high school principal or scientist than to a white construction worker. Furthermore, regardless of what people think of him or her, a high-achieving minority person may have more objectively measured power and economic life chances than some Anglos. Stated in more general terms, class and race may overlap to the extent that the life-chances, power, economic options, and prestige of a high-achieving black, Latino, or Indian person are greater than those of a low- or moderate-achieving white person.

One extreme version of the "open market" model suggests that race is but one kind of status that can be offset by socioeconomic achievement. That is, an industrial society functioning rationally will reward performance rather than skin color. Such an approach leads to the conclusion that high-status segments of racial minorities will become an undifferentiated part of the American middle class, or at least that skin color and ethnic status will pose no serious barriers. This option—assimilation—is more immediately open to middle-class Latinos and urban Indians than to middle-class blacks, largely because of the lower "visibility" of the first two groups.

A second version of the open market model appears to be far closer to reality for the majority of blacks, Latinos, and Indians. Although socioeconomic advancement increases the power and the economic life chances of minority persons, there are still likely to remain some racially-associated differentials between majority and minority persons holding the same degree of socioeconomic achievement. It is often observed that the high-achieving black person has difficulty in consistently "cashing in" on all power and status fronts. He or she may have the same education as the white person, but be paid less. Even with the same education and income as comparably trained white persons, he or she may have less power as a result of exclusion from social cliques in which policy decisions are made. Also, the status of black middle-class persons is multivalent. The status of black doctors will shift and vary as they move from group to group. Among their medical peers they may be fully respected as very competent doctors. They may easily enter into social relationships with other doctors, though among prejudiced white patients, the same physicians may receive minimal deference in the doctor-patient relationship and complete social exclusion in any other relationship. Indeed, one aspect of the marketplace model is that low status crystallization (a lack of fit or consistency among different statuses) in the combination of low ethnic position and high socioeconomic position creates very uncomfortable situations for the individual. The middle-class black or Latino is seen as laboring under conflicting expectations in contemporary society.[1] To what extent then does class achievement override racial barriers? The question has turned into a major debate in American Sociology.

*Open Marketplace and the Debate Regarding
the Declining Significance of Race*

In 1977, William J. Wilson, a black professor of sociology at the University of Chicago, asserted in a lecture at a professional meeting that the life-chances of Black Americans are now determined more by social class than race. One year later this thesis appeared in his book, *The Declining Significance of Race.*[2] Wilson's book set off one of the most heated and protracted debates in the field of Sociology.

Wilson argues that in present times race is receding in importance and economic class is becoming a far more important determinant of life-chances, i.e., ". . . The life-chances of blacks have less to do with race than with economic class affiliation."[3] He notes that talented and educated blacks are experiencing new job opportunities in governmental and corporate sectors that are at least as great as those of whites with comparable educational qualifications. This is not to say that Wilson ignores blacks living in poverty. On the contrary, in later articles and a follow up book, *The Truly Disadvantaged*, he focuses on the black underclass.[4] But again, he argues that anguish and frustration in the black underclass are determined less by racial discrimination than class factors such as inner city joblessness occasioned by shifts in the occupational structure. Structural dislocations in the economy such as de-industrialization—the shutdown of industrial plants located in central city areas of high black concentration—are the primary explanations for poverty, dependency, and the large increase in female headed households. Why exactly did this thesis produce such an uproar? Some argued that the conclusion (that there is a declining significance of race) is premature.

As Thomas Pettigrew states: "The fallacy seems to lie in the belief that an increase in the predictive power of one set of variables (class) necessitates a decrease in the predictive power of another set (race)."[5] Pettigrew notes that the black poor are much worse off than the white poor, and the black middle-class have a considerable distance to go before catching up to the white middle-class standard of wealth and economic security.[6] While social class may have an increased importance for the life-chances of blacks, race may remain as crucial as ever.

Another critic, Charles Willie, notes that the race gap in income persists at all levels of educational attainment.[7] Further, Willie suggests a counter hypothesis—". . . That the significance of race is increasing especially for middle-class blacks who, because of school desegregation and affirmative action and other integration programs, are coming into direct contact with whites for the first time for extended integration."[8] Willie cites his own case studies of black families who have moved into racially integrated neighborhoods and work environments: "Race for some of these pioneers is a consuming experience. They seldom can get away from it."[9] In a rejoinder, Wilson notes that he is talking in terms of degrees. He is not asserting that race has disappeared as a determinant of black life-chances, but rather that it is less important than it was historically. As to Willie's counter hypothesis, Wilson responds:

> "Many educated blacks do experience psychological discomfort in new integrated situations. Willie and I could probably draw many personal examples of this. We both are black and we both teach at elite universities. But I am sure that neither of us would trade places with a poor black trapped in the ghetto and handcuffed to a menial dead-end and poorly paid job. No cries about the psychological discomfort of the integrated black elite should distract our attention from the abominable and deleterious physical conditions of the isolated black poor."[10]

The Open Market Model constantly brings us to the question of the degree to which social class achievement changes, chips away, or overrides barriers based on racial status. Instead of an overarching assumption of a declining significance of race and concomitant rising importance of class, the relative importance of race or class in determining life-chances becomes an empirical question. For which outcomes does socioeconomic advancement neutralize racial barriers? And for which outcomes does race continue to make a difference in reduced life-chances?

The declining significance of race debate has focused entirely on African Americans. To what degree does class advancement reduce ethnic barriers for other minority groups who also suffered a conquest-colonial historical past, such as the Mexican Americans? Throughout this book we hypothesize that due to the extreme prejudice that blacks have faced, the high achieving black person is likely to encounter a greater residue of ethnic barriers and inconsistent treatment than the high achieving Mexican American.

Let me address the above questions with a few studies. Racial segregation in housing has proved to be one of the most intractable barriers for African Americans. That is, spatial assimilation illustrates the persistence rather than the decline of race as a factor. Massey and Mullan, in a comparative residential study of blacks and Hispanics, find that blacks have much more difficulty translating social mobility into residential mobility.[11] A follow up study comparing blacks, Hispanics, and Asians in residential segregation produced the same finding.[12] In other words, rising social status does not allow blacks to assimilate spatially like other groups. Thus, in comparison to Hispanics, middle-class and skilled working class blacks are often isolated within black or predominantly black neighborhoods, often near deteriorating inner-city areas. Massey and Mullan argue that "it is only possible to make the case that race is becoming less salient as a dimension of stratification if one ignores the fact that blacks are segregated by race not class."[13]

Research by Diana Pearce is consistent with these findings.[14] Black couples and white couples with identical economic and job history profiles (paid researchers) conducted a visit to ninety-seven randomly selected real estate agents. These visits were spaced several weeks apart so as not to arouse the suspicion of the agent. After looking at the written descriptions of a number of houses, each couple asked to see a house in desirable areas in the Detroit Metropolitan Area. The homeseekers had comfortable incomes. The males, in both black and white cases, had college degrees and white-collar jobs. In only 25 percent of the cases did the black couple get to see a house on the first visit to the real estate agent versus 75 percent of the cases for the white couple. Moreover, in those instances in which the black couple was shown a house, they were more likely shown a house close to areas of black concentration. Commonly known as *racial steering*, these real estate practices are one factor in the isolation of blacks (including middle-class blacks) in separate residential areas.

Research in the 1990s needs to continue to ferret out the resistance areas wherein class achievement does not override race. Preliminary trends in research suggest that racial barriers exist in terms of promotion to the highest positions of authority,[15] residential segregation,[16] and in the most intimate contacts such as racial intermarriage.[17] The Wilson debate has produced important contributions in the area of race versus class as determinant of blacks' life-chances. Historically race has receded in importance when compared with earlier periods, and this sweep of historical change is, in itself, interesting and important to note. Yet some racial barriers do remain.

The point, again, is that although a black, Latino, or Indian person who achieves a higher social class position is likely to have greater life-chances than a lower-class Anglo, ethnic differentials and barriers are still likely to remain at comparable levels of socioeconomic achievement. Further, the ethnic gap no doubt varies according to the minority group in question. Because of the uniquely high visibility, stigma, and prejudice that blacks have faced, the high-achieving black person is likely to experience a greater residue of ethnic barriers and inconsistent treatment than the high-achieving Latino or American Indian.

The Open Market Place and the White Majority

Not only does socioeconomic advancement bring greater control and privilege to minority persons but such advancement is beginning to have effects on the total society. It is important, therefore, to stress the term *open*. Although a great many studies have noted the increased differentiation within minority groups, the emphasis has been on differentiation in the encapsulated ghetto; the achievement of blacks and Latinos is not seen as having wide ranging effects on the society as a whole. Classic race-class formulations such as Warner's "class within a caste" and Drake and Cayton's "Bronzeville" are primarily intraethnic (e.g., black doctors only treat black patients).[18] The word *open*, then, is a purposeful attempt to break out of this tradition and note how the development of larger skilled and white-collar minority strata will have important effects on the broader society.

How does the socioeconomic advancement of blacks and Chicanos change the larger society? Small group research provides a vehicle for discussing such changes. Several studies involving black and white students in task-oriented game activities show that in "untreated" groups, equal status interaction is not likely to occur.[19] Even with social class held constant, white persons are consistently more likely to dominate game situations and to exert far more lasting influence on group decisions. The interpretation is usually that strong racist beliefs are still embedded in our sentiments, so that blacks are generally felt to be less competent than whites. Thus, in an open situation of status interaction, prior racist expectations structure the situation—white persons become more assertive, black persons more docile. One very "tight" study indicates that equal status interaction among black and white high school boys is possible, but only when the expectations of both whites and blacks are "treated" before the game.[20] In this experiment, black subjects were teachers and white subjects their students; the task was the building of a transistor radio. In addition, "clear evidence of black competence was presented to both black and white subjects by the use of video tapes, which recorded and played back the competent behavior of the black subjects . . ."[21] In a subsequent game situation (having nothing to do with radios), there was found a transferal of the treatment. Whites did not dominate the new situation; the flow of influence was equalitarian. A comparison or control group in which only black expectations were treated did not result in equalitarian interaction—white persons again dominated.

The small group research cited has wide-ranging societal implications. Specifically, it suggests how the development of skilled and white-collar strata in the minorities under discussion will effect broad change in race relations. Our thesis is that the socioeconomic advancement of blacks and Latinos into the dominant occupational structure means that there will be an increase in "conventional" role relationships in which black persons are dominant and white persons subordinate. By *conventional role relationships* we mean complementary roles in which rights, duties, prerogatives, and obligations are clearly spelled out, and where there is a clear dominance-submission pattern.[22] Examples would be:

SERGEANT	DOCTOR	POLICEMAN
Enlisted Man	Patient	Citizen
QUARTERBACK	FOREMAN	DEPARTMENTAL SECRETARY
Team Members	Worker	Students

When a minority group is largely impoverished, or when all mobility takes place only within the minority community, there will be no conventional role relationships in which blacks or

Latinos are in dominant positions. However, upward mobility into the more general occupational structure greatly increases the probability of blacks and Latinos being in at least some conventional role relationships in which they are dominant. When such role relationships occur, the results are likely to be striking for both minority and white participants. White persons are given a kind of stereotype-breaking "treatment" much like the white subjects in the Cohen-Roper small group study.[23] Black participants are likely to feel an increased sense of confidence and assertiveness. The reader may argue that such "treatments" would be extremely rare in a racist society. However, it is increasingly possible that many whites experience blacks in positions of authority in military institutions, as teachers of their children, as professors in their classes, as police officers giving them tickets. For those white persons not directly experiencing minority persons in the course of their work or in some kinds of formal organizations, many experience blacks in positions of authority indirectly, through the mass media.

The increased number of black and Latino newscasters is an interesting example of "treatment" through the media. A good newscaster is articulate, has good diction and presence, and, most important, is informing the audience. The increase of black quarterbacks in college and professional football is another case in point. When such role relationships occur, millions of viewers, both black and white, observe another black person in a position of dominance.

An interesting example of indirect experience with black ascendance was seen in the 1972 Democratic Convention. Yvonne Braithwaite, a black woman and chairperson for the convention, moderated it with great skill and confidence. It would be fascinating to know what was going on in the minds of millions of white viewers. No doubt many could never before have imagined a black women in such a role. In this case, although the viewers were not the direct subordinates in the role relationship, they were viewing subordinate role relationships between chairperson and delegates. We are postulating that the increase of role relationships in which blacks and Mexican Americans are in superordinate positions should have strong leverage effects on traditional race relations. Assessment of the exact effects of these "treatments," however, awaits further research. It is quite possible that the immediate effect will be to equalize the flow of power and influence in many interracial situations; this may or may not result in reduced social distance, or a greater willingness for or interest in social intimacy on the part of either majority or minority persons.

To summarize our thesis, black and Mexican American socioeconomic achievement in the dominant occupational structure is seen as having strong leverage effects on contemporary society. However, socioeconomic achievement per se is too gross a concept to measure all of the changes. The fact that there are more black foremen or electricians or teachers or parole officers does not, in itself, explain all of the recent changes in race relations. The conventionalization of occupationally linked role relationships, in which blacks or Latinos are in dominant roles (vis-a-vis whites), forms a crucial intervening link between minority occupational mobility and changed race relations. These include changes in attitudes toward black competence, greater tendencies toward equalitarian power, interaction in open non-structural situations, and greater confidence for the minority persons playing the dominant role. Diagrammatically, the picture looks like this:

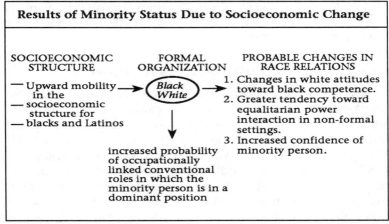

Results of Minority Status Due to Socioeconomic Change

SOCIOECONOMIC STRUCTURE — Upward mobility in the — socioeconomic structure for — blacks and Latinos → Black/White (FORMAL ORGANIZATION) → increased probability of occupationally linked conventional roles in which the minority person is in a dominant position

PROBABLE CHANGES IN RACE RELATIONS
1. Changes in white attitudes toward black competence.
2. Greater tendency toward equalitarian power interaction in non-formal settings.
3. Increased confidence of minority person.

Figure 3.1

Three additional points are crucial to this formulation.

- What gives the black person a dominant position in a conventional role relationship is most typically his or her position in some formal organization (e.g., civil service, school, hospital, military organization, or political office).

White persons do not willingly grant greater power to black persons as a matter of course. Rather, minority persons have fought and collectively pushed for increased racial representation in dominant positions. Such positions by definition grant the incumbents a certain amount of legitimate authority. As blacks and Latinos achieve these positions they automatically have authority over subordinates.

- For many years blacks have played prominent roles in television and cinema. In a few cases, the black actor or actress is the star of the show (e.g., Bill Cosby, Oprah Winfrey, or Arsenio Hall). However, we are not just emphasizing the increased number of blacks in TV and movie roles as "indirect treatments." Rather, we are stressing the increased frequency of role sets in which blacks and whites are both involved and blacks are in dominant positions.

- The small group research noted above suggests that equal status between black and white participants in games is not sufficient to upset traditional racial roles. White persons may exhibit no changes in attitudes when they experience blacks in the same occupational position that they have. Being exposed to minority persons in positions of greater power, however, is likely to upset traditional race roles and stereotypes.

II. THE MINORITY SUBCOMMUNITY PERSPECTIVE

The "open marketplace" model of race relations stresses the interaction of ethnicity and socioeconomic class in integrated situations and the common importance in both majority and minority communities of occupation, education, and income. However, it is likely that spatial segregation and isolation may have produced distinct black and Chicano subcultures which include different—even radically different—evaluations of status from those found in the dominant culture. The obvious implication of this possibility is that there may be a high degree of error in applying "uncorrected" white stratification theory or indices to the black or Latino communities.

Milder versions of the "minority subcommunity" perspective accept occupation, education, and income as important, but postulate that either a) there are significant differences in the relative importance of these factors between the black and the white societies,[24] or b) there are more limited ranges in each of these hierarchies in minority communities resulting in evaluations different from those of the white society for the same position— e.g., a high school principal may be middle-class in white society and upper class in black society.[25] The more extreme separatist versions of this perspective stress the need for a totally different set of criteria in understanding stratification in the black community. For example, family "respectability," unique ghetto life styles, and community participation in organizations have been suggested as alternatives.[26]

This last version of the race relations model has a strong black nationalist ring; it implies that the ghetto has generated its own status dynamics and that culturally unique criteria should be applied to the black community. All the issues that emerge from this approach cannot be discussed in this chapter; however, several points can be brought up which have special significance for the concept of race and class in interaction.

1. The minority subcommunity probably has its strongest effect on class and status evaluations made by lower-class blacks and Chicanos. When color and poverty unite one is likely to find a very high degree of spatial segregation, a low degree of participation in racially integrated institutions, and a somewhat separate set of status criteria. An updated version of Warner's "class within caste" model (see chapter 1) for blacks and Latinos may be helpful in conceptualizing this difference.

    In figure 3.2 the diagonal colorline represents the social distance between castes. It is not of uniform width, but is only thick at its lower-class end. At the middle- and upper-class end, the colorline funnels down to indicate a moderate barrier for middle- and upper-class blacks and an almost permeable barrier for middle-class Latinos. The greater the socioeconomic achievement, the more permeable is the caste line. The "open marketplace" model is more applicable at the middle and upper end of the color-caste line. But the lower-class stratum is likely to be so physically and socially segregated that intra-ethnic contacts are more crucial for one's status or identity. The indexes of occupation, education, and income, which are useful for determining status in the white world, may be incomplete measures of status, respect, or acceptance for lower-class blacks and Latinos.

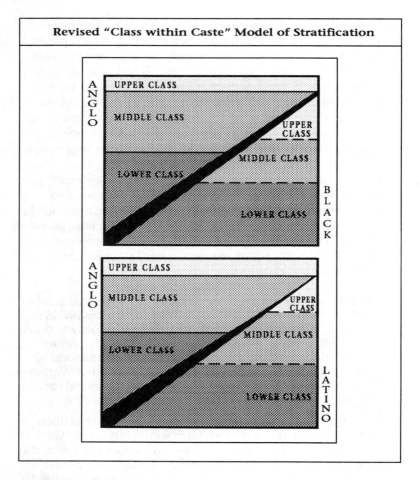

Figure 3.2

In a lower-class section of the Washington, D.C., black ghetto, Ulf Hannerz found that a number of status-graded life styles existed that are unknown to outsiders.[27] He found '"mainstreamers," "swingers," "street families," and "streetcorner men" who were assigned discrete ghetto-specific statuses. Hannerz found that blacks who are denied status and male ego satisfaction through steady employment and support of a family (the norms for the "mainstreamers") may alternately attain respect and status through a unique ghetto-specific masculinity (dressing well, talking well, fighting well, etc.). These alternative sources of identity and status-satisfaction have developed in the ghetto (especially in the lower-class sections) as a result of closed access to the dominant society. This is not to say that the minority subcommunity is only important at the lower-class end of the spectrum.

In analyzing Los Angeles data, Grebler, Moore, and Guzman found that not all higher-income Mexican Americans move away from the barrio. Some may choose to stay in the barrio for status-related reasons. One kind of person who may remain in the colony is the upwardly mobile Mexican American who has a relatively high income but low or moderate occupational prestige—that is, a person with imperfectly crystallized statuses. "For example, a highly paid truck driver of Mexican descent may be able to get more out of life by staying in a predominantly Mexican area, where both his income and his occupation receive deference because they are "above the norm."[28] Status inconsistency may be reduced by remaining in the barrio. Though black and Latino minority communities have developed and persisted because of residential segregation, they may offer certain kinds of desirable status definitions to both the moderate and the low achiever.

Of course there are reasons other than status gains that encourage identifiable minority persons to remain in the ghetto: there are warmer friendships, more sincere contacts in neighborhood shopping, and more helpful neighbors than the minority person is likely to find outside the ghetto

2. Given the strong possibility that alternative stratification systems exist in the minority subcommunity, some scholars have suggested that attempts at class comparisons across majority and minority communities—using the traditional measures of class, occupation, education, and income—are meaningless and futile. We do not agree. Such comparisons seem simply to be incomplete, or in need of further specification by the minority subcommunity. A number of studies have shown that occupation, education, and income are important measures of prestige in both black and white communities.[29] Money will enable an individual to attain many goals. Since it is the societal medium for the exchange of goods and services, money is important for both majority and minority persons regardless of subcommunity evaluations of honor. The minority person who is high on occupation, education, and income scales

objectively has more power to control his or her life than the lower-class minority person, and this holds regardless of microcultural evaluations.

3. Even if occupation, education, and income are accepted as important status determinants in both minority and majority communities, it is still quite possible that the three are weighted differently in different racial groups. A great many studies have shown that education has a uniquely important place in the black community.[30] (Black parents' stress on educational achievement perhaps originates from attitudes inherited from slavery. Unlike a job, education is something that whites can't take away). But in most widely used general indices of social class (e.g., Warner's ISC or Hollingshead's ISP), occupation receives the highest weight.[31] Research shows that blacks often do not receive the same occupational returns for their educational investment as white persons.[32] As a result of such job discrimination, it is quite likely that occupation is a less valid measure of socioeconomic status for black persons than for white persons. There appear to be serious problems in the comparability of occupations between races. One should be wary of studies that apply uncorrected indices across different racial groups.

4. The significance of the minority community is far greater than simply the physical space called a ghetto or barrio. There is, in addition, a psychological concept of a black or Latino community. For some, this may be simply an identification with others of the race who have suffered common oppression. For those blacks and Chicanos who have a more developed ideology, a separate community may symbolize the development of a unified group with a heightened sense of pride and cultural nationalism. The idea of community may mean that blacks, Chicanos, and Indians exert *collective* rather than individual power toward attaining their civil rights.

Harold Cruse, writing in support of a strong, unified black community, separates individual and collective mobility:

> If "we"—the great unskilled, uneducated, un-middle-class, unintegrated, and uninvited masses—staged an all-black-American super boycott merely to get a scattering of hand picked Negroes jobs in big corporations, it just would not be worth the bother. Such are *class* aims, integrationist class aims; they are not *group* economic aims.[33]

Similarly, Alfredo Cuellar, in discussing the growing ideology of Chicanismo, writes:

> *Chicano* ideologues insist that social advance based on material achievement is, in the final analysis, less important than social advance based on *la raza*; they reject what they call the myth of American individualism ... If Mexicans are to confront the problems of their group realistically they must begin to act along collective lines.[34]

The idea of a unified community is extremely important for understanding race-class interaction. To what extent does a strong identification with one's racial stratum outweigh class differences? Enough that lower- and middle-class segments of that stratum hold common outlooks and are willing to engage in common action? That is, how potent are the black and Chicano ideologies in uniting their respective races toward common outlooks and actions? Empirical explorations of race and class should, at a minimum, consider the possibility that a common racial ideology is more significant than a common class ideology.

III. Ethclass

The ethclass model is a third major construct on the way ethnicity and class interact. This approach is especially concerned with stratification outcomes and correlates, that is, the values, the primary group interaction, and the behavior that emerge from the joint occupancy of two hierarchies. According to the ethclass concept, it is fallacious to assume that either class variables or ethnicity variables will alone consistently predict values, interaction, or behavior. To assume that middle-class black persons will have outlooks identical to middle-class white persons is to accept the melting-pot ideology—i.e., that the functional goal of society is assimilation. However, to assume that race or ethnicity always sweeps aside class differences (especially in a united black community or a "black power" ghetto) is equally unsupported by data.

One of the more balanced presentations of this discussion is found in Milton Gordon's *Assimilation in American Life*.[35] Gordon views both class and ethnicity as powerful forces that profoundly affect identity, social participation, and cultural behavior. As a determinant of cultural behavior, life style, and taste, social class is likely to be more important than ethnicity. People of the same social class have similar interests, tastes, and occupational experiences, even if they are from different ethnic groups. However, when it comes to collective identity—a sense of peoplehood in which a common sense of destiny and heritage is shared with a large number of people of the same racial or national descent— ethnicity will be more salient than class position.

Ethnic identification is viewed as a powerful source of collective identity that does not disappear with class mobility. Many blacks, Chicanos, and Indians who make substantial gains will still retain a sense of shared fate with their respective ethnic or racial groups. However, just as class does not completely override race, the ethnic factor is not so powerful that it overrides all class differences. Instead, class outlooks and ethnic identification often unite or blend into what Gordon calls the ethclass or the "social space created by the intersection of the ethnic group with the social class."[36] This is illustrated by figure 3.3, in which the four ethnic populations of this discussion are cross-tabulated with social class.

Ethnicity and Social Class				
			Ethnicity	
	High◄————————————————————————► Low			
SOCIAL CLASS	Anglo	Mexican American	American Indian	Black
High Upper				
▲ Middle				
▼ Working				
Low Lower				

Figure 3.3

Each cell of the table represents a unique social space, a kind of sub-society. Gordon suggests that ethclass has the greatest salience for primary group participation.

> With a person of the same social class but of a different ethnic group, one shares behavioral similarities but not a sense of peoplehood. With those of the same ethnic group but of a different social class, one shares the sense of peoplehood but not behavioral similarities. The only group which meets both of these criteria are people of the same ethnic group *and* same social class.[37]

Following Gordon's logic, middle-class blacks would be far more likely to enter into relaxed, trusting relationships with other middle-Class blacks than with lower-class blacks or middle-class persons of other ethnic groups. Gordon hypothesizes that *cultural behavior* is best predicted by class, *sense of peoplehood* is most often a reflection of ethnicity, and *participation in primary* groups is confined to ethclass.[38]

Surprisingly, the concept of ethclass has received very little attention in race or stratification literature over the years. It appears to be an especially provocative concept for analyzing current race-class interactions among blacks and Chicanos. Class stratification within the black and Mexican-American populations appears to be developing rapidly while black pride and *la raza* are producing heightened ethnic identifications. A concept that posits that unique "social spaces" are determined by a blend of race and class has special relevance to the contemporary scene. Gordon's version of ethclass is chiefly confined to primary group participation. However, Gordon's concept may be expanded to suggest that an "ethclass effect" is any instance in which the behaviors or attitudes of individuals result from the joint effect of ethnicity and social class, this could be cultural outlooks or political behavior as well as the primary group interaction that Gordon suggests. Our expanded version of the concept means that the values and tastes of individuals are not necessarily due to their social class positions alone.

Since blacks, Chicanos, and American Indians are asserting their cultural uniquenesses, but at the same time have distinct class structures, it seems likely that there may be unique blends of ethnicity and class that will be reflected in attitudes and values. Many urban middle-class and working-class Mexican Americans may have an orientation toward mobility and materialistic success that is a blend of the ethnic tradition of family cohesion and solidarity and the middle-class orientation toward individualistic mobility. An often posed question is why lower-class blacks and Chicanos have not united into "Third World" coalitions, since their class interests are so similar. Ethclass would suggest that common class oppression (economic discrimination and unemployment) is not a sufficient condition to produce such unions; there must be commonality on both class and ethnic dimensions. There are many perceptions of the social system (such as feelings of ability to affect city government, distrust of government officials, and beliefs in the openness of the system) that may be profoundly affected by peculiar ethnic-class attitudes rather than solely by either ethnic or class attitudes. Working-class blacks sharing a common occupation (e.g., postal workers) may have an especially high potential for political protest since perceived class exploitation and racial identification reinforce each other in the direction of a unique sense of a shared fate and common grievances.

Ethclass can be a powerful tool for analyzing the society as a whole. The *white working class* (blue-collar workers) is one of the most widely discussed ethclass groups of recent years. White workers are seen as having unique complaints and grievances over the special reparations and dispensations granted to blacks. White workers who can barely afford to send their sons or daughters to college often feel that blacks or other minority persons are given an unfair advantage in both preferential admission and financial aid. They are expressing an ethclass outlook. Their intense grievances and anger are due to a combination of their race and their socioeconomic status.

An important feature of the ethclass model (in its expanded version) is that it takes into account two often discussed race relations outcomes—assimilation versus a separate united ghetto or barrio. We have frequently heard that the ultimate fate of minority groups in American society is upward mobility and assimilation into the dominant middle-class. More recently, with Afro-Centric ideologies there has been a call for control over ghetto institutions and a united black community. The concept ethclass suggests an outcome between these extremes. Class need not eradicate racial identification so that middle-class blacks become carbon copies of middle-class white. Rather, the ethclass perspective focuses attention on the retention of both race and class identities, a combination which produces unique joint effects for each distinct cell.

SUMMARY

A great many points have been covered in the discussion of three models of American race relations and a brief summary may be helpful to keep important points in focus. Figure 3.4 summarizes major perspectives that emerge from each of the three models.

1. Open Marketplace of Status Interaction

POSSIBLE OUTCOMES

a) *Assimilation*
Class achievement completely overrides racial status in terms of power, wealth, and honor (least likely alternative).

b) *Remaining Ethnic Differential*
Social class achievement greatly improves power and life chances of minority persons to the extent that middle-class blacks, Latinos and American Indians have greater power in the general society than lower-class whites. However, some racial barriers, strain, and inconsistencies remain.

c) *Changing Role Relationships*
Majority group's tendency to dominate racial interaction and to perceive minority people as incompetent is weakened by exposure to conventional role relationships in which minority person is in superordinate position.

2. Minority Subcommunities

POSSIBLE OUTCOMES

a) Subcommunity provides alternative sources of honor and prestige (especially for lower-class minority persons).

b) Persons completely identify with their respective ethnic communities. Ethnic position is more important than class.

3. Ethclass

POSSIBLE OUTCOMES

Race and class intersect to form subsocieties with unique attitudes, perceptions of the social system, and primary groups.

Figure 3.4

THE THREE MODELS AND PREDICTION

An important goal of this book is the prediction of attitudes, behavior, and social participation from the joint interaction of race and class. Chapters 5–8 will compare issues of whites, blacks, and Latinos of different socioeconomic levels. The three models—open marketplace, minority subcommunity, and ethclass—help in making these predictions.

It should be noted that the three models are not mutually exclusive, but rather focus on different aspects of race-class interaction. It is quite possible for individuals or groups to be shifting across these three "worlds." Mexican Americans or blacks employed in skilled or white-collar occupations may spend part of their time in an integrated or mostly Anglo work situation. Their jobs and positions in the hierarchy are crucial to their power, self-esteem, and their effect on whites.[39] Yet they may also be a part of a barrio stratification order and have thoroughly compartmentalized self-concepts in that "world." They may also have attitudes and self-concepts that could only be explained by ethclass. For example, they may feel that they are personally doing all right but that their race as a whole is not getting fair treatment.

Open Market and Prediction

The open market model constantly brings us to the question of the degree to which social class achievement changes, modifies, or overrides ethnic status. For example, chapter 7 will explore: to what extent does socioeconomic similarity reduce racial barriers to friendship? That is, does a common class position (similarity in education, tastes, and occupational experiences) reduce the social distance of the colorline such that many middle-class blacks, Anglos, and Latinos could enter into friendship contact?

Ethclass and Prediction

Although the concept of ethclass has great explanatory potential (and a kind of mystical ring) it has not been made operational or tested empirically. Several empirical directions for the concept are used in later chapters:
1) In chapter 5, it is suggested that the values, aspirations and outlooks of middle-class blacks often represent a complex blend of materialism, racial militance and racial identification;

2) Data in chapter 7, indicate that lower-class black and Mexican American children face a pile-up of ethnic and class barriers in obtaining a quality education.

To qualify as an ethclass analysis, there must be, at a minimum, a two-way comparison: a vertical comparison with persons of the same ethnic group and different classes, and a horizontal comparison with persons of the same class but different ethnic groups. However, if we take all the ethclass cells (figure 3.1) as our operational matrix, there are a great many horizontal and vertical comparisons to be made. That is, to be completely exhaustive in determining an ethclass effect we would need to show that middle-class blacks are different from middle-class whites, lower-class Chicanos, upper-class Indians, etc. For obvious reasons (such as the cost to include this many subgroups in a survey and the difficulty in locating certain subgroups in representative numbers) the complete study of ethclass effects would be nearly impossible. To trim the equation down to one essential comparison, a minority group ethclass (such as middle-class black or lower-class Chicano) should differ both from the same class in the Anglo majority and a different class in the minority group. For example, in figure 3.5 middle-class blacks (the ethclass under study) must be shown to be different from middle-class whites as well as from lower-class blacks.

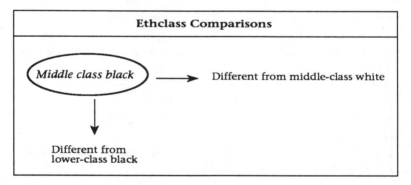

Figure 3.5

The horizontal comparison measures the class effect (middle-class black vis-a-vis middle-class white) while the vertical comparison measures the race effect. If middle-class blacks contrast with both comparison groups we can assume an ethclass effect.

A third and fascinating possibility of ethclass prediction would deal with race and class consciousness. Barely explored is the possibility of race and class consciousness uniting into special ethclass combinations. For example, a revised Marxian conflict perspective might lead us to the hypothesis that blacks or Chicanos who identify strongly with both their race and a working-class socioeconomic position will be especially radical in their outlook and behavior. In this example, a particular combination of subjective race and class are combining to determine political attitudes and behavior. Note, in this case, a single racial group is involved but both race and class are varying in terms of degrees of attachment and shared fate with the two strata.

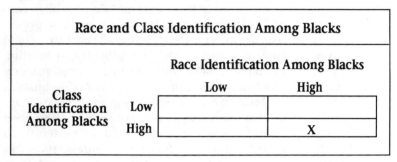

Figure 3.6

Minority Subcommunity as a Specification Variable

The minority subcommunity may provide important specifications in our race-class predictions as illustrated in figure 3.7.

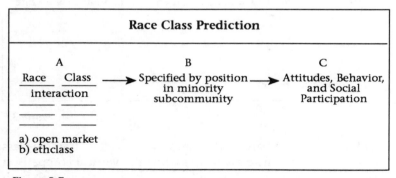

Figure 3.7

Suppose we were interested in the relationship between race, class, and self-esteem. Taking an ethclass approach, we might predict that lower-class blacks will be "uniquely low" in self-esteem. The prediction would involve the A and C components of figure 3.4. However, the minority subcommunity would provide an important specification. Lower-class blacks who are highly integrated into a minority subcommunity and have a very solid reputation in the street culture may not have low self-esteem at all. That is, the ghetto community serves as a strong buffer against reduced self worth due to being poor and black. Our revised prediction, taking into account A, B, and C, would be that lower-class blacks will have low self-esteem only when they have no alternative sources of self-respect from ghetto life. The ghetto community is a crucial specification variable in this prediction because the outcome of self-esteem is largely derived from social honor in various stratification orders. However, if we were predicting action such as willingness to file suit in the face of discrimination, class position in the dominant society (A) would be more directly related to the outcome (C) irrespective of the minority community (B). High occupation, education, and income increase the probability of filing suit regardless of ghetto honor.

NOTES

1. See Gerhard E. Lenski, "Status Crystallization: A Non-Vertical Dimension of Social Status," *American Sociological Review* 19 (August, 1954): 405–413.

2. William Julius Wilson, *The Declining Significance of Race: Blacks and Changing American Institutions* (Chicago: University of Chicago Press, 1978).

3. William Julius Wilson, "The Declining Significance of Race," in Norman R. Yetman and C. Hoy Steele (eds.), *Majority and Minority: The Dynamics of Race and Ethnicity in American Life*, 3rd edition (Boston: Allyn and Bacon, 1982), 391.

4. See William Julius Wilson, "The Black Community in the 1980s: Questions of Race, Class, and Public Policy," in Norman R. Yetman (ed.), *Majority and Minority: The Dynamics of Race and Ethnicity in American Life*, 4th edition (Boston: Allyn and Bacon, 1985) and William Julius Wilson, *The Truly Disadvantaged* (Chicago: University of Chicago Press, 1987).

5. Pettigrew, "The Changing—Not Declining—Significance of Race," in Charles Vert Willie (ed.), *Caste and Class Controversy on Race and Poverty: Round Two Of The Wilson/Willie Debate* (Dix Hills, NY: General Hall, 1989), 110.

6. Ibid.

7. Charles V. Willie, "The Inclining Significance of Race," in Norman R. Yetman and C. Hoy Steele (eds.), (Boston: Allyn and Bacon, 1982), 393–398.

8. Ibid., 398.

9. Ibid., 398.

10. William Julius Wilson, "The Declining Significance of Race—Revisited but not Revised," in Norman R. Yetman and C. Hoy Steele (eds.) *Majority and Minority: The Dynamics of Race and Ethnicity in American Life*, 3rd edition (Boston: Allyn and Bacon, 1982), 399–405.

11. See Douglas S. Massey and Brendan P. Mullan, "Processes of Hispanic and Black Spatial Assimilation," in Norman R. Yetman and C. Hoy Steele (eds.) *Majority and Minority: The Dynamics of Race and Ethnicity in American Life*, 4th edition (Boston: Allyn and Bacon, 1982), 352–367.

12. Douglas S. Massey and Nancy A. Denton, "Trends in the Residential Segregation of Blacks, Hispanics, and Asians 1970–1980," *American Sociological Review* 52 (1987): 802–825.

13. Massey and Mullan, "Processes of Hispanic and Black Spatial Assimilation," 368.

14. Diana M. Pearce, "Gatekeepers and Homeseekers: Institutional Factors in Racial Steering," *Social Problems* 26 (1979): 325–42.

15. James R. Kluegel, "Causes and Costs of Racial Exclusion From Job Authority," *American Sociological Review* 43 (June, 1978): 285–301.

16. See Pearce, "Gatekeepers and Homeseekers"; Massey and Mullan, "Processes of Hispanic and Black Spatial Assimilation"; Massey and Denton, "Trends on the Residential Segregation of Blacks, Hispanics, and Asians 1970–1980".

17. See Gunnar Myrdal, *The American Dilemma: The Negro Problem and Modern Democracy*. 2 vols. (New York: Harper and Brothers); Gerald David Jaynes and Robin M. Williams, A Common Destiny—Blacks and American Society (Washington, D.C.: National Academy Press, 1989).

18. St. Clair Drake and Horace R. Clayton, *Black Metropolis: A Study of Negro Life in a Northern City* (New York: Harcourt, Brace, 1945). See also W. Lloyd Warner's Introduction in Allison Davis, Burleigh R. Gardner, and Mary R. Gardner, *Deep South* (Chicago: University of Chicago Press, 1941).

19. See I. Katz, Judith Goldston, and L. Benjamin, "Behavior and Productivity in Biracial Work Groups, " *Human Relations* 11 (May, 1958): 123–141, and I. Katz and L. Benjamin "Effects of White Authoritarianism in Biracial Work Groups," *Journal of Abnormal Social Psychology* 61 (November, 1960): 448–456.

20. Elizabeth G. Cohen and Susan S. Roper, "Modification of Interracial Interaction Disability: An Application of Status Theory," *American Sociological Review* 61 (November, 1972): 643–657.

21. Ibid., 646.

22. This conception of "conventional role" is taken from Shibutani's discussion. See Tamotsu Shibutani, *Society and Personality* (Englewood Cliffs, N.J.: Prentice Hall, 1961), 46–54.

23. Cohen and Roper, "Modification of Interracial Interaction Disability: An Application of Status Theory."

24. See, for example, Norvel D. Glenn, "Negro Prestige Criteria: A Case Study in the Bases of Prestige," *American Journal of Sociology* 68 (May, 1963): 645–657.

25. See, for example, Andrew Billingsley, *Black Families in White America* (Englewood Cliffs, N.J.: Prentice Hall, 1968), 122.

26. An excellent summary of this separatist approach is found in Donald I. Warren and Patrick C. Easto's "White Stratification Theory and Black Reality: A Neglected Problem of American Sociology" (paper presented at the sixty-seventh annual meeting of the American Sociological Association, August 28-31, 1972), 8-15. See also, Billingsley, *Black Families in White America*, 124; Ulf Hannerz, *Soulside* (New York: Columbia Press, 1969), especially chs. 2 and 4; and Jay R. Williams, Social Stratification and the Negro American: An Exploration of Some Problems in Social Class Measurement" (Ph. D. diss., Duke University).

27. Hannerz, *Soulside*, chs. 2 and 4.

28 Leo Grebler, Joan W. Moore, and Ralph C. Guzman, *The Mexican American People* (New York: Free Press, 1970), 329.

29. For example, Siegel, after an exhaustive study of occupational prestige with Negro and white samples, concluded: "The assertion that there is a community-wide prestige hierarchy of occupations within the Negro community, based upon Negro experiences in occupations, just does not square with the facts. Instead, Negros appear to be evaluating occupations in the same world as everyone else evaluates them and to be employing essentially the same information and the same combination of criteria as everyone else." See Paul M. Siegel, "Occupational Prestige in the Negro Subculture," in Edward O. Laumann (ed.) *Social Stratification: Research and Theory of the 1970's* (New York: Bobbs-Merrill Co., 1970): 169.

30. Drake and Cayton, *Black Metropolis: A Study of Negro Life in a Northern City*, Glenn, "Negro Prestige Criteria: A Case Study in the Bases of Prestige," Seymour Parker and Robert J. Kleiner, *Mental Illness in the Urban Negro Community* (New York: Free Press, 1966).

31. W. Lloyd Warner, Marchia Meeker, and Kenneth Eells, *Social Class in America: Manual of Procedure for the Measurement of Social Status* (New York: Harper & Brothers, 1960); and August B. Hollingshead and Frederick C. Redlich, *Social Class and Mental Illness* (New York: John Wiley & Sons, 1958),

32. One of the most sophisticated studies on this point is Peter M. Blau and Otis Dudley Duncan's *The American Occupational Structure* (New York: John Wiley & Sons, 1967), ch. 6.

33. Harold Cruse, *The Crisis of the Negro Intellectual* (New York: William Morrow, 1967), 312.

34. Joan W. Moore with Alfredo Cuellar, *Mexican Americans* (Englewood Cliffs, N.J.: Prentice Hall, 1970), 153.

35. Milton M. Gordon, *Assimilation in American Life* (New York: Oxford University Press, 1964), especially chs. 2 and 3.

36. Ibid., 51.

37. Ibid., 53.

38. Ibid., 52–53.

39 See Alfred McClung Lee, *Multivalent Man* (New York: Braziller, 1964).

4

Social Mobility
The Rise of Middle Class and Skilled Working Class Strata for Blacks and Mexican Americans

To what extent has a middle class strata developed in the black population? Does the emergence of a middle class group mean that poverty has also been reduced among blacks? How do the trends in black mobility compare with those of Mexican Americans? These are the questions posed in this chapter.

Mobility of Blacks

Although black Americans often have been associated with poverty or working-class positions, recent data show a substantial and growing black middle class. Farley suggests four factors that account for these gains.[1] First, after World War I and in even greater numbers after World War II, blacks left the rural South and moved to urban industrial areas with their greater job opportunities. Second, since the 1950s, black demands for civil rights have increased. Third, more liberal court rulings and laws forbid discrimination in many areas of social life. And fourth, prejudiced attitudes of whites toward blacks have declined.

The emergence of a middle class from an oppressed minority group can be an extremely important development for the mobility and progress of that group as a whole. Middle-class black Americans have greater resources to fight discrimination. Middle-class blacks, in comparison with those in poverty circumstances, have greater organizational skills, political and business connections, more money, and knowledge of redress channels—skills and resources that are vital for breaking down discrimination barriers. In the black Civil Rights Movement, for example, the most involved participants were of middle-class origins.[2] One study found that in cities with a more developed black middle class, there is a greater probability of electing a black mayor.[3]

Middle-class resources are not always used to improve the status of an ethnic group, however. Many middle-class persons are assimilated into the mainstream, and their new skills and resources do not benefit the oppressed group to which they once belonged. One may frequently hear labels such as "bourgeois" or "Uncle Tom" applied to some successful blacks or "Tio Taco" and "Uncle Tomahawk" applied to some successful Mexican Americans and Indians.[4] A developing middle class within a subjugated ethnic group can either mean better resources and skills to fight discrimination or an increased tendency to assimilate into the cultural mainstream.

The potential of the middle-class segment of an ethnic group to improve the lot of the entire group depends on 1) the strength of ethnic ideologies favoring ethnic solidarity and ethnic involvement and 2) the permeability of the color line, or the ease with which middle-class ethnics can cross the color line to acquire resources and acceptance in the dominant white society.

The following hypothesis about the role of middle class status within ethnic minorities is advanced:

> If a rising middle class of an oppressed ethnic minority continues to face color stigma, social exclusion, and discrimination, the rising middle-class segment will often use its resources to attempt to change the system. But if the rising middle class of an oppressed racial minority faces a greatly reduced level of color discrimination, much of the potential for protest will be splintered or drained off.[5]

In chapter 2, for example, we noted that middle-class Mexican Americans face less ethnic prejudice in such areas as housing, integration, and marriage than do blacks. If the color line is more permeable for middle-class Chicanos, then we would expect less militance from them and more militance from middle-class blacks. This, of course, is an aggregate prediction referring to group probabilities. Some young Chicano individuals are entering professional schools for an expressed purpose of returning to the barrio and making available new channels of legal redress or health care to the Chicano poor. For these highly committed Mexican Americans, the ideology of their ethnic group would seem to override the possibility of assimilation based on their middle-class status.

Besides the possibility of middle-class skills aiding the group as a whole, there is another important reason to study the growth of the black middle class. Some accounts on the size of an emerging black middle class may have led to a belief on the part of whites that racial discrimination no longer exists. For example, one study announced that fully 52 percent of all blacks were in middle-class positions. One can only come to this sort of conclusion by using very low cutting points for "middle-class."[6] But such methodological details usually are not stressed in these reports. An image of a fairly large "new" black middle class has been created and whites as a result may no longer see a need for special programs for black Americans. "On the contrary, increasing numbers of whites are charging 'reverse discrimination' and are strongly resisting the use of their tax dollars for social programs on behalf of the poor and minorities."[7] If many of the accounts on the size of the black middle class are inflated or exaggerated, then it is important to study more carefully the size of this group 1) using a variety of measures and cutting points and 2) noting which segments of the black population have made gains, and which segments have not. This we propose to do in the following pages.

Proportion of Blacks in the Middle Group Income

A variety of data from 1970-1992 census reports present evidence for a moderate size black middle-income group. In 1991, black median family income was only $21,550 compared to the white median of $37,780. However, median income figures often lose or disguise dynamics within the black population. Family income of over $35,000 was often used as a fairly solid definition of middle income in the late 1980s and early 1990s. Using this cutting point, about 30 percent of all black families (compared to 54 percent of white families) were earning over $35,000 in 1991, 26 percent in the South, and 35 percent in the North and West.[8] This proportion of middle income black families varies considerably according to the composition of the family. In 1991, about 47 percent of all black families were married couple families. In many of these families, both husband and wife were in the labor force, and for these "married-couple-husband-wife-earner" families, fully 56 percent were in the middle-income category (compared with 70 percent of comparable white families). In short, when averaging all black families together, about 30 percent in the nation are in the middle income (or higher) category, and 35 percent of black families in the North and West are. However, for married couple families with both husband and wife in the labor force, the proportion of middle income families is a considerably higher 56 percent.

What about mobility? Has the middle income group changed through time? It is difficult to achieve perfect comparability in census reports over time. Earlier reports in the late 1960s and early 1970s noted a definite increase in the black middle-income group. Adjusting for inflation, the proportion of black families in the North and West in middle-income categories (above $15,000 at that time) increased from 14 percent in 1965 to 26 percent in 1974. What appears to be happening is that one segment of the black community (married couple families with two breadwinners) continue to move into middle categories and catch up with whites in earnings. But the proportion of families maintained by women with no husband present has also increased in the black population and the much lower incomes in these households depress the overall black income figures. These differences can be noted further in income gap analyses.

The Income Gap

Recent data show that there has not been a substantial closing of the income gap when black families as a whole are compared with white families as a whole. In 1947, the average black family income amounted to only 51 percent of the average white family income. By 1991, forty-four years later, the gap was a discouraging 57 percent.

There are, however, great variations in the black-white income gap according to region of the country, age of the respondents, whether it is a single parent or couple family, and whether one or both of the spouses works. If one locates certain subgroups within the black and white populations, the income gap is much smaller, that is, black family income is much closer to white family income. In analyses of the 1970 census, a very optimistic finding was noted: the income gap was completely eliminated (parity of earnings) between young black families residing outside the South in which both husband and wife worked, compared to comparable white families. "For these young families, the ratio of Negro to white income was about 96 percent in 1970, up from 78 percent in 1959."[9]

Similar findings can be noted in the more current 1991 reports. For married couple families with both husband and wife wage earners, black families made 76 percent of the income comparable white families in the South, and 92 percent in the North and West (age was not factored in as a variable in this report). Thus, from the standpoint of a rising black middle class, one segment of the black population (married couple families, both husband and wife earners, residing outside the South) is earning approximately the same income as a comparable segment of the white population. Some reports caution, however, that consideration of black working wives is crucial for the interpretation of the income parity findings. Young black wives in the North and West earned more than their white counterparts and thus made a greater contribution to household income. This was true because black wives were more likely to hold a job year round.[10]

Occupation

Besides income, occupation is a major index of social class. Many would consider it a superior measure to income, since it taps economic standing, prestige and authority over others. The data in table 4.1 show that substantial differences continue to exist between blacks and whites in the type of occupational positions they hold. About 31 percent of employed black males are engaged in the most physically exhausting, poorly paid and least prestigious jobs— operators, fabricators, and laborers—compared to 19 percent of white males. Similarly, higher proportions of black females than white females are in the operators category (12 versus 7 percent) as well as the service occupations (28 versus 16 percent). Many of these service occupations (such as house cleaning) are poorly paid and involve low status. On the other hand, from the perspective of a rising middle class, it can be seen that 31 percent of all employed black males are in white-collar occupations (executive/ managerial, professional, technical, sales and administrative support). Another 14.8 percent are in the skilled blue-collar positions (precision production, craft, and repair). Forty-six percent of employed black males, then, are in white-collar or skilled blue-collar occupations. Many skilled blue-collar and white-collar jobs provide at least a moderate degree of challenge, financial reward, and status in society.

Occupational Distribution of the Labor Force by Sex and Race, 1992					
Percentage of Employed Labor Force					
	Males			Females	
Occupational category	Total	White	Black	Total	White	Black
Executive, administrative, and managerial	13.5	14.3	7.1	11.4	12.0	7.2
Professional specialty	12.2	12.5	7.0	16.0	16.5	12.3
Technicians and related support	3.4	3.4	3.1	3.9	3.8	3.8
Sales occupations	11.4	12.0	5.7	12.4	12.9	8.7
Administrative support, including clerical	6.0	5.7	8.5	27.5	27.9	25.7
Service occupations	10.2	9.1	19.0	17.9	16.5	27.9
Precision production, craft, and repair	18.8	19.5	14.8	2.1	2.0	2.1
Operators, fabricators, and laborers	19.9	18.9	31.3	7.9	7.2	12.0
Farming, forestry, and fishing	4.6	4.7	3.6	1.0	1.1	0.3
	100.0	100.0	100.0	100.0	100.0	100.0

Source: U.S. Department of Labor, Employment and Earnings (January 1993), p. 194. Note: Figures may not add to totals because of rounding

Table 4.1

An even higher proportion of black females (58 percent) are in white-collar categories with a small proportion (2 percent) in precision production. Note that a higher proportion of black women (19 percent) than black men (14 percent) are in the two most prestigious white collar categories (executive, and professional specialty). Blacks have made considerable gains in moving into white-collar occupations. A comparison of 1966, 1977 and 1992 census data shows that the proportion of blacks (male and female combined) with white-collar jobs has greatly increased in this 22 year time period from 16 percent to 35 percent to 45 percent.

The above figures most likely give an exaggerated estimate of the size of the black middle class, especially so for black females where so many (26 percent) are concentrated in the administrative support (largely clerical) category. Clerical work typically means low salaries, little authority over others, and limited opportunity for advancement. Many in the administrative support category are in marginally middle-class clerical occupations.

An alternative way to categorize middle-class occupations is to combine white-collar jobs of high and mid-level prestige—executive/managerial, professional, technical and sales (but not administrative support-clerical)—with the more challenging and better paid blue-collar jobs (precision production/crafts). About 38 percent of employed black males and 34 percent of employed black females are in middle-class occupations, according to this definition.

The occupation index results in a slightly larger estimate of the size of the black middle class (36 percent middle class) compared to the family income index (30 percent middle class). One reason for this discrepancy is that the occupation data involve only employed persons, whereas the income data include families with very low incomes due to unemployment.

Educational Attainment

A very encouraging trend in black-white socioeconomic comparisons is that young black adults are continuing to narrow the gap in educational attainment. Table 4.2 presents educational attainment data for young blacks and young whites (25–34 years old) from 1960 to 1992. Note the dramatic increase in the proportion of blacks completing 4 years of high school or 1–3 years of college. In 1960, only 29 percent of young blacks had completed 4 years of high school or 1–3 years of college; this increased to 70 percent in 1992. Not only is this a very large change through time, but the 1992 black percentage is about the same as the white percentage (63 percent). The proportion of young blacks completing 4 years of college has also increased notably over time, from 4 percent in 1960 to 12 percent in 1992, though this percentage is considerably below the white percentage of 24.2 percent. It's important to note that while the percentage of blacks completing four years of college increased markedly between 1970 and 1980 (from 6 to 12 percent) and the college completion differential between blacks and whites narrowed, there is virtually no change in the black college completion rate between 1980 and 1992. At the time of this writing, there is a great deal of concern that black college enrollments across the country have declined notably from the 1970s. Quite likely, this is one reason the black rate has not significantly increased in the most recent period. However, the white rate also has not changed in the most recent eight year period, indicating that other (non-racial) factors such as ease of getting financial aid for college attendance may have changed.

	BLACK		WHITE	
	4 years high school or college 1–3	4 or more years college	4 years high school or college 1–3	4 or more years college
1960	28.9%	4.3%	49.4%	11.7%
1970	47.3%	6.1 %	59.5%	16.6%
1980	62.5%	11.7%	61.7%	25.1%
1992	69.8%	12.0%	62.9%	24.2%

Educational Attainment of Blacks and Whites 25 to 34 Years Old 1960 to 1992

Source: U.S. Bureau of the Census, *Population Profile of the United States, 1992*, Current Population Reports Series P-23, No. 185. U.S. Department of Commerce.

Table 4.2

Elected Black Officials

The increase in the number of elected officials can be used as a rough index of an increase in power or influence for a minority group. Beginning in the mid-1960s, there was a tremendous surge in the number of blacks elected to office. The total number of black elected officials in 1988 was 6,829, a large increase from 3,503 in 1975 and 1,469 in 1970. More specifically, the number of mayors increased from 48 in 1970 to 392 in 1985. The numbers are far lower at the national level. The number of U.S. Representatives increased from 9 in 1970 to 20 in 1985. The number of U.S. Senators has alternated between 0 and 1 during the same 15 year period. At the time of this writing, blacks have been elected to every elective public office except president and vice president. Nevertheless, the number of black elected officials is a small percentage of the entire American political system. "As of 1985, 4.0 percent of all elected officials in the South were black, as were 0.7 percent of those outside the South, and 1.2 percent of those in the nation as a whole . . ."[11]

From several studies Jaynes and Williams conclude that "the single most important determinant of black candidates' success is the racial composition of the electoral jurisdictions; the higher the black percentage of the voting-age population, the higher the probability of the election of a black to office . . ."[12] This helps to explain why the largest increases in elected black officials have come at the state and lower levels of government. In short, there has been a tremendous increase in the number of black elected officials overall, but the greatest increases are at the level of state and city offices, and black elected officials still constitute a small percentage of the American political system.

Mobility in Sports for Black Americans

It is widely stated that the institution of sport is one of the areas in American society in which blacks have found opportunity and equality. Obviously, there have been large increases in the number of black athletes in college and professional sports in the last several decades, and this increase in itself seems to attest to the view that sport is a major channel of upward mobility. More precise studies, however, have long noted racial inequalities in sports. For example, the concept of "stacking" refers to the fact that blacks, as compared to whites, have not been placed in key thinking positions on teams such as quarterback, pitcher, catcher, pointguard etc.[13] Another charge is that blacks are very unrepresented as head coaches, owners and general managers. In college sports programs, there has long been the charge that blacks, recruited with scholarships to perform that require their primary commitment to the athletic department, often wind up in four years with no degree. Have there been significant improvements in opportunity for blacks in the institution of sport?

On the issue of stacking, *Sports Illustrated*, in a 1991 article titled "The Black Athlete Revisited," notes that black quarterbacks were never seen on college teams in 1968 (the year of their first report).[14] By comparison, in recent seasons (e.g., 1990-1991), ". . . Auburn, Georgia, Michigan, Michigan State, Notre Dame, Tennessee, and USC—as well as last year's co-national champions, Georgia Tech and Colorado—have all started black quarterbacks."[15] In the National Football League (NFL) there were eight black quarterbacks at the end of the 1990 season. The *Sports Illustrated* (*SI*) writers, though noting definite improvements in numbers of black quarterbacks, argue that the figures are less impressive than they could be. For example, the Study of Sport in Society at Northeastern University notes that 61 percent of the approximately 1300 NFL players are black. The eight black quarterbacks made up only 9.8 percent of the

82 signal callers.[16] By contrast, in the National Basketball Association (NBA), 72 percent of the players are black "and the great majority of heroes and thinkers are black."[17] In basketball, SI notes, there has been a color-blind national admiration for highly personable and outstanding players such as Magic Johnson, Michael Jordan, and David Robinson. In baseball there were far fewer blacks holding pivotal "thinking" positions. SI reports only 12 black pitchers in the majors, and no black catchers.

The charge that black college athletes are used as sports commodities but not given the necessary support to graduate is borne out in 1980s statistics. An NCAA survey of graduation rates for black athletes shows that of athletes who entered college in the 1984–85 season, only 26.6 percent of blacks graduated compared with 52.2 percent of whites.[18] There has been a great deal of concern on this topic in the national Congress and on college campuses. SI reports that in House subcommittee hearings on athletes' graduation rates, one congressman stated that he was outraged that blacks

> . . . comprise only 7 percent of all college students while black athletes make up 56 percent on college basketball teams and 37 percent of football teams. It's time we highlighted the fact that it is simply no longer acceptable for athletes—and particularly black athletes—to be used up as sports commodities and then discarded when their eligibility is over.[19]

In terms of blacks in management, SI reports that the NFL had no black owners and general managers in 1968. In 1991, the League still had no black owners or general managers, and only one of 28 head coaches was black. By contrast, the National Basketball Association has far more blacks in management. At the end of the 1991 season, the NBA had one black co-owner, five black head coaches, and five black general managers. Baseball did not fare as well: there were no black owners and black general managers, and only two black field managers. The Center for the Study of Sport gave this report card on minority hiring in sports management for 1991: the National Basketball Association, a C+, and Major League Baseball got a C. In sum, the *Sports Illustrated* assessment of opportunity changes for blacks between 1968 and 1991 indicates overall progress but with continued inequalities.

This conclusion is in agreement with studies in sociology that note that sports provide a very limited channel of mobility for young blacks. Harry Edwards, a professor of sociology and a consultant on racial affairs to major league teams, notes that there is extreme competition for very few professional sports positions.[20] Young blacks can be eliminated at any point along this mobility channel. It is unrealistic, in aggregate terms, to think that large numbers of blacks will reach these positions. The unrealistic focus on pro sports prematurely shuts off a focus on studies or the pursuit of other career options. In a statement in 1991, Edwards in comparing the competition with the late 60s, notes that the competition is more fierce than ever. "Because there is much more money at stake and so much more pressure to get that money, kids are targeted earlier, cut off from reality earlier, immersed in the competition for the big prizes earlier. . ."[21] Edwards feels that both the black and white communities have exaggerated the opportunities in the sports institution for upward mobility. A small number of blacks have been incredibly successful, but less discussed are the numbers who do not receive college support after high school or, once in college, do not have a degree or a professional contract after 4–5 years of playing time.

The Division in Black America

The data summarized above suggest that a moderate-size middle class and upper working class group has developed in the black population and is likely to show continued growth in the future. However, a number of recent studies indicate that not all blacks are making progress; one segment of the black population has moved up, while another segment has made no gains or moved down. Many reports present data only for the *total* black population and thus mask these counter-trends.

About 30 percent of black families were below the poverty level in 1991, an increase from the 28 percent in 1979. The 1991 poverty rate for black families was over three times that of the white rate (9 percent). Children are especially affected by these high poverty rates. About 46 percent of all black children under the age of 18 in families were living in poverty versus 16 percent of white children.[22]

The poverty and downward mobility trend is exemplified by black unemployment rates that have increased in recent years. Usually the black unemployment rate is about twice as high as the white rate. However, in the late 1970s and during the recession of 1981–82, the unemployment gap increased considerably. In 1992, the unemployment rate for blacks was 2.3 times higher than for whites (14 percent of blacks were unemployed versus 6 percent of whites). The unemployment rate for blacks changed considerably with changes in the economy. In 1980, the black unemployment rate was 14.3 percent. The rate increased to an extremely high 19.5 percent in 1983, just after the end of the recession. The rate dropped to a low of 11.7 percent in 1988.

Of considerable concern is the very high unemployment rate for black teenagers (16–19 years). In the post recession period of 1983, the black teen unemployment rate was an incredible 48.5 percent, far higher than the white teen rate of 19.3 percent. By 1988 the rate for black teenagers had declined to 32.4 percent, which is still 2.5 times higher than the white teen rate of 13.1 percent.[23]

William Wilson maintains that the increases in black joblessness in the last two decades are due to deep structural changes in the economy or what he calls "de-industrialization."[24] Across the country, there has been a trend of plant shutdown in manufacturing and smokestack industries. These industries were usually located in central city areas, and were major employers of blacks. With the decline in smokestack industry jobs, there has been a concomitant increase in high skill service sector jobs (such as real estate planning and high technology computer jobs). But these are not jobs into which the unemployed can easily move. They typically require post high school training and experience. The shutdown in large manufacturing plants also leads to diminished job opportunities, because satellite stores surrounding the industrial hub are affected. That is, the restaurants, dry cleaning establishments and other small stores surrounding the industrial plant also close.

Wilson maintains that despair and joblessness has also increased as middle-class blacks have become more separated geographically from the lower class. Middle-class blacks have increasingly moved from central city areas to the more desirable suburbs. The flight of the middle class results in an absence of successful role models for black youth in the inner city. Moreover, there is an absence of networking in which successful blacks can help a young person find his or her first job or give them advice on how to break into a particular field.

Given evidence for a division in black America, with one segment clearly moving into middle class occupations and incomes, and another segment more firmly entrenched in poverty, what are the characteristics of those moving up or down? Moynihan argues that the "schism in black America" results in part from the black family structure.[25] Female headed families did not make substantial gains in income or occupational status, whereas two-parent families did. The proportion of families maintained by women alone has increased in all ethnic groups. However, the proportion is far higher for blacks than for whites or Hispanics. In 1992, 46 percent of black family households were maintained by women as contrasted with 13 percent of white families, and 24 percent of Hispanic families. There was an especially dramatic increase in the proportion of black female headed households between 1970 and 1980 (from 28 percent to 40 percent).[26] The rate of increase in female headed households reflects higher levels of divorce and separation as well as a rise in never married black women who maintain their own families. Wilson argues that the de-industrialization and resulting unemployment trends noted above is an important cause of the rise in female headed households in the black population. That is, joblessness leads to family instability. Obviously, income levels are likely to be lower in families maintained by women with no husband present, and these families are least likely to be moving into middle class occupations and income levels. In 1991, the median income of black-female householder families was only $11,410 compared with $19,550 for white-female householder families. The ratio of black to white median family income for female householder families was 58 percent.

In addition to family structure, blacks under thirty-five years old living in the North and West were more likely to make gains than middle-aged and older blacks living in the South. Education is linked with the up-down pattern. Blacks with any college experience made gains in income in recent years as contrasted with the small or non-existent gains made by those with no more than a high school education. Again, one segment of the black population has made substantial gains in the last twenty five years; another segment has made no gains and remains firmly entrenched in poverty.

The counter-trends in black mobility can be used to support opposite political views. Those arguing that special programs are no longer necessary for blacks can stress the "up" side of the mobility story, while those arguing for new programs to combat the unemployment, hopelessness and despair in inner city areas can stress the "down" side of the trends. Social planners should fully consider these data and not let the rising middle class create an illusion of overall black progress.[27]

MOBILITY OF MEXICAN AMERICANS

Although much data relevant to the mobility patterns of black Americans exist, it is much more difficult to note the movement of Mexican-Americans up or down the class structure. The biggest obstacle for the sociologist studying mobility is the changing Census Bureau classification of Hispanics over the last four decades. At first, Mexican Americans were classified as Caucasians and in no way distinguished from the white population. In 1960, "Spanish surname" was the term used to encompass Mexican Americans as well as all other Latinos. In 1970, the even broader category "Spanish language/Spanish surname" was used. Only in the mid-1970s census reports, are persons of Mexican origin separated from Cubans, Puerto Ricans, and other Spanish-speaking groups. Because of this diversity of classification, it is difficult to make systematic comparisons through time. We will have to settle for a much less precise overview involving some quantitative data and more general historical and qualitative summaries from several Mexican American scholars.

From Rural Farm Workers to an Urban Working Class

Mexican Americans are often depicted as rural, migratory farm laborers. This stereotype of the Mexican American has probably been reinforced by the widely publicized grape and lettuce boycotts led by United Farm Workers and Cesar Chavez. Although migratory farm laborers are an extremely important population, especially when considering issues of justice and ethnic solidarity, they are a minority of Mexican Americans. Most Mexican Americans are concentrated in urban areas and employed in urban occupations.

The 1990 census shows that nine-tenths of the Mexican American population lived in urban areas. The typical occupations of Mexican Americans are blue-collar semi-skilled jobs (males), or clerical and service jobs (females) in an urban setting, not migratory farm labor. A middle-class segment has also emerged. This does not mean that all discrimination battles have been won, for as Penalosa explains ". . . to assert that Mexican Americans have largely left behind the problems associated with migratory agricultural labor is not to say that they have no problems. It is rather that now their problems have become those of an under privileged urban minority group."[28]

As was true of the black American experience, World War II brought a dramatic shift from rural to urban occupations for Mexican Americans. During World War II, young Mexican

Americans gained new skills in the military and in war-production plants, skills which they transferred to urban industrial jobs when the war ended.[29] World War II also served to highlight the unequal status of Mexican Americans, who fought and gave their lives in defense of the United States, yet continued to face discrimination as returning civilians.

In urban industrial environments there is typically an emphasis on skill, merit, and rational efficiency rather than family lineage or race. The rigidity of caste barriers declines and there are more opportunities for employment. The large-scale migration to urban industrial areas meant that the Mexican American population was changing from a lower ethnic caste to a lower and working class group.

Geographical mobility is as important as class mobility when discussing Mexican Americans. To move from South Texas to Los Angeles is to change dramatically one's style of life and life chances.[30] South Texas is an area where Mexicans have always faced the most consistent and rigid racial barriers. In contrast, California (particularly Southern California) is a relatively open society with a larger working and middle class, a lower degree of traditional Mexican folk-culture, a more highly rationalized economic system, and a more permeable color line for upwardly mobile Chicanos. This characterization of California, however, must be balanced with the realities of the urban barrio of East Los Angeles, where one finds a high degree of poverty, tense police-community relations, and an educational system that fails to educate large numbers of Latino children.

The Size of the Mexican-American Middle Class
Income

The median income of Mexican-American households in 1991 was $22,477. Thirty two percent of Mexican-American families are in the $25-49,999 category, and 13.1 percent of households are in the $50,000 or more category. The closest comparisons with black families is from 1991 data which shows 29.2 percent of black families in the $25–49,999 category, and 14.9 percent in the $50,000 category. The most recent, (at the time of this writing) 1992 report on Hispanics categorized income groups in a way that did not allow a comparison of Mexican Americans and blacks for the over $35,000 middle-income bracket.[31] Instead, the above income breaks of $25,000–49,999 and $50,000 or more are used.

From these comparisons, Mexican-American family incomes appear to be slightly higher than those of blacks. However, it has been suggested that because Mexican-American families are more likely to remain intact and to have extended family members living together for a long period of time, they have more potential wage earners than black, or, for that matter, Anglo families. Thus, the somewhat higher income for Mexican-American families is probably caused by the fact that they have two or more wage earners.

About 27 percent of families of Mexican origin were living below the poverty level in 1991, compared with 10 percent non-Hispanic families. The high rate of poverty among Hispanics may be related, in part, to female headed families without a spouse present. About half of all Hispanic families headed by a female were living in poverty, compared with 25 percent of non-Hispanic white families.

Occupation

The 1992 occupational distribution for Mexican American males and females, compared with non-Hispanic males and females, is present in table 4.3.

Occupational Distribution of Mexican-American Males and Females and Non-Hispanic Males and Females, 1992

OCCUPATIONAL CATEGORY	MEXICAN ORIGIN MALE	MEXICAN ORIGIN FEMALE	NON-HISPANIC MALE	NON-HISPANIC FEMALE
managerial and professional	9.3%	14.0%	28.6%	29.7%
technical, sales, and administrative support	14.0%	39.3%	21.9%	45.6%
precision production, craft, and repair	20.0%	3.1%	18.8%	1.9%
service occupations	16.6%	24.6%	9.0%	15.4%
farming, forestry and fishing	10.9%	2.8%	3.7%	.9%
operators, fabricators, and laborers	29.2%	16.2%	18.0%	6.5%

Source: U.S. Department of Labor, The Hispanic Population in the United States: March 1992, Current Population Reports Series P-20, No. 465 RV. U.S. Department of Commerce

Table 4.3

Mexican-American males are most likely to be found in lesser skilled blue collar jobs (29 percent are operators, fabricators and laborers), and skilled blue collar jobs (20 percent precision production). Mexican-American females are especially concentrated in the occupational categories of technical, sales and administrative support (39 percent) and service (25 percent). Mexican-American males are far less likely to be in the top white collar jobs (managerial and professional) than non-Hispanic males (9 percent versus 29 percent). It is interesting that Mexican-American females are more likely to be in these top white collar jobs than Mexican-American males (14 percent versus 9 percent).

Using the two white collar occupational categories as index of middle-class position, about 23 percent of Mexican-American males are in white collar jobs versus 53 percent of Mexican-American females. The finding that over half of Mexican-American females are in white collar (middle class) positions is misleading since many in the Administrative Support category are clerical workers with low pay and little opportunity for advancement. The data for males is likely to be a better estimate of the size of middle class stratum, since most males in the second category are technical and sales workers, not administrative support (clerical) workers.

Are black males more likely to be in white collar positions than males of Mexican origin? Comparing the first column of table 4.3 with the third column of table 4.1, it can be seen that black males are represented in higher level occupations more than Mexican American males—31 percent of black males are in white-collar positions, versus 23 percent of males of Mexican origin. At the other end of the scale, black males and Mexican-origin males are equally represented in the lowest skill blue-collar jobs—31 percent of black males are operators, fabricators, or laborers, versus 29 percent of Mexican-origin males. Thus, while both groups have large proportions concentrated in the poorest paid, most physically exhausting jobs, black males are more represented than Mexican-American males in the more prestigious and better paying white collar jobs.

In terms of occupational mobility over time, it appears that Mexican American males and females are somewhat more likely to be in white collar jobs in 1992 than in 1976 (23 percent versus 18 percent for males, and 53 percent versus 44 percent for females). There has been some degree of occupational mobility over time.

Educational Attainment

The educational attainment of Hispanics in the United States has, by all measurements, been well below that of Anglos as well as black Americans. Among the Hispanic population, Mexican Americans, in particular, have had lower attainment. One frequently reads of a 45–50 percent drop-out rate of Mexican-American youth in California school districts. Simplistic accounts often "blame the victim" by assuming that Mexican American families place less emphasis on educational attainment than other groups. Other, more structural accounts, note that the typically lower attainment of Hispanic children is a failure of our schools, rather than a failure of the children or their families. For example, studies of Mexican American children indicate that they are more often misclassified and mislabeled with IQ tests, and incorrectly placed in slow learner tracks (see chapter 7).[32] Many of the problems associated with Hispanic childrens' higher rates of educational failure can be attributed to language problems. Bilingual programs remain controversial and have only been able to claim limited success. Moreover, many Hispanic children (estimates as high as 40 percent) are somewhat bilingual, but more proficient in English than Spanish. These English dominant children place out of bilingual programs. Typically, they are in Spanish speaking households where their English speaking and writing skills are not reinforced. Such children often fall between the cracks in the system. They are not eligible for specialized remedial instruction, and they fall behind in their achievement in small increments each year as the curriculum becomes more demanding in English skills.[33]

Table 4.4 shows the educational attainment of Hispanics (Mexican, Puerto Rican, Cuban, Central and South American, and other Hispanic combined) for the years of 1970, 1980, and 1992. In 1970, only 32 percent of Hispanics 25 years old and over completed four years of high school or more, compared with 44 percent in 1980 and 53 percent in 1992. Despite these improvements, the educational attainment of Hispanics remains well below the comparable percentages for non-Hispanics—53 percent (1970), 68 percent (1980), and 82 percent (1992). Moreover, the percentages for Mexican Americans are lower than those for the Hispanic category as a whole—46 percent of Mexican-origin males and 43 percent of Mexican-origin females (25 years and older) completed high school or more in 1988. The percentages are somewhat higher if one focuses on young Mexican Americans in the 25-34 year old age bracket; 53 percent of Mexican- American males, and 56 percent of Mexican-American females completed high school or more in 1988. Still, these percentages suggest that a very high proportion of Mexican American young persons (perhaps, 45 percent) drop out of high school. The 55 percent of Mexican-American young persons (25–34 years old) completing high school or more is far lower than the 82 percent of comparable young blacks completing high school or more. These differences in educational attainment make it more understandable why black males and females are more often represented in upper white collar jobs than Mexican-American males and females.

Completion of four or more years of college is increasingly essential for entry into the highest paying and most prestigious white-collar jobs. Table 4.4 shows that Hispanics (as a whole) have made some gains over time in terms of increased proportions completing college. Five percent in 1970 completed college versus 9 percent in 1992. The proportions for non-Hispanics were twice as high—11 percent and 22 percent. However, Mexican Americans have lower college completion rates than other Hispanics. Only 6 percent of Mexican Americans (25 and older) had completed college in 1992.

Educational Attainment of Hispanics and Non-Hispanics of Persons 25 Years and Over 1970 to 1992

	HISPANIC		NON-HISPANIC	
	4 years high school or more	4 or more years college	4 years high school or more	4 or more years college
1970	32%	5%	53%	11%
1980	44%	8%	68%	17%
1992	53%	9.4%	82%	22%

Source: U.S. Bureau of the Census, Population Profile of the United States 1992, Current Population Reports Series P-23, No. 183. U.S. Department of Commerce.

Table 4.4

The Chicano Generation

Alvarez [34] speaks of a Chicano generation that first emerged in the 1970s. The majority are sons and daughters of urban working-class parents. Compared with earlier generations of Mexican Americans, they are more affluent and have the highest aspirations. But middle-class status is escaping them. Although they have achieved higher levels of education than their parents, the occupational structure of the larger society has become so technical, bureaucratized, and professionalized, that young Chicanos are being excluded from middle-class positions. Many have been eliminated from entrance into a good four year college because their barrio high school education is so inferior compared to the education in middle-class Anglo schools. Chicanos also lack the credentials for middle-class status because they have not had separate institutions for higher learning. There are more than one hundred black colleges and universities, and although some people question the quality of separate institutions, black colleges have played an important role in certifying large numbers of blacks for middle-class positions.

Large corporations are interested, for the first time, in hiring Spanish-surname people, in order to meet federal Affirmative Action regulations. Chicanos, however, often lack the credentials for obtaining such jobs. "The irony is that as discrimination disappears or is minimized those who have historically suffered most from it continue to suffer its after-effects."[35]

Another circumstance against the development of a Chicano middle class is the emigration of technically skilled and educated middle-class persons from Latin American countries to the United States, who are lured by the higher pay of United States corporations. This further threatens to displace opportunities for young Chicanos because United States corporations can meet federal demands by hiring any Spanish-surname person. Alvarez concludes that there are substantial barriers for many Chicanos, and there is not likely to be a dramatic growth of a middle-class sector in the immediate future.

SUMMARY

Solid data show that some segments of the black population have made progress in bettering their occupations, education levels, and incomes in the last twenty five to thirty years. The proportion of blacks in white-collar and skilled blue-collar positions has increased. About 31 percent of employed black males are in white-collar positions in 1992, and a larger 46 percent are in white-collar or skilled blue-collar jobs. Not all of the jobs lumped into white-collar and skilled blue-collar categories have substantial incomes, high prestige and good opportunities for advancement, but many do. A conservative estimate is that about 35 percent of employed black males are in middle class or upper class occupations. However, a fairly large race differential remains by occupation—48 percent of white males are in white-collar positions; 67 percent are in white collar or skilled blue collar positions.

The income gap has not reduced through time when black families are compared with white families overall. However, some segments of the black community have made notable family income gains. The families showing the greatest gains are young black families in the North and West with two working spouses. The income of these families is now equal to comparable white families.

The sports institution has provided opportunity for a number of talented black athletes. Moreover, blacks are much more likely to be placed in key "thinking positions" today such as quarterback and pointguard. However, there is extreme competition for a very few positions; the chances for upward mobility in sports, have been exaggerated.

The data indicate a clear socioeconomic division in Black America. While one segment is moving into middle class occupations and incomes, another segment is locked into poverty. About 30 percent of black families were below the poverty level in 1991 Almost 50 percent of black children under the age of 18 were living in poverty in 1991. Traditionally, the black rate of unemployment is twice that of the white rate; in the late 1980s, the ratio of black to white unemployment increased to 2.5 times greater. Following the writings of William Wilson,[36] de-industrialization (the shutdown of smokestack and manufacturing industries) was advanced as a major reason for the increased black unemployment rate and a concomitant increase in female-headed households without husbands present.

There is growing evidence for a white-collar and skilled blue-collar stratum among Mexican Americans. In 1992, about 23 percent of employed Mexican American males were in white collar jobs and another 20 percent in skilled blue-collar jobs. Although only 9 percent of Mexican-American males were in top (managerial and professional) white-collar jobs, a larger 14 percent of Mexican origin females were in these positions. For Mexican American males, the phenomenon of a rising middle class appears to be more a case of moving into skilled blue-collar and lower white-collar positions.

As in the case of blacks, there is a notable division in socioeconomic attainment in the Mexican American community. While some have moved into middle class positions, a substantial 27 percent were living in poverty in 1991. Almost half of employed Mexican American males were in unskilled blue-collar occupations or service occupations in 1992.

The educational attainment of Hispanics has increased notably over time, especially for young persons in the 25–34 year old category. Still the high school and college completion rates are far lower for Hispanics, as a category; 52 percent of Hispanics are high school graduates or more in 1992 versus 82 percent of blacks and 91 percent of non-Hispanic whites.

Further Meanings of the Rising Middle Class.

Statistics that show a developing middle class among blacks and Mexican Americans must be carefully interpreted. They do not mean that society now is as open for the conquered minorities as for the population as a whole. Mexican Americans and blacks still face many ethnic barriers and must expend more effort to overcome these barriers than their white counterparts. For example:

- Mexican Americans and black families often achieve their middle-class incomes only when both husband and wife work full time, year round. They make the same income as a white family in which only the husband works full-time. In short, black and Mexican-American middle-income families often have to invest a much greater household input of time and effort to get the same economic outputs as white middle-class families.

- Data suggest that blacks in white-collar positions in organizations are less likely to be promoted into positions of high authority.[37] Accounting for experience, education and skill, blacks continue to face racial barriers in reaching positions such as manager and district supervisor.

- Black and Chicano professionals entering private practice (medical doctors, veterinarians, dentists, and lawyers) may be forced into a segregated marketplace with a smaller and poorer clientele from which to draw. The black professional in private practice is missing the more lucrative marketplace from which the white professional benefits.

- Middle-income blacks often live on the periphery of inner-city ghettos. In such areas families have difficulty in converting their middle incomes into the same privileges that the white middle class enjoys automatically. Many "peripheral" neighborhoods have higher crime rates, more police stop-and-search contacts, poorer schools, and economic zone changes (more liquor stores and motels) that detract from the beauty and economic stability of the neighborhood.

NOTES

1. Reynolds Farley, "Trends in Racial Inequalities: Have the gains in the 1960s disappeared in the 1970s?" *American Sociological Review* 42 (April, 1977): 189–208.

2. See Gary T. Marx, *Protest and Prejudice* (New York: Harper & Row, 1967); and Ruth Searles and J. Allen Williams Jr., "Negro College Students Participation in Sit-Ins," *Social Forces* 40 (March, 1962): 215-220.

3. Harvey Marshall and Deborah Meyer, "Assimilation and the Election of Minority Candidates: The Case of Black Mayors," *Sociology and Social Research* 60 (October, 1975): 1–21.

4. Stan Steiner, *The New Indians* (New York: Dell Publishing Co., 1968).

5. Vincent Jeffries and H. Edward Ransford, *Social Stratification: A Multiple Hierarchy Approach* (Boston: Allyn & Bacon, 1980), 524.

6. Ben J. Wattenberg and Richard M. Scammon, "Black Progress and Liberal Rhetoric," *Commentary* (April, 1973): 35–44.

7. Robert B. Hill, *The Illusion of Black Progress* (Washington D.C.: National Urban League, 1978).

8. U.S. Bureau of Census, "The Black Population in the United States: March 1992," *Current Population Reports* Series P-20, No. 471.

9. U.S. Bureau of the Census, "Differences Between Incomes of White and Negro Families by Work Experience of Wife and Region 1970, 1969, and 1959," *Current Population Reports* Series P-23, No. 39.

10. Ibid., 1–8.

11. Gerald David Jaynes and Robin M. Williams Jr., *A Common Destiny: Blacks and American Society* (Washington, D.C.: National Academy Press,

1989). The quoted statement is based on the following studies: James E. Conyers and Walter L. Wallace, *Black Elected Officials: A Study of Black Americans Holding Governmental Office* (New York: Russel Sage Foundation, 1976); Richard L. Engstrom and Michael D. McDonald, "The Election of Blacks to City Councils: Clarifying the Impact of Electoral arrangements on the Seats/Population Relationship," *American Political Science Review* 75 (June, 1981): 344-354; and Albert K. Karnig and Susan Welch, *Black Representation and Urban Policy* (Chicago: University of Chicago Press, 1980).

12. Jaynes and Williams, *A Common Destiny: Blacks and American Society*. 239.

13. Stanley Eitzen and Norman B. Yetman, "Immune from Racism?," *Civil Rights Digest* 9 (3, 1977): 3–13.

14. William Oscar Johnson, "The Black Athlete Revisited: How Far Have We Come?" *Sports Illustrated* 75 (August 5, 1991).

15. Ibid., 40.

16. Ibid., 40.

17. Ibid., 40.

18. Ibid., 40.

19. Ibid., 40.

20. Harry Edwards, "The Collegiate Athletic Arms Race: Origins and Implications of the 'Rule 48' Controversy," *Journal of Sport and Social Issues* 8 (1984); 4–22; see also W. M. Leonard II and J. M. Reyman, "The Odds of Attaining Professional Athlete Status: Refining the Computations," *Sociology of Sport* 5 (1988): 162–169.

21. Johnson, "The Black Athlete Revisited: How Far Have We Come?", 40.

22. U.S. Bureau of the Census, *Current Population Reports* Series P-20 No. 471, 15.

23. U.S. Bureau of the Census, "The Black Population in the United States: March, 1992," *Current Population Reports* Series, P-20, No. 442, 9.

24. See William Julius Wilson, "The Black Community in the 1980s: Questions of Race, Class, and Public Policy," *The Annals of the American Academy of Political and Social Science* 454 (1981); William Julius Wilson, The Truly Disadvantaged (Chicago, University of Chicago Press, 1987).

25. Daniel P. Moynihan, "The Schism in Black America," *The Public Interest* 27 (Spring, 1972): 3–24.

26. U.S. Bureau of the Census, "Household and Family Characteristics: March 1990 and 1989," Series P-20, No. 447.

27. Hill, *The Illusion of Black Progress*.

28. Fernando Penalosa, "The Changing Mexican-American in Southern California," in Norman R. Yetman & C. Hoy Steele (eds.), *Majority and Minority* (Boston: Allyn and Bacon, 1971).

29. Rodolfo Alvarez, "The Psycho-Historical and Socioeconomic Development of the Chicano Community in the United States," *Social Science Quarterly* 53 (March, 1973): 920–942.

30. Joan W. Moore, *Mexican Americans* (Englewood Cliffs, N.J.: Prentice Hall, 1970).

31. U.S. Bureau of the Census, "The Hispanic Population in the United States: March 1992," Series P-20, No. 471.

32. Jane R. Mercer, "IQ: The Lethal Label," *Psychology Today* (September, 1972).

33. *Los Angeles Times*, "Latino Students Advance, Only to Fail," August 1, 1983.

34. Alvarez, "The Psycho-Historical and Socioeconomic Development of the Chicano Community in the United States."

35. Alvarez, Ibid.

36. Wilson, 1981, "The Black Community in the 1980s: Questions of Race, Class, and Public Policy"; Wilson, 1987, *The Truly Disadvantaged*.

37. James R. Kluegel, "Causes and Costs of Racial Exclusion from Job Authority," *American Sociological Review* 43 (June, 1978): 285–301.

PART II

SELECTED REVIEWS OF RESEARCH ON RACE, CLASS, AND GENDER INTERACTIONS

Black and Latino Perceptions of Inequality

Ghetto Rebellions and the Anger of the Black Middle Class

Dual mobility trends for blacks and Latinos was a central theme in the data presented in chapter 4: in the last 30 years, a rising black and Latino middle class has moved into white collar or skilled blue collar occupations, while at the same time the black and Latino lower classes, residing in inner city areas, are facing increased joblessness, poverty, and isolation. This chapter deals with the perceptions of inequality and discrimination on the part of blacks and Latinos of different social classes and the reactions of these groups to discrimination. How have minority persons reacted to the pressure cooker situations in inner city areas? Under what conditions do we find extreme reactions like ghetto rebellions?

We begin with an analysis of the tensions in inner city areas. The 1992 Los Angeles Civil Disorder, the largest civil disturbance in recent history, is discussed as a reaction to ghetto tensions. To give historical perspective and background to this event, the 1992 civil disorder is compared with the Watts riot of 1965. Later in this chapter, we note perceptions of inequality on the part of the black and Latino middle class groups and their propensities to engage in protest activity.

MINORITY GROUP PROTEST: COMPARISONS OF THE 1992 LOS ANGELES CIVIL DISORDER AND THE 1965 WATTS RIOT

On April 29, 1992, a jury in Simi Valley California, a white suburban community located 50 miles from Los Angeles, announced not-guilty verdicts for four police officers in one of the most visible and sensational cases of police force in history—the beating of Rodney King. Anger and shock waves were felt across the nation, especially among minorities in inner cities. The verdicts of "not guilty" seemed incomprehensible to many. In *Understanding the Riots*, The Los Angeles Times reports the angry reaction of one resident:

> In South Central Los Angeles, 24-year-old Marcus had had enough. Raised in an inner city home but bussed to suburban schools, he could appreciate the impulse to put your faith in the system. But this was too much. The King beating was on videotape, Marcus knew. They had beaten the man senseless. They had mistakenly believed that he was on PCP, then one of them had joked about the beating. How could they not be guilty of something? It brewed inside him, the fury.[1]

For three days and nights the world watched in horror as rage, destruction, and violence swept Los Angeles. Police cars were overturned, innocent persons were yanked from their cars, hundreds of stores were destroyed and looters swarmed the stores and markets. By the end of the uprising there were 45 dead and at least a billion dollars in damages, making it the largest U.S. civil disorder of the century.

Two interpretations of the disorder were commonly voiced. The first was the view that this was a *riot*, a more spontaneous breakdown in law and order, fueled by a lack of police presence and participated in by persons taking advantage of a situation. The second view was that the disorder was a *rebellion* or *uprising* set off by the "King verdicts" but in response to long standing grievances in the community including a lack of jobs, poverty and a view that the police, and more broadly the criminal justice system, were unfairly wielding justice to minority residents. By this view, many of the participants were striking out in anger, the King verdict being a final straw to long standing community tensions. Moreover, the "rebellion" interpretation was seen as a predictable reaction to ghetto isolation and a worsening of conditions.

The explosion of anger in the April '92 disorder was not the first time. Reports indicate that the conditions that fueled the unrest were virtually the same as those that led to the Los Angeles Watts riot in 1965. In the discussion that follows, similarities and differences between "Watts" and the current Los Angeles disorder are noted. The ways in which race and class compound and intersect will be frequently noted.

THE WATTS RIOT: FIVE VARIABLES

During the summer of 1965, as a graduate student at UCLA, I conducted a study on the reactions of Los Angeles Black Americans to the Watts riot.[2] The research began as a study in civil rights activism. I was interested in the new forms of militant protest such as sit-ins and demonstrations, which, at that time seemed outside the mainstream of politics. It appeared that for the first time, black Americans were building an independent power base and coercing the white majority into concessions by means of economic boycotts and demonstrations that called attention to discriminating institutions. I wanted to know who these more militant civil rights activists were. A random sample survey methodology was utilized with black interviewers doing the interviewing. Ironically, the dissertation research involved the question of why Los Angeles had been so quiet. Why so few demonstrations? Was Los Angeles so much better off? The Watts riot occurred in the middle of the study! We, on the research team, were stunned. South Central Los Angeles had exploded into flames, sirens and looting. The study goals were immediately expanded. Civil Rights militance, as I had originally conceived it—programmed organized demonstrations—was expanded to include the raw anger of riot violence. The whole study took on an air of excitement. We felt we had a chance to gather historical data since we were in the field so fast in the aftermath of a riot. Respondents were interviewed as buildings were still smoldering. The sample consisted of 312 black males, randomly selected by residence, living in the Watts, South Central and Crenshaw areas of Los Angeles. The Watts and South Central areas are primarily lower class, while the Crenshaw area is more middle class in composition.

Already in the survey was the question, "Would you be willing to use violence to get Negro rights?" and "Have you participated in violence to get Negro rights?" Added to the interview schedule were the open-end questions, "What were your reactions to the riot,?" "What do you think caused the riot,?" and "How well do you think you're represented by leaders in this (South Central) area?" Figure 5.1 summarizes five variables that were important in explaining willingness to use violence, or were perceived by the respondents as a cause of the rebellion.

An alienation theoretical scheme had been developed in the original study. The concept of alienation has a long history in sociology. The concept refers to a separation or disengagement from groups or social systems important to the individual such that the person feels a sense of isolation, powerlessness or meaninglessness.[3] Alienation logically related to riot participation. It was expected that individuals who were more alienated from the system would have more likely participated in violent protest, would be more willing to participate in violent protest, and would be more supportive of the Watts riot as necessary and legitimate.

Three forms of alienation were studied: *Racial isolation, political powerlessness,* and *racial dissatisfaction.* Racial isolation was defined as a lack of intimate equal status contact with whites. Though interracial contact between blacks and whites may be frequent, it often involves such wide status differentials that it does not facilitate candid communication, nor is it likely to give the minority person a feeling that he or she has some stake in the system. In short, racial isolation is viewed as a weak normative bond to the system. It was reasoned that blacks who are more racially isolated will have fewer channels of communication to air their grievances and will feel little commitment to the leaders and institutions of the community. This group, which is blocked from meaningful white communication should be more willing to use violent protest than groups with greater involvement with white society.

Five Variables That Were Important inExplaining Riot Participation or Support for the Riot	
ALIENATION VARIABLES	RIOT VARIABLES
1. *Racial Isolation.*Viewed as a weak normative bond or low commitment to system channels. Measured by low degrees of equal status social contact with whites.	• Willingness to use violence to get black rights.
2. *Political Powerlessness.* Viewed as a low expectancy of exerting control in the political system—perception of closed redress channels.	• Have used violence to get black rights. • Approval of Watts riot.
3. *Racial Dissatisfaction.* Perceived racial discrimination in the community, compared to blacks in the South, and whether respondent has benefitted from the Civil Rights Movement.	
WIDELY BASED COMMUNITY PERCEPTIONS OF CAUSES OF THE RIOT REBELLION	
4. *Long Standing Police Tension.* Perceived verbal discourtesy or excessive force.	
5. *Economic Discrimination.* Perceived joblessness, discrimination in hiring, and consumer exploitation.	

Figure 5.1

Political powerlessness (defined as a low expectancy of exerting control in the political system) was the second measure of alienation. Persons scoring high in powerlessness appeared to be perceiving closed redress channels in major institutions, such as voting, the courts, and the criminal justice system. *Racial dissatisfaction* (the third measure of alienation) is the perception that blacks are treated unequally and unfairly because of their race. Questions dealt with overall treatment in the community, housing discrimination, employment discrimination, and whether the person felt any gains from the civil rights movement. These three measures of alienation were each correlated with willingness to use violence and approval of the riot. The tandem effect of all three (combinations of isolation, powerlessness, and racial dissatisfaction) produced a very strong relationship with violence and approval of the Watts riot. For example 65 percent of those high in all three measures of alienation reported a willingness to use violence versus only 12 percent of those low on all three measures.

Alienation only had a clear significant impact on violence and riot approval among lower SES blacks. An ethclass effect was evident (chapter 3) in the sense that alienation in the context of minority status and lower class inner city area was highly related to violent protest. Middle class blacks were not willing to use violence and tended not to approve of the riot even if alienated. In short, the alienation disaffection only converted to violent protest action or riot sympathy in lower class areas where living conditions were objectively very bad. It could be argued that middle-class blacks had too much to lose, that is too much stake in the system in terms of good jobs and home ownership, to risk involvement in radical protest.

What did the black community view as major causes of the Watts riot? Figure 5.1 lists two widely held community perceptions. Two thirds of the respondents spontaneously mentioned long standing police tension as a cause. Some referred to verbal discourtesy; others spoke of excessive police force. The other widely perceived cause of the riot was economic discrimination (partially overlapping the racial dissatisfaction variable noted above). Forty-five percent spoke of economic factors, citing joblessness, poverty, and consumer exploitation, i.e., being overcharged for inferior goods.

The findings of this study lean toward a conflict-rebellion interpretation. These five variables—isolation, political powerlessness, racial dissatisfaction, perceptions of unequal treatment from the police and perceptions of economic discrimination are an important backdrop for understanding the current Los Angeles uprising. They are conditions that have festered largely unchanged.

NON-CHANGE SINCE WATTS

Not only have conditions not improved, but it could be argued that conditions in the inner cities have worsened in the last thirty years (see chapter 4). Plant shutdown or de-industrialization has brought widespread unemployment to blacks and Latinos. Moreover, the exodus of middle-class and working-class blacks from deprived inner city areas has resulted in a new class isolation, somewhat distinct from the isolation from white society discussed in the above Watts survey. There is a lack of job networking, middle-class role models, and middle-class community organizations. Young persons growing up in the inner city no longer have a successful role model living on the block. The whole fabric of social connections (advice, encouragement, introductions) so necessary for upward mobility has been removed from the inner city.[4] Street life alternatives, such as drug distribution, become the alternate success routes for minority youth.

Racial isolation has remained somewhat constant from the 1965 period. The major effort to combat isolation was a series of court orders to integrate Los Angeles public schools. Given the geographic spread of the Los Angeles district, school bussing was necessary to distribute students in more racially balanced proportions.

> Though it affected only about 10 percent of all students in the school system, the integration program was still one of the largest ever attempted: 1,200 buses moving 64,000 fourth-through eighth-graders among 260 schools. Some white parents boycotted the schools in protest, keeping an estimated 10,000 children home the first day.[5]

Apparently, white parents were less worried about black and Latino students being bused into their neighborhood schools than about their own children being bused into inner city schools. A year after busing began in Los Angeles, California voters approved a constitutional amendment forbidding state courts to use busing orders to desegregate the public schools. The legality of the amendment was upheld in 1980. The Los Angeles experiment to reduce racial isolation by court had failed.

Nor has police tension declined significantly from the '65 Watts climate. Although there have been some police initiated community outreach efforts, the 1970s and 80s had numerous instances of police-community tension in Los Angeles: for example, the Eulia Love incident, in which a black woman was shot and killed by two LAPD officers during a violent confrontation dealing with an unpaid gas bill; the charge that the choke hold was more often used in ghetto arrests of minority persons and frequently resulted in the death of the arrestee. On January 14, 1989, Long Beach Police Officers were videotaped arresting a suspect and apparently pushing the arrestee through a storefront window. The arrested person was a black Hawthorne police sergeant on administrative leave. The case received wide coverage in the media. Another symbol of legal injustice that occurred before the '92 civil disorder was the Latasha Harlens case. A fifteen year old black teenager (Harlens) argued with store owner Soon Ja Du over whether she was trying to steal a bottle of orange juice. As the 15 year old walked away, the grocer shot her fatally. Soon Ja Du received probation for the case. Black residents were outraged and there was a boycott of the store. The perceptions of excessive police force and legal injustice clearly existed in the black community in the decade prior to the Rodney King beating. Although there are striking similarities between Watts and the '92 civil disorder, the differences are also interesting and informative. An important difference is that the 1992 disorder had a much broader participation base. Both blacks and Latinos were involved in the protest and Asians (especially Korean Americans) were very involved in protecting their property.

DEMOGRAPHIC CHANGES IN LOS ANGELES

As a national trend, inner city areas have become more diverse in ethnic composition. Latino and Asian-American increases are especially notable in many cities. In particular, Los Angeles has become the new Ellis island or port of entry for immigrant groups. In the 1980–1990 decade the L.A. central city area was transformed from a mostly black area to one with a large Latino resident population and a sharp increase in Korean American owned businesses. The influx of Latinos to the Los Angeles area has been truly astounding. Civil wars were driving new waves of immigrants to Los Angeles. Though the majority of these Latinos were Mexican in origin, there was also a sharp increase in Salvadorians and other Central Americans.[6] The sheer number of Latinos altered Los Angeles from one end to the other, but in particular, they were remaking Black South Central Los Angeles. "Their very neighborhoods, blacks saw, were being transformed into the West Coast's fastest growing Latino barrio. By the end of the '80s, Watts—a name synonymous with black Los Angeles—would become almost 50 percent Latino and begin holding Cinco de Mayo Parades."[7]

The Latino new arrivals to Los Angeles experienced the same inner city tensions that blacks had. A national immigration bill (Simpson-Mazoni bill) was passed in 1986. The bill guaranteed amnesty or citizenship to immigrants who had been in the U.S. prior to January 1, 1982, i.e., to those with equity or a long term job history in the United States. Many of the new illegal immigrants arriving between 1980 and 1990 did not qualify for this amnesty cutoff, and, as a result, faced inner city joblessness with the added stigma of being undocumented. Thus Latinos and blacks were highly exposed to the same inner city tensions of joblessness, poverty, political alienation, race and class isolation and abrasive police contacts.

Asian American increases to the Los Angeles area were also notable. Between 1970 and 1980, the Asian Pacific population increased 92 percent and has continued to grow in the 1990s. "Los Angeles County is the port of entry for the largest number of Korean immigrants and the home of the largest Korean community outside of Korea."[8]

MINORITY GROUP PROTEST
RATHER THAN BLACK-WHITE CONFRONTATION

Who participated in the Los Angeles disorder? Many may have assumed that blacks were most involved given the fact that the Rodney King incident involved the beating of a black male. Recent statistics of 6,000 arrestees[9] indicate that both blacks and Latinos were highly involved, reflecting the demographic changes noted above. Latinos were more involved (or, at least, more likely to be arrested) than any other ethnic group.

The arrestee data show that for the six days of riots, 51 percent of all arrestees were Latino as compared with 36 percent black (the remaining 13 percent were primarily Anglo). Blacks and Latinos combined represent 87 percent of all the arrestees.

If the King verdicts had somewhat less salience for Latinos than blacks, one might guess that Latinos would be more involved in the later looting stages rather than the early confrontation stages of the disorder. Not so! The number arrested was higher for Latinos than blacks each day of the riot.

The arrest report developed broad categories of arrest. Latinos had higher proportions in each category. In the case of *property crimes* (looting, theft, burglary and auto theft), 55 percent of the arrestees were Latino versus 36 percent black. For *civil disturbances* (e.g., curfew violations, disturbing the peace, and disorderly conduct) 48 percent of the arrestees were Latino versus 41 percent black. Finally, for *violence* (e.g., assault, homicide) 48 percent were Latino versus 40 percent black. Clearly, the Latino edge in arrests is in property crimes, and these are most likely to be looting arrests. However, Latinos show higher numbers arrested in all three categories. Do the high Latino arrest numbers reflect that group's *participation* rate? Not necessarily. The numbers could also reflect a reluctance on the part of Latinos to flee or resist arrest, a concentration of police efforts to arrest Latinos more than blacks, or a greater reluctance on the part of the police to arrest blacks more than Latinos. Though the high Latino arrest numbers are subject to different interpretations, it is very clear that both blacks and Latinos were highly involved in the disorder. These are important data. They indicate that the disorder was more a minority protest than a black-white confrontation. Most likely, the five variables noted earlier (isolation, powerlessness, dissatisfaction, perceived police malpractice, and joblessness and economic discrimination) are just as salient for Latinos as blacks. Moreover, there may be special discrimination tensions experienced by Latinos that need to be examined further. for example, Central American immigrants have shown an almost 100 percent increase into the Los Angeles central area in the last decade.[10] As noted above, most of these immigrants missed the amnesty clause of the immigration bill and are likely experiencing very marginal employment. Further research is needed to better understand the unique discrimination and acculturation strains experienced by Latinos residing in inner city areas.

KOREAN AMERICAN STORE OWNERS
AND BLACK AND LATINO CUSTOMERS

Tensions between Korean Americans and African Americans have been evident in the impoverished inner city areas of Los Angeles, New York, Chicago and Washington D.C. The clashes have often been violent. A mother of four (Bo Hua Cha) was shot as she stood behind the counter of her dry cleaning store in Washington D.C. In 1993, eight robbery murders of Asian shopkeepers in Washington D.C. drew the outrage of the Korean American community.[11] The Soon Ja Du/Latasha Harlins case, that occurred before the Rodney King beating, was a major source of tension in Los Angeles. Why have Korean American merchants acquired small businesses (commonly known as "mom and pop shops") in inner city areas? It should be noted first that Korean immigrants represent a very diverse population in terms of social class. A bi-modal distribution would be the best way to describe the recent immigrants. One large segment is upper-middle class in terms of professional and other white collar occupations. The media often portrays these highly successful Korean (and other Asian) Americans as the "model minority"—hard working, industrious, high achieving. However, other segments of the Asian immigrant population are working class in terms of occupational background and economic resources. These Korean Americans have attempted to gain a foothold by purchasing the stores in the inner city once held by Jews, Italians, Greeks, and other ethnic whites. The inner city markets and small stores are the only businesses that many Korean Americans can afford. The small dry cleaning store or grocery store became the main hope to realize the American Dream—to afford a college education for one's children. Korean American store owners are stereotyped as workaholic upwardly mobile entrepreneurs. Quite typically, family members take different shifts in operating the shop. As a result, few residents in the surrounding community are hired. It should be emphasized that Korean Americans are not the first to take on this immigrant entrepreneur role. Moreover, there has commonly been economic tension between small shop merchants and the community. Prices are typically higher in small inner city stores because the volume of goods is so much lower than a supermarket and because there is the need for more security devices and greater insurance coverage. Although Korean immigrants viewed the city as somewhat unsafe in terms of crime and violence, they were willing to take the risk because it was the only place they could afford to launch a business.

Koch and Schockman[12] in an analysis of the Los Angeles civil disorder offer additional reasons why Koreans settled in inner city areas: (1) there is little competition from the large chain stores which have proportionally abandoned this area after the Watts riot (2) low rents and overhead (3) access to the *kye* system for capitalization of their enterprises (a system in which a group of families pools their investment money and acts as an informal banking system) (4) relative ease of skirting state labor enforcement laws by the high utilization of unpaid family labor. Sociologists have given more structural reasons for the concentration of Korean immigrant entrepreneurs in the inner city. Bonacich argues that "Korean small business is not business *per se* but a form of utilization of cheap immigrant labor by American capitalism.[13] The immigrant entrepreneur can be described as a "middleman minority" sandwiched in between large corporations whose products they sell, and inner city residents whom they serve. "Large corporations use Korean small businesses to fill in the marketing gaps in the economy, especially in blighted ghetto areas."[14]

In addition to viewing Korean immigrants as a middle man minority, it has been argued that interpersonal contacts between Korean merchants and black customers have been strained. Although some customer-merchant contacts have been positive, many blacks have expressed resentment that the profits from these stores flow out of the community, and that Korean American merchants have not usually hired African Americans or Latinos; rather, all the store managing and operating positions are occupied by family members. There is a clash of perceptions. Many blacks and Latinos see the Korean American shopkeeper as the oppressor. Korean American merchants, by contrast, see themselves as bringing vital services to the community. Who else, they ask, is supplying food stuffs and vital services? Tension and misunderstandings in interaction styles may also contribute to the clashes. "The Korean who opens a store in a poor neighborhood may speak little English and know nothing of American-style customer relations. His perception of blacks may be skewed by pimp and prostitute videos he watched in Asia . . . His mostly black or Hispanic customers may see him as disrespectful and unresponsive. They wonder how he can open a business when they can't. They assume he's making scads of money—and taking it home to the suburbs."[15] This image is further perpetuated by the "model minority" stereotype. Although they may own small stores, they are believed to be quite rich. A variation on this theme is that Korean American store owners have received special low interest loans from the government. Contrary to these popular stereotypes, Korean American store owners have not been given special loans and privileges, and many are barely making it in a fragile and precarious economic position.

Korean Americans suffered more than one-half of all the economic losses in the '92 civil uprising—two thousand businesses worth more than 400 million. One year after the disorder, only 28 percent had rebuilt their stores. The destruction of stores was the breaking of the American Dream for many Korean American families.

A survey of elite Korean and black business persons was conducted by Koch and Schockman one year after the uprising.[16] The survey found that Korean merchants felt victimized and politically unrepresented. They felt they were first victimized by rioters during the uprising, then, by bureaucratic disregard as they tried to seek help and get loans to rebuild their stores. In comparison to black business persons, Koreans had little faith in the REBUILD L.A. efforts and less hope that the new chief of police would make a significant difference in community relations. Korean respondents seemed to be expressing a kind of malaise and powerlessness in the sense of being politically unrepresented. In another study, involving Korean Americans who lost businesses,[17] two-thirds of the respondents said they have not recovered from the riots and one-half said they were pessimistic about the future and viewed rebuild efforts as a "hopeless cause." It is ironic that both the participants and the victims in the riot expressed political powerlessness. Both groups are operating in a context of limited economic resources, limited power and closed redress channels. it is indeed unfortunate that the Korean immigrant entrepreneur became a convenient target for the enormous multifaceted grievances in ghetto life.

To summarize, there were many similarities in the Watts and '92 disorders, however, the '92 uprising involved more complex race and class dynamics than the 1965 Watts riot. Joblessness was more acute; both race and class isolation were operating; the structure of the inner city was changed with the flight of middle class black

Americans, who took jobs, social services, and cultural networks with them; Latino immigrants were arriving in larger numbers, many being excluded from the legitimate job market; both Latinos and blacks were highly involved as participants; and special tensions had developed between immigrant Korean American merchants and black and Latino customers.

BLACK MIDDLE CLASS PERCEPTIONS OF INEQUALITY

The demographic data in chapter 4 clearly indicates the rise of black and Latino middle-class populations employed in white-collar or skilled blue-collar occupations. What happens to racial discrimination with socioeconomic advancement? Do middle and upper class blacks experience unique barriers and racism? This section addresses the attitudes of privileged blacks in white collar occupations. We begin with an overview history of the black middle class, followed by studies of middle-class black encounters with prejudice in public settings and in professional occupational settings.

Historical Background

Until the mid-1960s, middle-class black persons in America were profiled as individuals who accepted unconditionally the values of white people—"their canons of respectability, their standards of beauty, and their consumption patterns."[18] Middle-class blacks were also seen as maintaining social distance from lower-class members of their own race, and were afraid to endorse or participate in militant action that might jeopardize their precarious position in the general society. E. Franklin Frazier's last publication of *Black Bourgeoisie* is perhaps the classic account.[19] He maintains that middle-class blacks (those in white-collar and craft occupations) are ambivalent, both toward the wider black community and the white middle class with which they tend to identify. They disassociate themselves from the masses of their own group because they view lower-class black behavior as the reason for prejudice and blocked mobility. Frazier makes an important distinction between the "old" and the "new" middle class. Members of the old middle class are predominantly descendants of house slaves or free Negroes—"men and women who had purchased their freedom by diligent effort or who had been set free by some liberal planter, because of some heroic deed, or more frequently because of long years of faithfulness."[20] Due to sexual exploitation of black women under the slavery system, many of these blacks were lighter in skin color. A very special segment of the Negro group was created, in which lighter skinned or more Caucasian appearing blacks were given special privileges and freedoms. The descendants of this group were unusually careful to marry someone of the same class level and skin color. The behavior of this old bourgeoisie, Frazier notes, was based on a "genteel tradition" patterned after the ideal of the Southern lady and gentleman. They placed great stress on stable and conventional family life, and on frugality and industry in economic matters. However, a major new segment of the middle class emerged in the 1940s and 1950s. Unlike the old bourgeoisie, the new recruits to white-collar occupations came from the black masses. These were the actors, entertainers, and professionals who managed to fight their way into better positions. It is this "new" middle class of which Frazier is most critical. This new class rejected both the folk culture of the Negro masses (e.g., the singing and preaching styles found in the Baptist church) as well as the stable standards and genteel tradition of the old bourgeoisie. The new class was rootless, lacking a cultural or economic base. Bennett summarizes Frazier well when he notes:

> Frazier is critical of the manners, morals, and political views of the new class which, he says, is characterized by its psychological insecurity, its material dependence on the white propertied classes and its frantic quest for status. Worse yet, the new class composed essentially of "the successful members of the rising black masses," lacks a base in the economic system. Its wealth is too inconsequential, he says, for it to wield any political power. It is a lumpen, a fake bourgeoisie . . .[21]

Moreover, Frazier asserts that the new middle class suffers from an inferiority complex that leads to a fear of competing with whites on an equal level, a conspicuous display of wealth, and an escapism in which black achievements, wealth and business success are greatly exaggerated. Finally, Frazier (and many others) stresses the fact that middle- and upper-class blacks may have vested interests in perpetuating the segregated ghetto since black professionals and businessmen often service the separate and unequal institutions of the ghetto as doctors, teachers, morticians, etc. The black professionals in private practice, for example, may be unable to establish a large clientele in both black and white communities. A racist society combined with personal ambition thus leads the black professional to search for success by maintaining an exclusively black practice. According to this view the middle-class black stratum has not been active in breaking down discrimination barriers since many have a stake in the continued survival of the ghetto.[22]

No doubt there are life-style residues of Frazier's "old" and "new" middle classes; however, as will be suggested in this chapter, neither group is an accurate characterization of middle-class blacks in more current times. The class interest of acquisition, exemplified by a display of wealth and status, has been reshaped and modified by an intense movement of ethnic identification. Empirical evidence indicates that the black middle class is a complex blend of individualism, careers, militant attitudes (and sometimes action), and racial identification. In ethclass terms, there is a complex blend of class interests and race interests in the black middle class of today.

Changes in the Composition of the Labor Force

As the demographic data discussed in chapter 4 show, there is a growing upper-blue-collar and white-collar segment in the black population. Much of the growth of this new middle class is due to upward mobility from manual occupations rather than to a growth of the light-skinned aristocracy of which Frazier spoke. In one study of the black middle class, two-thirds of the white-collar respondents were sons whose fathers were in blue-collar manual occupations.[23] Many of the newer arrivals to the middle class have not come from a tradition of separation or social distance from the black masses. Further, the skin-color composition of the middle class is changing. Edwards, in a study of Negro professionals, finds that the most common skin color is brown, rather than very light or very dark.[24] Similarly, Kronus reports that three-fourths of his middle-class sample were brown or dark brown.[25] Increasingly, the black middle class is not a highly visible (light-skinned) sub-group anxious to protect its color status.

Another major change in the last twenty years is that upwardly mobile blacks have moved in increasing numbers into occupational categories that were formerly exclusively "white," rather than remaining in specific "ghetto" occupations. There has been an increase in the number of black professionals, managers, and sales and clerical persons. Many of the new black middle class are salaried, white-collar workers who have no special stake in segregation or in the establishment of an exclusively black clientele.

Action in the Face of Discrimination

There is now overwhelming evidence that the Civil Rights movement had its birth and most consistent support in the black middle class rather than the lower class.[26] The earliest activists tended to be students from fairly comfortable middle-class homes, though there was some participation from older segments of the black middle-class population.[27] Many accounts of the Civil Rights struggle speak of a generation gap between the direct protest tactics of the well-educated young and the more moderate intra-system methods of their parents.[28] However, once the Civil Rights (and later Black Power) movements were in motion, new constraints toward racial identity, action and loyalty were generated that spread the base of support both age- and class-wise.

There are good reasons why the black middle class should be most active in both individual and collective protest of the organized, programmed variety. When a person attains a middle-class position, he or she has greater resources with which to fight discrimination than has the lower-class person. The attainment of wealth, education, and high occupational position is clearly related to increased personal influence, knowledge of available channels of redress, enough money to hire a good lawyer, or enough knowledge to file suit, and adequate personal connections for affecting the system. Empirical support for the notion of increased resources can be seen in table 5.2 in which black respondents (interviewed by black interviewers shortly after the Watts riot) were asked, "What would you do if you went into a restaurant and were refused service because of your race?"[29] Placed in this hypothetical situation of race discrimination, blacks in white-collar jobs, those with incomes over $7,000, and those with some college education, were far more likely than those lower in SES to say that they would take definite action such as "organize a demonstration," "tell all my friends to boycott the restaurant," "report it to the NAACP or CORE," or "sue." Lower-class blacks were more likely to make statements such as "I would walk away," or "there's nothing you can do in situations like that."

Action in the Face of Discrimination by Education, Occupation, and Income

Item: *What would you do if you went into a restaurant and were refused service because of your race?*

	NON-ACTION RESPONSES (e.g., walk away)	ACTION RESPONSES (e.g., sue or boycott)
Education		
Less than High School	71%	29%
High School Graduate	58	49
Some College	28	72
Occupation		
Unemployed	61	39
Blue collar	53	47
White Collar	34	66
Income		
Under $5,000	59	41
$5–7,000	59	41
Over $7,000	29	71

Source: Ransford, Watts study. Three hundred twelve black males (ages 18–65) were interviewed after the Watts riot. Data in this table are unpublished. For further specifications on the sample and data collection procedures, see note 15 and H. Edward Ransford, "Skin Color, Life Chances, and Anti-White Attitudes," *Social Problems*, 18 (Fall, 1970), 167–168.

Table 5.2

Studies conducted in the 1990s indicate that middle-class blacks continue to face chronic and burdensome discrimination in public places and must frequently use middle class resources to combat that discrimination. Feagin studied discrimination cases in detail using thirty-seven in-depth interviews taken from a larger sample of one hundred and thirty-five middle class blacks interviewed from 1988–1990.[30] Respondents came from a variety of cities—for example, Boston, Buffalo, Baltimore, Washington D.C., Dallas, and Los Angeles. Feagin notes that discrimination varies from private to public sites. In the workplace, middle class status provides some protection against discrimination. A black professor at a predominantly white university comments ". . . if I'm in the university where my status as a professor mediates against the way I might be perceived, mediates against the hostile perception, then it's fairly comfortable."[31] This protection weakens as the person moves into public accommodations such as large stores and restaurants and is interacting with white strangers. Racial rebuffs and insults are more likely in these public situations. Historically, blacks have had to face discrimination in public places with resigned acceptance. The interviews show how middle-class blacks in the 1990s use their connections and power. A black news director at a major television station experienced poor restaurant service. She and her date were not seated. She directly confronted the manager noting that she had money and three major credit cards ". . . And then I took out my card and gave it to him and said, 'If this happens again, or if I hear of this happening again, I will bring the full wrath of an entire news department down on this restaurant'."[32] Feagin notes that this example provides insight into the character of modern discrimination. The discrimination was not blatant, but rather involved rejection in the form of poor service. The black middle class news director responds by assertively articulating a statement of rights: " . . . she has worked hard, earned the money and credit cards, developed the appropriate middle-class behavior, and thus has under the law a *right* to be served."[33] The civil rights laws of the 1960s and 1970s legitimized this kind of response and deeply affected the thinking of middle-class blacks.

Rage and the Invisibility Syndrome

Highly successful black Americans often experience infuriating situations of racism in their daily lives. In chapter 3, we noted that black middle class persons move between some situations in which their achieved status is salient and other situations in which their ascribed status (race) is most important. "The struggle today is particularly poignant for middle-class black men who have successfully jumped through the academic and corporate hoops that society promised would guarantee respect. They may go for days before a random encounter reminds them once again of their 'place'."[34] A number of publications in the early 1990s speak of the rage and invisibility felt by the black middle class. A major family therapy journal (*The Family Therapy Networker*) devoted an entire issue to the unique strains and stresses experienced by the black middle class. An article by Franklin gives an example of the invisibility syndrome. A highly paid manager in a major corporation describes a disturbing incident. He had taken a white business client to an expensive restaurant. When Bill (black manager) told the maitre d' they were there for dinner, the man had looked past him and asked his white guest if they had reservations. "When the meal was over, the waiter placed Bill's American Express Gold Card and the charge slip in front of Bill's client." Fearful of creating an embarrassing scene, Bill reached over and signed the slip, continuing to talk with his client. Later, after they had parted, Bill was at curbside while cab after cab passed him in favor of white couples or business persons. "Finally, after yet another cab passed him in favor of a white couple, Bill flung himself across the hood, swearing and flailing his attaché case at the driver's window."[35] The author of this article (a black family therapist) notes that all evening Bill had struggled with his sixth sense "that he was not being seen for himself but as a stereotype—first, as too insignificant to host a client at an expensive restaurant, and then as too dangerous to be let into a cab. Franklin adds that black middle class men often do not speak of these things with their wives and children, wanting to present themselves as strong and capable. Other research reports work strains on the job. Black managers with white subordinates may have their directives questioned or second guessed, with a common assumption among whites that the black manager reached his position only by affirmative action policies."[36]

Ellis Cose in a book titled *The Rage of the Privileged Class* summarizes interviews of highly successful blacks with this statement: "I heard a plaintive declaration—always followed by various versions of an unchanging and urgently put question. 'I have done everything I was supposed to do. I stayed out of trouble with the law, gone to the right schools, and worked myself nearly to death. What more do they want? Why in God's name won't they accept me as a full human being?'"[37] In short, black middle class persons (especially males) often face daily insults, rebuffs, and avoidance. Although racism has declined notably over historical time, class achievement does not override race for middle-class black Americans.

Black perceptions of inequality and job discrimination are borne out by workplace studies. A 1991 Urban Institute study involved teams of black and white job seekers with identical qualifications applying for 476 jobs advertised in newspapers in Washington and Chicago.[38] In essence, matched pairs of black and white men were applying for the same jobs. White applicants were three times more likely to advance in the hiring process than black applicants. "Employers were caught in the act," commented a senior researcher in the study. The study somewhat discredits arguments that affirmative action has produced reverse discrimination or preferences for minority applicants. The researchers conclude that " . . . despite extensive legislative and regulatory protections and incentives to hire minorities, unfavorable treatment of young black men is widespread and pervasive across firms offering entry level jobs in Washington D.C., and Chicago Metropolitan areas."[39] It was of interest that black men encountered more discrimination when applying for sales or service jobs that involved public contact than when they applied for blue collar positions. Discrimination against black males appeared to be highest in jobs offering the greatest future income potential.

There are important linkages between the problems of the black poor in the inner city and the continuing prejudice experienced by middle-class blacks. The problems of the black middle class pale by comparison with those of lower-class blacks. Yet, the nation cannot afford to ignore the "incomplete mobility" of middle-class blacks. Moreover, the continuing barriers and discrimination experienced by the middle class does not send an encouraging message to black youth that hard work and achievement pays off. As Cose notes " . . . one must at least consider the possibility that a nation which embitters those struggling hardest to believe in it and work within its established systems is seriously undermining any effort to provide would-be-hustlers and dope dealers with an attractive alternative to the streets."[40]

RACE, CLASS, AND DISCRIMINATION
Comparison Between Mexican Americans and Blacks

Compared with the numerous mass demonstrations, ghetto rebellions, and black power demands of blacks in the 1960s, most Mexican Americans have been less militant. It would be a great mistake, however, to depict Mexican Americans in the last several decades as silent. There are many signs of growing moods of militant protest and a willingness to bargain with the white majority using power tactics rather than simple persuasion. To mention but a few examples, we can note the highly effective grape and lettuce boycotts led by Cesar Chavez to bring union representation to farm workers, the militant claims to land rights led by Reies Tijerina in New Mexico, the numerous protests among Chicano college students for establishment of quotas for Chicano entrants, the young activists who walked out of several East Los

Angeles high schools protesting what they called the inability of the educational system to deal with language and cultural differences, and the East Los Angeles riot of 1970 that left two dead and hundreds injured. However, much of the Chicano militance of the last decade has been overshadowed by black protest. The anger and grievances of Chicanos have not been burned into the public consciousness to the same extent as blacks. In several interviews following the East Los Angeles riot these comments were recorded: "The authorities didn't listen. They didn't believe that the frustrations in the Mexican-American community would ever boil over . . ." "Issue after issue has been laid to rest with nothing done about them because the feeling has been that the Mexican American would never be a violent person."[41]

The Chicano Movement

The "Chicano Movement" was an example of the attempt of Mexican Americans of the Southwest to redefine their common identity and their relations to the white majority. The "movement" began with some middle-class students in the summer of 1966, but it spread quickly to others who were not middle-class. According to Cuellar the major force of the movement is the ideology—*Chicanismo*. To quote briefly from his discussion:

> Chicanos assume that along with American Indians and black Americans, Mexicans live in the United States as a conquered people. This idea allows *chicanismo* to explain the evolution of the Chicano as essentially conflictful. In each conflictual relationship with Anglos, the Mexicans lost out and were thus forced to live in the poverty and degradation attendant upon those with the status of a conquered people . . . *Chicanismo* emphasizes that the Mexican was transferred into a rootless economic commodity, forced either to depend on migrant farm work or to sell his labor in the urban centers, where his fate depended upon the vicissitudes of the economy . . . It is argued that Anglo racism denies the Mexican his ethnicity by making him ashamed of his "Mexican-ness." Mexican ancestry, instead of being a source of pride, becomes a symbol of shame and inferiority. As a consequence, Mexicans spend their lives apologizing or denying their ancestry to the point that many dislike and resent being called "Mexican," preferring "Spanish American," "Latin," "Latin American," and similar euphemisms. For these reasons, the term "Chicano" is now insisted upon by activists as a symbol of the new assertiveness. Advocates of chicanismo therefore hope to reconstruct the Mexican Americans' concept of themselves by appeals to pride of a common history, culture and "race". . .

> Chicano ideologues insist that social advance based on material achievement is, in the final analysis, less important than social advance based on la raza, they reject what they call the myth of American individualism . . . if Mexicans are to confront the problems of their group realistically they must begin to act along collective lines. Hence the stirrings of new spirit of what *chicanismo* terms "cultural nationalism" among the Mexican-Americans of the Southwest.[42]

There appears to be a growing mood of cultural nationalism in the Southwest that is felt especially by young people identifying themselves as "Chicanos." However, Chicanismo has not embraced the Mexican-American population to the same extent that: Black Power and African-American identity has the black population. It would seem logical that actual and perceived discrimination would be an important variable affecting ethnic consciousness for the group. To what extent do Mexican Americans perceive an ethnic stratification system in which they are disadvantaged? Some research, comparing black and Mexican-American adults, indicates that blacks are more likely to perceive discrimination in housing, education, and jobs.[43] Although about half of the Mexican Americans did report some inequality in these areas, they perceived their situation to be far better than blacks did theirs. To what extent do discrimination barriers, and perception of discrimination vary by *class* and *ethnicity*? Do middle-class Mexican Americans perceive less discrimination than middle-class blacks?

The evidence indicates that middle-class Mexican Americans face fewer barriers and have more integration-assimilation options than do middle-class blacks, especially so in the area of housing or spatial assimilation. Finding desirable housing and locating in a good residential area represents the epitome of the American Dream. Massey and Denton state "as a minority group's socioeconomic status increases, its members seek to improve their spatial position in urban society, which typically involves moving into neighborhoods with greater prestige, more amenities, safer streets, better schools, and higher value homes."[44] In the last decade, studies have examined the segregation of blacks and Hispanics using measures of spatial isolation or segregation and inter-ethnic contact, i.e., the probability of residential contact within and between groups.[45] The conclusion from these studies is that blacks, regardless of socioeconomic status, experience a high degree of spatial isolation or segregation from whites. By contrast, spatial segregation varies from modest to moderate levels for Hispanics.

Socioeconomic mobility for Hispanics is more often associated with spatial assimilation and contact with Anglos. The pattern holds for a variety of metropolitan areas across the country. In some areas of rapid immigration, Hispanic segregation has increased but the levels of segregation are invariably lower than for blacks. Massey and Denton argue that *suburbanization* is a crucial intervening process between changes in socioeconomic status and acculturation.[46] That is, racial integration has usually been associated with moving to the suburbs. For Hispanics, spatial assimilation does take place through the suburbanization process, but not so for blacks. Some blacks are, no doubt, moving to the suburbs but this movement has no effect on segregation. "Either blacks are moving to suburbs in numbers too small to make a difference, or suburbs and central cities are equally segregated."[47] Anglos appear to share residential space with Hispanics more readily than with African Americans. We have seen in chapter 4 that blacks have developed a substantial middle class and skilled working class in recent years. But the Massey and Denton analysis indicates that blacks have not achieved the freedom to move wherever they want. The level of black segregation in housing is not affected by blacks' socioeconomic status. "Because rising social status does not allow blacks to assimilate spatially in the manner of other groups, they are isolated within all-black or nearly all-black neighborhoods located disproportionately within declining inner-city areas."[48]

The greater assimilation options for Mexican Americans are also apparent from intermarriage data. High rates of intermarriage for a minority group indicate assimilation or a merging of minority and majority group. Anglo-Mexican intermarriage rates differ a great deal by generation, region of the country, and socioeconomic status. There has been a substantial increase in the Hispanic intermarriage rate. Intermarriage rates for Mexican Americans were highest in California, averaging a 50 percent out-marriage rate. In small towns and cities in south Texas, the exogamy rates were far lower, averaging 10–27 percent. A person most likely to intermarry outside the Mexican American group is a Mexican-American woman, born in the United States and living in California and of higher occupational status.[49] Although the black rate of out-marriage has also increased recently, the rate is far lower (2.5–3 percent outgroup marriage) than the Mexican-American rate.[50]

The above data on spatial assimilation and intermarriage rates fit John Howard's distinction between "partial" and "total" minority groups.[51] Partial minority groups (illustrated by Mexican Americans) means that the dominant group does impose impediments to group mobility, especially among lower-class members of that group, but individuals who manage to acquire the mannerisms, education, and occupational status of the dominant group are often accepted as members of the dominant group. By contrast, "total minority" (illustrated by African Americans) means that the group more consistently faces prejudice and discrimination even with socioeconomic mobility. Though Howard's distinction may be a little too sweeping for the 1990s, in the specific areas of residential segregation and intermarriage rates it does seem to be operating. Further, the distinction between partial and total minorities leads to an interesting proposition: lower-class Mexican Americans probably face the same barriers as lower-class blacks, but middle-class Mexican Americans often fare considerably better than middle-class blacks. Thus, the quality of life experienced by lower-class Latinos in an urban barrio may be very similar to that experienced by lower-class blacks in the ghetto, involving the same components of joblessness, consumer exploitation, inferior schools and hostile police contacts. Middle-class Latinos, however, may face far less color prejudice than middle-class blacks.

MEXICAN AMERICAN FARMWORKERS*

Though "partial" minority may be a useful label for some of the options open to middle-class Latinos, there is no more "total" or thoroughly oppressed minority group than lower-class Mexican-American farmworkers. The plight of the present-day farm workers is likened to pre-Civil War conditions of blacks on the plantations. As late as 1966, there was evidence that hundreds of farmworkers were kept in virtual serfdom on remote ranches all over the southwestern United States, financially and physically unable to leave.[52]

Why is it that when this very small fraction of one of the conquered minorities (about 6 percent of the Mexican-American population) ask for so few and such reasonable changes (like minimum wages and portable toilets on the job), that management reacts with such widespread, oppressive measures, thwarting the self-development of a rather unobtrusive power base?

---

*This discussion of Mexican-American farmworkers in the Southwest should be regarded as one interpretation of events.

The attempts to undermine the farmworkers' peaceful efforts to organize for benefits accorded other American industrial workers are not just isolated incidents or even a matter of deliberate consensus and planned action among agri-businessmen across the country. It is much more than that. It is not force and coercion that sustain, through time, one group's power over another, rather it is the institutionalization of that power—building into society a particular pattern of interaction. The farmworkers and growers are locked into a very old, traditional labor pattern. Agribusiness in the United States depends upon a massive, continuous, snag-free flow of cheap laborers.

Beginning with the Chinese immigrants in the 1870s, there have always been enough desperate, poverty-stricken people (either citizens already in this country, or people from abroad) willing to work in the fields without questioning the conditions. Mexican Americans have been particularly available. For years, they were imported or deported, depending on whims of economists, lawmakers, and businessmen. Other industries were not allowed to import foreign workers. (Farmers can still use "green-carders" to fill in if American farmworkers raise their voices in protest of working conditions. "Green-carders" are Mexican citizens with special work permit visas). Other industries were forbidden to use child labor, were required to pay minimum wages, to make working conditions safe, to allow for the development of unions and worker representations. Farmworkers were excluded from these legal protections. They do not come under the jurisdiction of the National Labor Relations Board.**

Governmental exceptions and special privileges abound in agriculture. Farmers are given billions in Federal subsidies to protect them from fluctuations in the economy, to reimburse them

---

**For years there have been suggestions by politicians and growers that farm workers should now be included under NLRA, but few people realize that the time they should have been included was somewhere between 1935 and 1947. After the 1935 Wagner Act, unions became more and more organized and gained tremendous strength; the 1947 Taft-Hartley Amendment was aimed at curbing union power, and now would prevent the farm workers from developing *any*. The Taft-Hartley Amendment limits the right to strike and to boycott—farm workers would be caught with many conditions remaining unchanged once stripped of this kind of economic muscle. The farm workers feel that they need a little catching-up with other industries. They liken the NLRA to Civil Rights legislation—unless a group has enough power to demand enforcement of laws, the laws mask the real, existing conditions of inequality.

for empty fields, but farm laborers receive nothing. Farmworkers, without any economic safeguards or rights guaranteed to other American workers are clearly at the bottom of the stratification system, class-wise. What about *eth*class?

> You see, says Cesar Chavez, the farm worker is an outsider, even though he may be a resident worker . . . His is an outsider economically, and he is an outsider racially. Most farm workers are of ethnic backgrounds other than white.[53]

Though growers are seldom heard referring publicly to farmworkers as "ignorant Mexicans," many paternalistic statements are still made, which imply a belief in inferiority. ". . . The idea that farmworkers are a different breed of people—humble, happy, built close to the ground—still prevails," according to Chavez.[54] Growers often refer to "my boys" in a manner very similar to that of plantation owners talking about "their" Negroes.

> The Mexican is a child by nature, a grower explains. He has no sense of the future. He likes to enjoy himself. Sing. Dance. Drink. So he loves all those parades and flags and singing the union has. It's a fiesta to him, the damn union . . . He doesn't know anything about farm economics.[55]

The Mexican-American farmworkers remain the last minority group which still offers direct economic payoffs for exploitation. For example, it has become costly to exploit blacks. The costs, in terms of welfare rolls, national image, riots, and crime, increasingly has made large-scale, systematic exploitation of blacks unprofitable. There is no longer a nation-wide, systematic attempt to keep blacks economically "in their place." But any organization of power among farmworkers is seen as a threat to the highly lucrative business of agriculture, as well as a threat to the whole economic system. The implication of farmworkers with power does not mean just slightly higher wages and a few benefits: it suggests that the power elite might have to yield some of its exclusive hold on power over to a heretofore docile, predictable work force upon which the economy is dependent.

In the 1960s farmworkers, for the first time, exerted a significant amount of counter-power. Under the leadership of Chavez, farm workers and their supporters appealed to consumers not to buy table grapes. *Boycott Grapes!* became an effective means to force growers to recognize the strength and legitimacy of the United Farmworkers' union and to sign contracts that would bring improved wages and benefits. A consumer boycott of a perishable crop has great power potential, yet such a boycott can only be successful when there is wide scale support in middle-class America.

How could such a voiceless minority as farmworkers ever organize a world-wide boycott against table grapes—the only world-wide boycott in history? Traditional Marxian class conflict theory would tell us that a totally powerless population often widely dispersed rather than in close proximity, disengaged from the conventional economic structure, with little hope or rising expectations for change would be overcome with hopelessness and despair, rather than ready to actively to change the system through class action.[56]

There are probably three special aspects of the farm worker movement that account for its tremendous support and publicity, and help to explain why it is an exception from theoretical suppositions.

1. Cesar Chavez, the leader of the United Farm Workers Union (UFW), is to some, a saint, and to others, a dangerous power-monger. All who know of him are impressed by his outstanding ability to organize and his quiet charisma. Cesar Chavez is unequivocally dedicated to change through non-violence. He explains that though violence would certainly have won some union contracts, violence never wins respect.

2. The United Farmworkers have won respect—respect from some very respectful segments of our society—the National Council of Churches and many middle-class lay people. No other lower-class minority movement has managed to secure support from such groups. One reason for middle-class support is the safety of non-violence. Probably the timing of the movement too, helped. During the 1960s (the beginning of the table grape boycott) our nation was fraught with riots and war. Aside from the moral and religious appeal of non-violence, a group pushing for change through peaceful means seemed, to many people, an isolated, perhaps vanishing, alternative to bloodshed, one that needed support and encouragement.

   The grape boycott was a "safe" action, allowing for wide-spread support for farmworkers among middle-class segments of the society. Asking people not to buy grapes was a very small favor with which many people were able to comply. The farmworkers movement included millions of "mini-activists." The California Migrant Ministry (formerly under the direction of the Reverend

W. C. Hartmire, and supported by representatives of all faiths) asked for food and clothing and small donations of time and money from parishioners and friends. These were items that middle-class people could give safely, but were very important for widely based support and subsequent public pressures for change.

3. The third aspect of the farmworkers' struggle that made it unique was its powerlessness. That this low ethclass has been kept politically and economically powerless has been demonstrated. But, led by Cesar Chavez, they turned powerlessness—the very condition that should have spelled despair and apathy—into their most dynamic asset. The utter powerlessness and oppression of the Mexican-American farm worker is used as a device for extracting sympathy and support from middle-class Americans. More importantly, the rock-bottom feelings of powerlessness of the farm worker actually account for his patient, unswerving, push for change. The poverty-stricken Mexican American could say, "What have I got to lose? Things can't be worse."

Powerlessness became the very source of the farmworkers' power, the ability to endure unbelievable opposition to requests for change and to persist in those demands against all odds. This third aspect of powerlessness as the most powerful non-violent weapon for change cannot be separated from the (1) leadership of Cesar Chavez. Neither can it be separated from (2) the unusual widespread support of so many non-Mexican-American, non-farm-working, non-lower-class people. Cesar Chavez's words may best illustrate the uniqueness of the farm worker movement that seems to touch all of those who have been involved even slightly.

> When we are really honest with ourselves, we must admit that our lives are all that really belong to us. So it is how we use our lives that determines what kind of men we are. It is my deepest belief that only by giving our lives do we find life. I am convinced that the truest act of courage, the strongest act of manliness, is to sacrifice ourselves for others in a totally non-violent struggle for justice. To be a man is to suffer for others. God help us be men.[57]

In 1970, many large farm growers finally signed contracts with the United Farm Workers. The contracts brought health and retirement benefits for the first time as well as higher minimum wages. It appeared that self determination was at last becoming a reality for the powerless worker. However, in 1973, when contracts were to be renewed, California growers ignored or refused requests by farmworkers to hold elections for union representation. Completely bypassing UFW, growers secretly signed contracts with the Teamster's Union. Although the Teamster contracts were not without benefits (some of the benefits were comparable to the UFW contracts) the Teamsters were not oriented toward the unique problems of the farmworkers (the need for on-site medical facilities, pesticide protection for workers etc.) and their contracts reflected it. The issue became far more than the relative benefits of the two contracts; workers were once again not allowed to express their collective voice—the issue was self determination. Growers apparently found the Teamsters more appealing; they have in common a more business-like, less emotional, English speaking, middle-classness. More important, Teamsters have a vested interest in a constant, uninterrupted flow of produce from the farm to the supermarket. Teamsters wanted crops harvested under any conditions so that they could be guaranteed pay for transporting those crops.

The term *co-optation* is used when powerful organizations absorb the demands of dissidents in such a way that the social organization is not significantly altered. Contracts with Teamsters represented a kind of co-optation of worker demands. Such contracts did not alter the agribusiness equation. Two powerful groups (growers and Teamsters) worked together for their common economic interests. Farmworkers, though given some increased material benefits, remained essentially outside and powerless to effect change.

In California, in the mid-1970s, there was state legislation that recognized farm worker rights, including that of selecting their own union, but these rights have not been systematically enforced. As a result, boycotts of head lettuce and grapes continue, with the focus now on health conditions and use of pesticides. The present boycotts tie directly into the health consciousness of the 1990s. Middle-class segments of the population are now also concerned about cancer clusters, contamination of the environment and pesticide residues in their food supplies. Farmworkers are making a powerful appeal to the public, pointing out that a boycott of grapes will force growers (and, in turn, legislators) to provide safer health conditions that will directly benefit consumers.

Farmworkers are striving to convert their lower-class status only to working-class position. This seemingly minor shuffling at the bottom of the hierarchy, however, threatens to shake the giants at the top—not enough to change noticeably the life styles of middle or upper-class persons but enough to demand a significant redistribution of power in a huge industry that is institutionalized about the total power of those at the top and the total voicelessness of those at the bottom. In their modest demands for traditional rights and privileges—self-determination, a voice in their future, secret ballot elections, choosing their own representatives, freedom from hunger and dangerous working conditions—farmworkers threaten another cluster of traditional American patterns: huge corporate power and bureaucratic insensitivities. Parallels of similar battles can be heard from the rumblings of consumers, the homeless, from welfare recipients, and from American Indians. So far, indications of change, or redistribution of power (of even a tiny tokenism of power trickling down from the top) are more potential than actual. Success of the farm worker movement may mean not just the correction of injustices in that particular labor pattern, but application of a new economic pattern that could well affect other ethclass or lower-class or powerless people as well.

NOTES

1. Los Angeles Times Staff, *Understanding the Riots*, (Los Angeles: Times Mirror Company, 1992): 46.

2. H. Edward Ransford, "Isolation, Powerlessness, and Violence: A Study of Attitudes and Participation in the Watts Riot," *American Journal of Sociology*, 73 (March, 1968): 581–591.

3. Melvin Seeman, "On the Meaning of Alienation," *American Sociological Review*, 24 (1959): 783–791.

4. William Julius Wilson, *The Truly Disadvantaged* (Chicago: University of Chicago Press, 1987).

5. Los Angeles Times, *Understanding the Riots*, 26.

6. David Heer and Pini Herman, *A Human Mosaic: An Atlas of Ethnicity in L.A. County, 1980–1986* (Panorama City, CA: Western Economic Research Company, 1990).

7. Los Angeles Times, *Understanding the Riots*, 28.

8. Nadine Koch and H. Eric Schockman, "Riot, Rebellion, or Civil Unrest? Perspectives of the Korean-American and African-American Business Communities in Los Angeles," Paper delivered at the Fifth Annual Asian Pacific American Community Research Roundtable, California State University, Los Angeles, April 16, 1993.

9. Tim Delaney, "Fragmentation and the 1992 Los Angeles Riots," Paper delivered at the Annual Pacific Sociological Association Meetings, Portland, Oregon, April, 1993.

10. Heer and Herman, *A Human Mosaic: An Atlas of Ethnicity in L.A. County, 1980–1986.*

11. John Ritter, "Brutal Realities Dashing Korean Dreams," *USA Today*, (Tuesday, October 12, 1993): 9A.

12. Koch and Schockman, "Riot, Rebellion, or Civil Unrest? Perspectives of the Korean-American and African-American Business Communities in Los Angeles," 28.

13. Edna Bonacich, "The Present, Past, and Future, of Split Labor Market Theory," Research in Race and Ethnic Relations 1 (1979): 49. See also Edna Bonacich, "Making it in America," *Sociological Perspective* 30 (October, 1987): 446–465.

14. Koch and Schockman, "Riot, Rebellion, or Civil Unrest? Perspectives of the Korean-American and African-American Business Communities in Los Angeles."

15. Ritter, "Brutal Realities Dashing Korean Dreams."

16. Koch and Schockman, "Riot, Rebellion, or Civil Unrest? Perspectives of the Korean-American and African-American Business Communities in Los Angeles."

17. Recent survey conducted by Yeong S. Jyoo with the Korean American Inter-Agency Council as reported in Connie K. Kang, "Korean Riot Victims Suffer Stress Disorder," *Los Angeles Times* (March 3, 1992).

18. Tamotsu Shibutani and Kian M. Kwan, *Ethnic Stratification* (New York: Free Press, 1962).

19. E. Franklin Frazier, *Black Bourgeoisie: The Rise of a New Middle Class* (New York: Free Press, 1962).

20. Sidney Kronus, *The Black Middle Class* (Columbus: Charles E. Merril, 1970).

21. Lerone Bennett, Jr., "Black Bourgeoisie Revisited," *Ebony* 28 (August, 1973): 52.

22. See, for example, Shibutani and Kwan, *Ethnic Stratification*, 498; Frazier, *Black Bourgeoisie: The Rise of a New Middle Class*, 108.

23. Bart Landry, *The New Black Middle Class* (Berkeley: University of California Press, 1987).

24. G. Franklin Edwards, *The Negro Professional Class* (Glencoe, III: Free Press, 1959).

25. Kronus, *The Black Middle Class*, 21.

26. See, for example, Gary T. Marx, *Protest and Prejudice* (New York: Harper & Row, 1967), 55–70; Ruth Searles and J. Allen Williams, Jr., "Negro College Students Participation in Sit-Ins," *Social Forces* 40 (March, 1962), 215–220.

27. Searles and Williams, Ibid., 215–220; Edwards, *The Negro Professional Class*, 5–16.

28. Harry Edwards, *Black Students* (New York: Free Press, 1970).

29. This is the same Watts survey described earlier in this chapter.

30. Joe R. Feagin, "The Continuing Significance of Race: Antiblack Discrimination in Public Places," *American Sociological Review*, 56 (February, 1991): 101–116.

31. Ibid., 109.

32. Ibid., 105.

33. Ibid., 105.

34. Anderson J. Franklin, "The Invisibility Syndrome," *The Family Therapy Networker*, 17 (July/August, 1993): 35.

35. Ibid., 34.

36. Richard Lacayo, "Between Two Worlds," *Time* (March 13, 1989): 58–68.

37. Ellis Cose, *The Rage of a Privileged Class*, Harper-Collins Forthcoming. Pre-release book excerpts in *Newsweek*, "The Hidden Rage of Successful Blacks," 122 (November 15, 1993): 56–57.

38. See summary of Urban Institute Study (1991) on Black and White Job-seekers (Raymond Struyk, senior researcher), *Los Angeles Times*, (Wednesday, May 15, 1991).

39. Ibid.

40. Cose, *The Rage of a Privileged Class*, as quoted in *Newsweek*, "The Hidden Rage of Successful Blacks," 57.

41. *Los Angeles Times*, (August 31, 1970): 1.

42. Alfred Cuellar, "Perspectives on Politics," in *Mexican Americans* by Joan W. Moore, 1970. Reprinted by permission of Prentice-Hall, Inc. Englewood Cliffs, N.J.

43. Chandler Davidson and Charles M. Gaitz, "Ethnic Attitudes as a Basis for Minority Cooperation in a Southwestern Metropolis, *Social Science Quarterly* 53 (March, 1973): 738–748.

44. Douglas S. Massey and Nancy Denton, "Trends in the Residential Segregation of Blacks, Hispanics, and Asians," in Norman R. Yetman (ed.) *Majority and Minority: The Dynamics of Race and Ethnicity in American Life*, 5th edition (Boston: Allyn and Bacon, 1991)

45. Ibid. See also Douglas S. Massey and Brendan P. Mullan, "Processes of Hispanic and Black Spatial Assimilation," in Norman R. Yetman (ed.) *Majority and Minority: The Dynamics of Race and Ethnicity in American Life*, 4th edition (Boston: Allyn and Bacon, 1985).

46. Massey and Denton, "Trends in the Residential Segregation of Blacks, Hispanics and Asians," 371.

47. Ibid., 377.

48. Massey and Mullan, "Processes of Hispanic and Black Spatial Assimilation," 368.

49. Joan Moore and Harry Pachon. *Hispanics in the United States* (Englewood Cliffs, New Jersey: Prentice Hall, 1985), 108.

50. Sylvester Monroe, "Love in Black and White: The Last Racial Taboo," *Los Angeles Times Magazine* (December 9, 1990): 14.

51. John Howard, *Awakening Minorities*, (New Brunswick, N.J.,: Transaction Books, 1970): 6.

52. Stan Steiner, *La Raza: The Mexican Americans* (New York: Harper and Row, 1970): 247–248.

53. Ibid., 261 and 1970s conversation with Rev. W. C. Hartmire, Director California Migrant Ministry: "In the Southwest, where most of the pioneering in organizing a farmworkers' union is taking place, about 70 percent of the farmworkers are Mexican American, others are Filipino, black, and a few Anglos."

54. Steiner, *La Raza: The Mexican Americans*, 264.

55. Ibid., p. 260.

56. For an excellent summary of the Marxian class conflict approach, see Reinhard Bendix and Seymour Martin Lipset, "Karl Marx's Theory of Social Classes," in Reinhard Bendix and Seymour Martin Lipset (eds.) *Class, Status, and Power* (New York: Free Press, 1966): 6–11.

57. Peter Matthiessen, "Profile: Cesar Chavez, New Yorker (June 21 and June 28, 1969). This excerpt appeared subsequently in Peter Matthiessen, *Sal Si Puedes* (New York: Random House, 1970.)

6

Adding Gender to the Equation
Race, Class, and Gender

The primary focus of this book is the interaction of social class and race/ethnic background. Gender inequality—that is, patterned inequalities between men and women in power and privilege—is viewed now as another important stratification order.[1] Over the last thirty years, in particular, women from all parts of public and private life have challenged old gender role assumptions and attempted to change their status in their jobs and families. Demands for fair, equal treatment have included a variety of gender role negotiations for shared power and resources.

Adding gender inequality to class and race-ethnic inequalities produces a multiple hierarchy model. This is illustrated in figure 6.1. Note that the arrows connect each hierarchy with power, privilege, and prestige. A stratum or position in each hierarchy (such as upper class, black, or female) represents an aggregate of people who share the same access to power, privilege, or prestige. The higher the position in each hierarchy, the greater the access to power, privilege and prestige. The lower the position, the greater the discrimination barriers in acquiring these social rewards.

Gender may independently determine access to power, privilege, and prestige. A woman may be in an advantaged position on other hierarchies (she may be white, well-educated and from an influential, wealthy family) but be denied a management position because of her gender. In most societies, men have had far greater shares of resources, life chances and social honor than women.

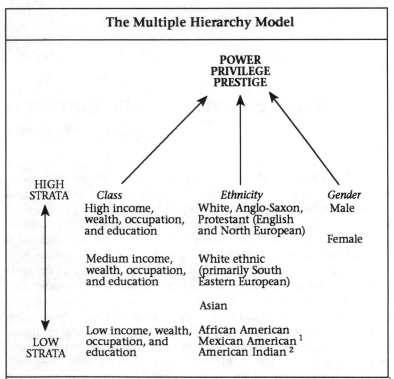

[1]Although *Hispanic* is the term used most widely to include Mexican Americans or Chicanos, Cubans, Puerto Ricans, South Americans, and other Spanish-speaking people, lumping together all Spanish-speaking people under the term *Hispanic* would blur sociological analysis. Language often is all that Hispanic people share. Chicanos or Mexican Americans are discussed most in this book because 1)they represent 60 to 70 percent of the Hispanic population of the United States, depending on the inclusion of illegal aliens, and 2) their historical experiences fit a model of conquest and colonization—important factors when power inequality determines positions in the ethnic hierarchy.

[2]The terms American Indian and Native American are used interchangeably in this text.

Figure 6.1

INDIVIDUAL AND INSTITUTIONAL SEXISM AND SEX DISCRIMINATION

As with race/ethnic discrimination, an important distinction can be made between individual and institutional discrimination.

Employers who discriminate against women because they believe women to be unfit for the job (saying "women are too emotional, . . . not physically strong enough, . . . lack the presence to be in supervisory posts") are holding individual sexist attitudes and are engaging in individual discrimination. In many cases, however, gender inequalities and discrimination may be embedded in the system itself. That is, every day routines and practices may impact harmful consequences on women even if there is very little personal, sexist bigotry involved. For example, women are expected to work the same hours as men. Yet child care is often assumed to be the responsibility of a woman. Most work organization do not provide day-care facilities or after school care, or allow flexibility in work hours that would allow men and women to pick up a child after school. Showering and sleeping facilities in fire stations formerly were constructed with only one gender in mind. Architects, designers, and business owners do not consciously discriminate against women when they build large recreational or entertainment centers with equal numbers of restrooms for men and women. There is a traditional institutional insensitivity to women's needs. Both individual and institutional sexism are operating in our society today. Consider, for example, three aspects of gender inequality: income, occupational status, and household labor.

Income

Income is an important variable when discussing the concept of privilege because many services, rights and immunities are purchased. There are substantial differences in the median incomes of men and women. In 1987, the median annual earnings of women who worked year-round full-time was 65 percent that of men.[2] That is, women earned 65 cents for each dollar earned by men. At every level of education, women have much lower incomes than men who have achieved the same educational level. For example, among those with four years of high school, women employed full-time, year-round earned 65 percent of male earnings; for those with four or more years of college, the gap was about the same—68 percent.[3] Some of the explanation for the gender gap in income can be explained by qualifications and work experience. Men and women differ in educational attainment and fields of specialization chosen. Once employed, women are more likely to have job interruptions and to spend less time in the labor force. "For instance, in 1984, among full-time, year-round workers (aged twenty-one to sixty-four), 42 percent of the women experienced one or more work interruptions lasting six months or more over the course of their labor market careers, as compared to 12 percent of the men."[4] Also men, on average, have accumulated more labor market experience; 40 percent of men compared to 23 percent of women have over 20 years of work experience.[5] But a number of studies have indicated that when all income-relevant factors are held constant, such as education and work history, there is still a significant gender differential and this remaining gap is believed to be a result of sex discrimination. Research suggests that one half or more of the income gap between men and women is due to discrimination.[6]

There is some encouraging news that the gender gap in earnings has narrowed slightly over time. In 1970, the gender gap was 59.4 percent for full-time, year-round workers compared with 65 percent in 1987. The gap has narrowed the most for cohorts of younger women 25–34 years old: from 62.2 percent in 1967 to 74 percent in 1987.[7]

Occupation

Although women have moved into management and professional occupations in record numbers in the last decade, most women are still confined to a relatively few low to middle status occupation categories. Table 4.1 (see chapter 4) shows that 45 percent of the female labor force is found in the administrative support (including clerical) and service occupations. Men are slightly more likely than women to be found in executive, managerial, and administrative positions (13 versus 11 percent) and much more likely to be found in the best paying, most prestigeful blue-collar jobs (19 versus 2 percent precision production). Surprisingly, a higher proportion of women than men are classified "professional specialty." However, Blau and Winkler note that about half of the women in this professional category are concentrated in traditionally female dominated fields of librarian, registered nurse, prekindergarten and kindergarten teacher, elementary-school teacher, special-education teacher, dietician, and speech therapist.[8] By contrast, male professional workers are more concentrated in better paying occupations of engineer, lawyer, architect, chemist, announcer, and physician.

Women are highly concentrated in roughly twenty occupations while men are more widely distributed throughout the occupational structure. Not only is there a high degree of occupational segregation, but the twenty occupations dominated by women involve low income and prestige and poor chances for advancement. Clerical jobs are the classic example. Approximately one-third of all women in the labor force are employed in clerical jobs.[9] Although some clerical jobs involve work challenge and responsibility, many involve routine tasks; most are, at best, moderately well paid and practically all are sealed off as a separate hierarchy with virtually no possibility of crossing over into better paying management positions. The segregation of male and female jobs is commonly referred to as the dual labor market. Collins notes that men and women are not only occupying different positions, but typically women work in occupations in which they receive orders from men and give orders only to other women or to children (clerical work, nursing, elementary school teaching).[10] Thus, the distribution of men and women in occupations is an example of unequal power.

The last two decades have brought notable changes in the occupational mobility of women. The prestige occupations of medicine and law are two cases in point. Kaufman notes that for the first seven decades of this century the proportion of women among active physicians remained at about 7 percent.[11] In the last two decades changes in federal law and gender roles has led to a remarkable increase in the proportion of women in medical schools. In the academic year 1964–65, 7.7 percent of the first year medical students were women. In 1987, women constituted 19.5 percent of all practicing physicians and 27 percent of all medical residents.[12] Despite these impressive increases, it should be noted that female physicians are more concentrated in lower paying specialties such as pediatrics and public health, while male physicians are more often found in higher paying surgical specialties.

Women have also made impressive gains in the legal profession. In the academic year 1976–77, 22.5 percent of those receiving law degrees were women, compared to 38.5 percent in 1984–85. Approximately 20 percent of lawyers were women in 1987.[13]

Not only are women entering male-dominated occupations (architecture, law, medicine, business management, police enforcement, and the military) but increasingly they are in positions in which they give orders to both male and female subordinates, thus overturning the traditional power inequality gender pattern that has so pervaded the occupational structure. Even with these recent changes, women as an aggregate are highly concentrated in traditionally female occupations. The dual labor market is still very much alive.

Non-division of Household Labor

Privilege involves not only access to the good things in life, but also immunity from the unpleasant things in life. Much of the household labor may be considered unpleasant. Household labor—meal preparation, laundry, cleaning—is a never-ending chore involving often dirty and monotonous tasks. Rarely is housework described as a source of fulfillment or satisfaction. In addition, child care, though involving many satisfactions, is extremely time consuming. With recent developments, such as the increase in the number of working women and the rise of the feminist movement, one gets the impression that there has been a more equitable division of household labor. Numerous articles on two career families and 50/50 marriages have appeared in newspapers and magazines. Such articles suggest that the drudgery of household labor is becoming more equally shared by husband and wife. A number of recent studies challenge this assumption.[14] In particular, a study by Berk and Berk involves a very thorough set of observations on work tasks.[15] To capture fully the household division of labor, the study involved a variety of methods: a one-hour interview of 309 married women, participant observation in 40 households, and a diary of the activities of 158 women covering twenty-four hour periods. (The women were paid for making these detailed accounts.) The study found that women perform 75–85 percent of all household labor. Even more provocative was the finding that a woman's contribution to household labor (1) did not change significantly if she worked full-time outside the home, (2) became only slightly more equal when she was employed in a more prestigious and better paying job, (3) did not change for older and younger couples (4) was unaffected by the presence of preschool-age children, and (5) was not affected by the education or income of a couple. That is, even among younger, well-educated, working-wife families, where presumably the goals of feminist equality would be most strongly held, women did the majority of household tasks. Such findings point to a conclusion that career women are holding down two full-time jobs.

GENDER IN INTERACTION WITH RACE AND CLASS

Gender inequality combines or interacts with race and class inequality in a number of interesting ways. Chapter 3 outlined several models of race-class interaction that can also be applied to gender. For example, the Open Marketplace Model suggests that social class achievement greatly improves the power, income and life chances of minority persons and women. However, some remaining racial and gender barriers and discrimination are likely to remain. For example, the term "glass ceiling" is increasingly used to describe the instance in which minority persons or women encounter an invisible ceiling to their mobility into top positions. The organization may welcome minority persons or women at entry level managerial positions yet prevent their ascendance into top decision making positions. Discrimination against women seeking these positions may occur as a result of stereotypical judgements that a woman's career commitment is likely to be in competition with child care or that a female candidate for promotion lacks the aggressiveness or toughness necessary for the job. Moreover, if she reaches a relatively high position in the organization, she may face a situation of role encapsulation. Rosabeth Kanter, in her book *Men and Women of the Corporation,*[16] notes that token women (often in high positions) were placed in limited roles that gave them the security of a "place" but constrained their areas of permissible behavior. Tokens were perceived in terms of stereotypical roles that preserved familiar gender role interactions. For example, a token woman in the organization was sometimes treated as a "mother" (one to whom men brought their private troubles and expected comfort), a "seductress" or sex object, a "pet" (one adopted by the male group as cute and amusing; a cheerleader), and an "ironmaiden" (a tough or dangerous, strong woman). Thus, even with achievement, there were strong gender constraints operating. The mobility is incomplete. *Incomplete mobility* refers to instances in which people who have attained high status in occupation, authority over others, or education are denied the full prerogatives of that status because of their race or gender. That is, mobility in the class hierarchy is not accompanied by full access to power, privilege, and prestige. The person has "made it" from a class achievement standpoint, but inequalities remain because of the person's ascribed status. Research documents the incomplete mobility of high achieving women. Miller et al. found that inequalities remained for women in high authority positions in formal organizations.[17] Women of all ranks were more likely to be rated low by co-workers in perceived influence and professional respect and to be more isolated from persons in positions of authority. One would logically expect that women who had reached higher positions in organizations would be more favorably rated. Especially important was the finding that women in higher positions of authority, education and occupational rank faced the greatest inequities in respect, influence, and access to information. Although they had reached a higher position, their access to power and influence was less than that of men in the same position. One interpretation is that these women were isolated from informal male peer groups and activities (golf games, informal talk in locker rooms etc.) in which vital information is shared. Hughes writes that when women are the first of their kind in organizational positions, they are often marginal because they are not included in the "informal brotherhood in which experiences are exchanged, competence built up, and the formal code elaborated and enforced."[18]

There are similar barriers to women's advancement in the professions such as law, medicine, dentistry and engineering. These professions involve a high degree of informal interaction. They are closed worlds in which colleagues develop many interdependencies, such as exchanging information essential to the performance of the job, or giving opinions and feedback to each other's work. In many professions a sponsor-protegé system exists. A senior colleague (usually male) in a profession may be eager to pass his knowledge and skills to a younger protegé. Epstein notes that male sponsors may hesitate to accept a female protegé because of a belief that she is less committed to the profession or because the husband of the female protegé or wife of the male sponsor resents the close, intense work relationship between student and sponsor.[19]

Ethclass is another race-class interaction model noted in chapter 3. In this case, race and class intersect to form subsocieties with unique attitudes and perceptions of the social system. The combined effects of race and gender also present another instance of special social spaces. For example, white men, black men, white women, and black women can be viewed as "ethgender" groups with distinctive experiences and outlooks. The double burden of work and household responsibilities is a fairly new situation for white middle-class women, yet the burden has a long history for women of color. Black men have historically experienced high degrees of discrimination and unemployment. Almquist[20] and Terrelonge[21] note that black women have responded by developing an alternative form of family. Many black families are characterized by extended households (with grandmothers and aunts present) and pooled resources. Patricia Hill Collins speaks of the intense oppression that black women have faced as a result of the combined effects of race and gender.[22] She discusses the strategies that black women have developed. Black women have "found their voices" in the church, and black women's organizations. Consuelo Nieto makes similar points when speaking of the Mexican-American women. She argues that Chicanas wishing to express feminism face a unique set of constraints. The gender roles of Mexican Americans tend to be traditional. The woman is expected to be the nurturer and the emotional caregiver of children. The Catholic Church's conception of *Marianismo* or idealization of the Virgin Mary reinforces these expectations of nurturing mother and wife.[23] These traditions allow little room for individual expression or roles outside of the home.

Empirical studies of the interaction of gender and race or gender and class are commencing. My colleague, Jon Miller, and I were interested in the intersections or joint effects of race, class, and gender on feminist outlooks. The following reprinted article from the *American Sociological Review* is our attempt to note race-class-gender interactions in predicting feminist outlooks.

Race, Sex, and Feminist Outlooks

by H. Edward Ransford and Jon Miller
University of Southern California
American Sociological Review 48 (February, 1983): 46–59.

Introduction

In the climate of womens' liberation, the equal rights amendment, and the ascendance of some women into political and business positions formerly dominated by men, there has been special interest, in the last decade, in new definitions of women's roles. The study of sex-role outlooks represents one important way of gauging the overall degree of sexual inequality in a society. Sex-role attitudes and beliefs provide the cultural ideological context in which relations between the sexes are acted out. Conflict between the sexes and upward mobility for women in the class structure are more likely to occur when traditional sex-roles are challenged.

Despite numerous studies on sex-role attitudes in the last decade comparative sex-role research on blacks and whites has been far less common. One would expect that attitudes towards changing roles of women would continue to be profoundly affected by past and current racial oppression. However, comparisons of sex-role outlooks of black and white women have produced inconsistent, even contradictory findings (Ladner 1971; Weitzman 1979; Gump 1975). Moreover, almost completely absent is comparative information on the outlooks of black and white men toward changing women's sex-roles. This lack of focus on the attitudes of men toward women's roles is a prominent omission in the literature. The Black Nationalism of the 1960s and the early 1970s often involved an emphasis on black masculinity: black men need to take charge of their families, protect their women from white male sexual exploitation, and take on positions of leadership and power in the black community and the larger society (Staples 1973). We know very little about the effects of this "new" black masculinity ideology on the sex-role outlooks of black males.

This study attempts to address some of these omissions and inconsistencies by comparing black and white women and black and white men of different socioeconomic levels on a number of measures of feminist sex-role outlook. It is hypothesized that black females will be more sex-role feminist in outlook than white females, and that black males will be more sex-role traditional in outlook than white males. A multiple hierarchy stratification approach provides a general conceptual background for these expectations (Jeffries and Ransford 1980; Lenski 1966; Gordon 1964). According to this view, socioeconomic status, ethnicity/race and gender are somewhat separate hierarchies, each affecting the distribution of power, privilege and prestige. Jeffries and Ransford (1980: 265–93) argue that more accurate predictions and a fuller theoretical understanding often result from a consideration of the intersections or joint effects of SES, race and sex. These intersections of status positions represent unique social spaces within which persons construct explanations of reality. We maintain specifically that the intersection of race and gender will create unique aggregates which might be called "ethgenders," the life chances and experiences of which assume patterns that cannot be anticipated simply by adding the effects of race to those of gender. Further, we argue that the joint effects of race and gender will lead to distinctive sex-role outlooks[1a]. Black women, for example, who are in a subordinate position on two stratification hierarchies (race and gender) are expected to be quite distinct in their outlook from white women. Moreover, the literature which we will review points to the likelihood that the differences in sex-role outlook between black and white men and black and white women are likely to be especially pronounced at particular points in the class structure. In short, combinations of race, gender and class will be examined in this paper with the expectation of more fully explaining differences and similarities in sex role outlooks. Past research and theoretical rationales guide us most immediately to two paired comparisons: differences in sex-role outlooks between black females and while females, and differences in outlook between black males and white males.

Black Females Compared with White Females

A number of writings suggest a unique tradition for the black female, one that evolved out of slavery and race-sex discrimination:

1. Historically, American plantation slavery made no distinction between the work roles of men and women. The weak, soft, delicate image of white women during this period (and to some extent currently) did not apply to black women. "Instead of being viewed as too weak to work out of doors, black women were most likely though of as strong and as bearers of heavy burdens" (King 1975: 121). In the post-slavery period black men faced extreme job discrimination in the market place and were unable to provide for the economic well-being of their families. The black working woman was essential to the survival of the family. Black women, then, have historically worked longer, harder, and made a more significant economic contribution to the household than have white women. The model of the hardworking black female that can be traced to a slavery heritage is reinforced in current times.

2. Ghetto life requires a special kind of sex-role socialization that emphasizes independence and self-reliance for black women. Joyce Ladner presents a persuasive case for this independence model based on open-ended qualitative interviews of young black adolescent women (Ladner 1971). The young women in Ladner's sample expressed the need to be self-reliant and not dependent on a man for support. Ladner suggests that the female emphasis on hard work and economic self-sufficiency

has persisted because black males continue to face job market discrimination and welfare discrimination (welfare disincentives which lead to absence from the household). Very young black girls initially speak of a Prince Charming supporter and protector, but as they grow older they become more skeptical of living their lives through the success or failure of a man. In general, Ladner notes that ghetto life requires aggressiveness and toughness. To survive, a black woman needs to be able to fend for herself. A dependent, passive, middle-class housewife is almost unimaginable in this ghetto context (Ladner 1971, Weitzman 1979: 174).

From this discussion, one line of reasoning would suggest that racial discrimination has forced black women to take on independence roles now idealized by the feminist movement. Thus, in one sense black women are "already liberated" and should voice more consistent support of sex-role emancipation than white women. Based on this, it could be hypothesized that black women will be more likely to hold a feminist sex-role outlook involving: 1) rejection of negative female stereotypes (women are excessively emotional, illogical, etc.); 2) rejection of the view that women are suited only for a homemaking role; and 3) support of the view that women can be just as capable as men in positions involving autonomy, such as positions of political leadership[2a].

It should be noted that some studies have not supported these assertions. In two comparative studies of black and white college students (Hershey 1978, Gump 1975), black women are just as likely to hold traditional female stereotypes as white women. Similarly, Gurin and Gaylord (1976) find that black college women choose the same traditionally feminine occupations that white women do. Only in one recent study is there partial support for Ladner's theme of self-reliance among black females. Epstein (1973) reports that some highly successful black women have used their two negatively evaluated statuses as an impetus for achievement.

A multidimensional view of sex-role traditionalism may help to resolve these contradictory findings. Black women may be more independent and self-reliant than white women on some aspects of sex-role outlook and just as traditional as white women on others. With the four measures of sex-role traditionalism used in this study (women's place in the home, women working, and two items on women in political leadership positions), we can explore this possibility in our data. It is also true that the black women in the surveys that question Ladner's view are college women and are, therefore, likely to come from middle-class households where there are special resources for educational attainment. They may not have been socialized to the same ghetto survival self-reliance norms that Ladner found among lower-class adolescents (Weitzman 1979: 176).

What is needed is a systematic comparison of black and white women's sex-role attitudes with a large sample that allows for differentiation among lower and higher socioeconomic positions. The NORC sample employed in this study will allow us to make such comparisons. Drawing from the above literature review, our working hypothesis is as follows: black women will be significantly more sex-role feminist than white women, especially so at lower points in the class structure.

Black Males Compared with White Males

Hannerz (1969) among others, has argued that black males have been denied the traditional avenues of masculine expression—economic success, career achievement, and upward mobility. In America, the dominant cultural pressure on the male is to be the major bread winner. Yet, lower-class black males face both race and class discrimination and have few opportunities and resources to be adequate breadwinners. The public welfare system further emphasizes the male's economic inadequacy by awarding funds to mothers rather than fathers and, in many states, paying funds only when the man is out of the home. Lower-class black males have developed "ghetto-specific masculinity," Hannerz argues, as a creative adaptation to discrimination. Working with what is available to them, they have developed a masculine role that provides an alternative source of dignity and self-respect based on strong overt concerns with sexual exploits: toughness and ability to command respect, personal appearance with an emphasis on male clothing fashions, liquor consumption and verbal ability (Hannerz 1969: 79).

The ghetto-specific male role obviously has many qualities of sexual exploitation and dominance over females. It may also introduce tensions into a marital relationship. If the wife subscribes to the dominant model of husband as economic provider and faithful husband, but the male continues to act out ghetto-specific masculinity roles (drinking, gambling, uncertain loans to friends, extramarital sex), the stage is set for conflict. In short, in both marital and nonmarital situations, ghetto-specific masculinity involves a male dominance ideology—an ideology that would not encourage autonomy and independence for a woman. It should be noted that Hannerz's thesis makes sense only at the lower end of the class structure. Schematically:

The combined impacts of race and class discrimination
lead to
inadequate resources to play economic provider, husband dominant role
lead to
black males asserting alternative expressions of masculinity.

But many research findings indicate that white lower-class males are also more traditional on the topic of sex-roles and male dominance (Komarovsky, 1962). To demonstrate empirical support to the thesis of ghetto-specific masculinity, it must be shown that lower-class black males are significantly more traditional in sex-role outlook than lower-class white males; a demanding hypothesis indeed.

At higher points in the class structure it could be argued that stably employed working-class and middle-class blacks have the economic resources to play the role of economic provider successfully and, therefore, have no need for ghetto-specific masculinity. From this view. there should be no difference in sex-role traditionalism between white males and black males at higher points in the socioeconomic structure. Some recent evidence suggests, however, that black males may have a more traditional outlook *regardless* of SES position. The Black Power and Black Nationalist movements of the 1960s and early 1970s represented a new assertion of black masculinity, and one that likely cut across the class hierarchy (Staples 1973). Thus, Black Muslims (Nation of Islam) note that black men, under slavery, could not protect their women from the sexual advances of the white master. The message is clear: black men must regain a leadership position and take control of their households (Essein-Udom, 1962). Moreover, the Islamic religion of the Black Muslims preached that it was normal and right for men to hold authority over women (Staples 1973, 1975).[3a]

As the Civil Rights and Black Power movements took hold in the middle and late 1960s, far more attention was paid to the liberation of black men than black women (Stone 1979: 584). If the black male, in particular, has been disadvantaged by racial discrimination with its blend of *white supremacy* and *male dominance*, then black rights has for women become tantamount to the need for greater male control and leadership in general. Murray (1975) points out that: "When the nationally known civil rights leader James Farmer ran for congress against Shirley Chisholm in 1968, his campaign literature stressed the need for a 'strong male image' and a 'man's voice' in Washington."

To summarize, the above discussion supports the expectation that lower-class black males will be more sex-role traditional in outlook than lower-class white males. However, at higher points in the socioeconomic structure, there are competing rationales. One view postulates that at higher positions in the structure, the difference between black males and white males on feminist outlook will be smaller (decline of ghetto-specific masculinity). The other view (reassertion of black masculinity during the Civil Rights and Black Power movements) suggests that black males will be more traditional than white males at all points in the socioeconomic structure. We will explore these two possibilities in the data.

Control Variables and the Interaction Model

In addition to the control for socioeconomic status, three other variables, highly relevant to sex-role outlooks, will be utilized in both the male and female analyses: *mother's labor force participation, work status of the woman of the household,* and *age* of the respondent.

Respondents whose mothers were employed were directly exposed to a nontraditional female role modes, a model that should challenge stereotypes of women as dependent and passive (e.g., see Vogel et. al. 1970). Of special interest is the effect of the interaction of ethgender and mother's work status on feminist outlook. If it has been normative or expected historically that black women will be gainfully employed, then "working mother" as a variable should have less effect on liberalizing the sex-role outlooks of black respondents than white respondents.

Similarly, a household in which the woman is employed brings constraints toward equality in roles between husband and wife. Household power derives, in part, from labor force participation (Blood and Wolfe 1960). Again, we are interested in the effect on sex-role outlook of the interaction between female work status and ethgender. For example, if black males are more traditional than white males (as predicted), is this so in wife-employed households as well as households in which the wife does not work?

Ethgender may also interact with age in the prediction of feminism. If black male traditionalism was intensified by the Civil Rights and Black Power movements of the 1960s and early 1970s, then younger black respondents (18–30) who typically had a more active participation in those movements may be especially traditional in outlook, given our 1974–1978 sample time frame.

Each of the above inquiries involves an interaction or specification mode of analysis: ethgender differences in feminist outlook need to be examined within successive categories of other variables. Accordingly, the basic empirical question of this paper can now be stated as follows: In terms of their levels of feminism, are black men significantly more traditional than white men, and black women significantly more feminist than white women, and are these differences intensified within certain categories of SES, employment status of the woman of the household, age, and labor force participation of the mother?

THE SAMPLE AND MEASUREMENT OF VARIABLES
Sample

Our data came from the National Opinion Research Center General Social Surveys. The NORC surveys are stratified, multistage, area probability samples of clusters of households in the Continental United States. Four samples (1974, '75, '77, '78) that involved the same measures of feminist outlook were pooled to increase the case base for blacks. Following are the Ns for the four ethgender groups: white male = 2,397; white female = 2,920; black male = 277; black female = 392.

Measurment of Feminist Outlook

Four items were used to measure feminist outlook:
1. Women should take care of running their homes and leave running the country up to men. Agree___ Disagree___

2. Do you approve or disapprove of a married woman earning money in business or industry if she has a husband capable of supporting her? Approve___ Disapprove___

3. If your party nominated a woman for president, would you vote for her if she were qualified for the job? Yes___ No___

4. Tell me if you agree or disagree with this statement: Most men are better suited emotionally for politics than are most women. Agree___ Disagree___

For brevity we will refer to these items as "feminism home," "feminism work," "feminism president," and "feminism politics," respectively. Intercorrelations among the items range from .19 to .54. Instead of combining the measures into a scale, we prefer an item-by-item analysis since we view each as a separate component of the feminist outlook. Item 1 measures "the woman's place" a concentration on marriage, home, and children is the primary focus of female concern. Item 2 measures favorability toward women working even if household income is adequate. It controls for the economic necessity of working, leaving a measure that more purely measures desirability of women working. Item 3 can be seen as an index of favorable attitudes toward women in top leadership positions. Item 4 is another political question, but it also suggests an additional difference in masculine and feminine traits. The terminology "better suited emotionally" appears to be measuring sex-role stereotypes in which men are viewed as unemotional and rational, and women are viewed as emotional, sentimental, romantic and illogical (Chafetz 1974). Given our decision to treat these items separately, we are dealing with four single-question scales of indeterminate reliability and unknown validity, and the findings should be judged with this in mind.

Measurement of Specification Variables

Socioeconomic Variables. The following variables are included in the analysis: education, occupation. perception of present family income, subjective class identification, whether or not the respondent has ever received government aid such as welfare, and respondent's perception of household income at the time he/she was 16. The latter measure should help to untangle time priority questions by demonstrating whether or not past class circumstances affect present attitudes on sex-role feminism.

Mother's Labor Force Participation. An index was constructed from two questions on the NORC survey:

1. Did your Mother ever work for pay as long as a year after she was married? Yes___ No___

___If yes,

2. Did she work for as long as a year around the time when you
    were 16? Yes___ No___

We argue that a strong impact toward feminist outlook was in effect
if the respondent had a working mother and, in addition, one who
worked when the repspondent was 16 (score of 3). Our reasoning
is that a working mother may especially have an impact if she was
working during the respondent's teenage years, at a time when the
young person was focusing his or her own career goals. Medium
impact was expected if the mother worked, but not when the
respondent was 16 (score of 2); and low impact was anticipated if
the mother never worked as long as a year (score of 1).

Female Employment Status. Whereas mother's labor force
participation reflects past household experiences that may affect
present sex-role outlook, fema*le employment status* deals with the
present circumstances of the household. In the case of males,
spouse's working status is the measure, whereas for female
respondents, her own working status was the measure. Though
they are separate variables, both record the presence of a working
woman in the household.

FINDINGS
Black Females versus White Females

Overall, the data do not support the thesis that black females are
more sex-role feminist in outlook than white females. The black
female response is within a few percentage points of the white
female response on all four items and none of the differences was
statistically significant. On the item dealing with political
participation by women, 51 percent of the white women and 56
percent of the black women rejected the view that women are
emotionally unsuited for politics. (Note that this means almost
half of both groups endorsed the traditional response on this item).
Seventy-one percent of the whites and 69 percent of the blacks
endorsed the idea of women working, while 79 percent of the
whites and 82 percent of the blacks reacted favorably to the idea of
a qualified woman president. Finally, 65 percent of the white
females and 63 percent of the black females rejected the idea that
women should take care of running the home and leave running
the country up to men.

The pattern of no difference between black and white females
does not change when controls for social class, work status,
socialization, and age are introduced. A separate regression analysis
for women was performed involving these variables plus a dummy
for race (0=white; 1=black).

Comparing the relative sizes of the Betas in table 6.1A, note that education and age are the strongest predictors of feminist outlook, but effects are also apparent for mother's employment, government aid, and employment status of the woman in the household. By contrast, race did not approach statistical significance for any of the feminism variables. It is of course possible that a difference between black and white females would emerge within some category of the SES, employment, or age variables. This will be examined in the section of the paper below that deals with interaction effects. However, at this juncture it can be stated that for women there is a clear pattern of nonassociation between race and feminist outlook.

Black Males versus White Males

We have just shown that black females are not significantly more feminist than white females. But black males are significantly more traditional than white males, especially on the first item, dealing with the woman's place in the home, and the fourth item, dealing with the emotional suitability of women in politics. Emphasizing the traditional side, 49 percent of the black males agreed that a woman's place is in the home, compared to only 33 percent of the white men (p<.001). Sixty percent of black males agreed that women are emotionally unsuited for politics versus 44 percent of white males (p<.001). On the remaining two items, 37 percent of the black men rejected the idea of women working, compared to 31 percent of the white men (p<.05); and 24 percent of the blacks would not vote for a qualified woman for president, compared to 17 percent of the whites (p<.01). The pattern of results was corroborated by the regression analysis in table 6.1B, which again used race (white=0, black=1), female employment, mother's labor force participation, age, and the SES measures as regressors. Race had a significant effect on feminism, net of all other independent variables, but only on items 1 and 4 dealing with the woman's place in the home and the emotional stability of women in politics (p<.01 in both cases). As in the female analysis (table 6.1A), education, age, and work status of the woman were also important predictors of feminist outlook for the males.

Analysis of Interaction Effects

Black men are more sex-role traditional in these data than white men, but does ethgender interact with socioeconomic status, mother's employment, age, or work status of the spouse in the prediction of sex-role outlook? For example, are black males especially more traditional than white males at the lower end of the class structure as the ghetto masculinity thesis would suggest? The most straightforward method for detecting interaction effects would be to add nine product terms to the regression variables in table 6.1 (race x mother's employment, race x education, etc.). However, given the high intercorrelations among these product terms (the average intercorrelation was .84, with some coefficients as high as .95) and the resulting problem of multicollinearity, we opted for an equivalent technique that avoids the collinearity problem and at the same time gives more precise data on the form of the interactions. In table 6.2 separate regression analyses for black men and white men are presented. The black-white differences in slopes for each of the independent variables were tested for statistical significance using T-tests. The results are presented in the Interaction Summary at the bottom of table 6.2. Parallel analyses for black and white women appear in table 6.4.

Interaction Effects for Males. The analysis in table 6.2 revealed that, among males, race interacts significantly with subjective class (.01) and mother's employment (.05) in the prediction of feminism politics. The interaction effect involving perceived family income at age sixteen barely misses significance (p=.051). In addition, race interacts with mother's employment in the prediction of feminism work (.05).[4a]

The form of the interaction effect involving subjective class identification runs contrary to Hannerz's ghetto-specific masculinity thesis. The direction of the slopes indicate that for black males, the higher the subjective class identification the greater the *traditional* outlook, while for white males, subjective class has no effect on sex-role outlook (the relevant slopes are -.135 and .002). We were especially concerned with the effects of the interaction of race and the SES variables because of their theoretical importance—they provide the primary test for the ghetto-specific hypothesis. This argument stressing special black male adaptation is controversial and demands care and precision in analysis. Accordingly, the data in table 6.3, a cross-tabular analysis, have been generated to give more interpretive detail on the form of the interaction effects. In discussing these data we will be especially concerned with how lower SES blacks differ from lower SES whites. For consistency with our discussion, the percentages in this table represent those high in traditional sex-role outlooks.

Regression of Attitudes toward Feminism on Indicators of Race, Mother's Employment, SES, Age, and Women's Employment Status for Men and Women

| | A. WOMEN | | | | | | | | B. MEN | | | | | | | |
| | 1. Feminism Home | | 2. Feminism Work | | 3. Feminism President | | 4. Feminism Politics | | 1. Feminism Home | | 2. Feminism Work | | 3. Feminism President | | 4. Feminism Politics | |
	b	Beta	b	Beta	b	Beta	b	Beta	b	Beta	b	Beta	b	Beta	b	Beta
Race	-.001	-.00	.013	-.00	-.002	-.00	.027	.01	-.106	-.07**	-.029	-.01	-.039	-.03	-.156	-.09**
Mother Employed	.052	.09**	.028	.05*	.033	.07**	.046	.08**	.015	.02	.018	.03	.001	.00	.029	.05
SES																
Occupation	.035	.05*	.035	.05*	-.007	-.01	-.001	-.00	.062	.09**	.014	.02	.020	.04	.019	.02
Education	.109	.22**	.063	.13**	.051	.12**	.083	.16**	.079	.18**	.083	.19**	.029	.08*	.047	.10**
Government Aid	.039	.04*	.050	.05*	.026	.02	.042	.04*	.009	.00	.012	.01	.009	.01	.037	.03
Perceived Income	.014	.02	.027	.04*	.009	.01	-.009	-.01	.018	.03	.027	.04	.019	.04	.008	.01
Family Income When 16	.021	.03	.005	.01	-.000	-.00	-.009	-.01	.011	.01	.004	.00	.002	.00	.008	.01
Subjective Class	-.000	-.00	.016	.02	-.010	-.01	-.012	-.01	-.011	-.01	.006	.00	.009	.01	-.021	-.02
Age	-.004	-.17**	-.005	-.19**	-.005	-.23**	-.004	-.14**	-.004	-.15**	-.004	-.16**	-.002	-.11**	-.003	-.10**
Woman Employed	.028	.08***	.026	.08***	.009	.03	.015	.04	-.030	.08***	.054	.16**	.008	.02	.014	.03
R^2	.18		.14		.11		.09		.14		.15		.04		.05	
Intercept	1.72		1.25		1.05		1.62		1.74		1.43		1.16		1.82	

*p<.05.
**p<.01.

Table 6.1

Table 6.2

Regression of Attitudes toward Feminism on Indicators of Mother's Employment, SES, and Age for White Men and Black Men

	White Men								Black Men							
	1. Feminism Home		2. Feminism Work		3. Feminism President		4. Feminism Politics		1. Feminism Home		2. Feminism Work		3. Feminism President		4. Feminism Politics	
	b	Beta	b	Beta	b	Beta	b	Beta	b	Beta	b	Beta	b	Beta	b	Beta
Mother Employed	.013	.02	.015	.02	.008	.01	.041	.07**	.043	.08	.073	.14*	-.011	-.02	-.052	-.09
SES																
Occupation	.058	.09**	.012	.02	.021	.04	.014	.02	.123	.14	-.033	-.03	-.011	-.01	.076	.08
Education	.080	.18**	.093	.22**	.027	.08*	.042	.09	.088	.16*	.065	.12	.062	.13	.069	.13
Government Aid	.009	.01	.016	.01	.015	.01	.038	.03	-.022	-.02	-.035	-.03	-.037	-.04	.000	.00
Perceived Income	.027	.04*	.031	.05*	.023	.05*	-.005	-.00	-.024	-.03	-.028	.04	-.012	-.02	-.038	-.06
Family Income When 16	.014	.02	.005	.00	.005	.01	.003	.00	.012	.02	.021	.03	.001	.00	-.071	-.12
Subjective Class	-.002	-.00	.007	.00	-.017	-.02	.002	.00	-.080	-.10	.011	-.01	-.035	-.05	-.135	-.18*
Age	-.004	-.17**	-.004	-.18**	-.002	-.11**	-.003	-.10**	-.004	-.15*	-.005	-.21**	-.004	-.18**	-.004	-.17*
R^2	.13		.13		.04		.04		.13		.12		.07		.12	
Intercept	1.76		1.33		1.16		1.78		2.13		1.34		1.16		2.16	

*p<.05.
**p<.01.

INTERACTION SUMMARY
Significant Differences Between Slopes (T-test, one tail) for Black and White Men:
(1) Subjective Class (Feminism Politics, p<.01)
(2) Mother Employed (Feminism Politics, p<.05)
(3) Mother Employed (Feminism Work, p<.05)
(4) Income 16 (Feminsm Politics, p<.051)

Differences between White and Black Males on Four Measures of Sex-Role Outlook, With Controls for Measures of Socioeconomic Status and Mother's Employment

VARIABLES INDICATING ATTITUDES TOWARD FEMINISM

	1. Percent Who Agree Women Should Take Care of Home				2. Percent Who Believe Women Should Not Work				3. Percent Who Would Not Vote For Female President				4. Percent Who Agree Women Unsuited Emotionally For Politics			
	White		Black		White		Black		White		Black		White		Black	
Control Variables	%	N	%	N	%	N	%	N	%	N	%	N	%	N	%	N
Education																
Some College	18	(869)	27	(55)	14	(882)	22	(58)	11	(875)	12	(58)	37	(721)	41	(53)
High School Graduate	32	(684)	41	(64)	30	(702)	26	(68)	16	(697)	14	(65)	43	(597)	66**	(53)
Less than High School Graduate	52	(755)	62*	(141)	49	(768)	48	(144)	25	(757)	32	(146)	54	(624)	65*	(116)
Occupation																
Professional	20	(708)	18	(28)	19	(718)	28	(29)	11	(714)	13	(30)	40	(598)	40	(25)
Manager/Sales	26	(236)	50*	(16)	26	(236)	27	(15)	16	(234)	38*	(16)	44	(200)	64	(14)
Blue Collar	41	(863)	46	(96)	37	(883)	36	(98)	20	(874)	20	(98)	45	(724)	55	(84)
Unemployed	32	(114)	40	(25)	32	(118)	42	(26)	14	(117)	15	(26)	43	(97)	55	(22)
Subjective Class:																
Middle Class	28	(1124)	49**	(78)	26	(1143)	36	(81)	14	(1135)	26**	(82)	42	(959)	69**	(67)
Working Class	39	(1179)	50**	(182)	35	(1202)	38	(189)	20	(1187)	22	(187)	47	(975)	56	(155)
Perceived Family Income:																
Above Average	20	(600)	46**	(28)	18	(614)	36*	(28)	11	(601)	14	(28)	41	(513)	62*	(26)
Average	37	(1156)	52**	(118)	33	(1188)	32	(122)	18	(1179)	28	(120)	46	(955)	66**	(95)
Below Average	40	(542)	47	(114)	39	(542)	42	(120)	22	(539)	22	(121)	46	(963)	33	(102)
Perceived Family Income When Respondent 16:																
Above Average	21	(383)	40*	(20)	21	(391)	19	(21)	14	(383)	10	(19)	38	(331)	79**	(20)
Average	35	(1239)	49*	(77)	31	(1266)	37	(82)	17	(1254)	23	(81)	46	(1031)	59*	(69)
Below Average	38	(678)	51**	(158)	35	(688)	39	(162)	20	(685)	25	(165)	46	(574)	37*	(130)
Mother's Work Status:																
Did Not Work	40	(1076)	57**	(79)	37	(1093)	45	(82)	21	(1087)	27	(81)	49	(891)	44	(66)
Worked When Respondent 16	25	(612)	43**	(102)	22	(622)	28	(107)	14	(618)	26**	(105)	36	(525)	61**	(87)
Worked, But Not When Respondent 16	28	(354)	61**	(28)	22	(362)	52**	(29)	13	(356)	23	(30)	42	(301)	64*	(25)

*p<.05.
**p<.01.

Table 6.3

Table 6.4

Regression of Attitudes toward Feminism on Indicators of Mother's Employment, Socioeconomic Status, Employment Status of Woman, and Age for White Women and Black Women

	WHITE WOMEN								BLACK WOMEN							
	1. Feminism Home		2. Feminism Work		3. Feminism President		4. Feminism Politics		1. Feminism Home		2. Feminism Work		3. Feminism President		4. Feminism Politics	
	b	Beta	b	Beta	b	Beta	b	Beta	b	Beta	b	Beta	b	Beta	b	Beta
Mother Employed	.027	.06**	.014	.03	.015	.04*	.031	.07**	-.010	-.02	-.009	-.02	.008	.02	.021	.05
SES																
Education	.123	.25**	.084	.18**	.050	.12**	.090	.18**	.123	.23**	.048	.09	-.004	-.01	.004	.00
Government Aid	-.029	-.02	.032	.03	.014	.05	.049	.05*	.098	.10*	.161	.17**	-.046	-.05	.000	.00
Perceived Income	.015	.02	.021	.03	.008	.01	-.009	-.01	.013	.02	.097	.15*	.010	.01	-.022	-.03
Family Income When 16	.030	.04*	-.007	-.01	.011	.02	.017	.02	.020	.02	.052	.06	-.055	-.07	.005	.00
Subjective Class	.016	.02	.029	.04	.007	.01	-.003	-.00	-.064	-.10*	-.060	-.09	-.089	-.14*	-.044	-.06
Age	-.005	-.19**	-.005	-.22**	-.005	-.26**	-.004	-.16**	-.006	-.23**	-.003	-.12	-.006	-.25**	-.005	-.19**
Woman Employed	.027	.08**	.028	.09**	.008	.03	.011	.03	.051	.15**	.011	.03	.021	.06	.068	.19**
R²	.17		.14		.11		.08		.22		.11		.08		.09	
Intercept	1.52		1.31		1.02		1.65		1.76		1.24		.76		1.81	

*p<.05.
**p<.01.

INTERACTION SUMMARY

Significant Differences Between Slopes (T-test, one tail) for Black and White Women:
(1) Subjective Class (Feminism Home, p<.02) (Feminism Work, p<.02) (Feminism President, p<.01)
(2) Education (Feminism President, p<.05) (Feminism Politics, p<.01)
(3) Mother Employed (Feminism Home, p<.05)
(4) Woman Employed (Feminism Politics, p<.01)
(5) Government Aid (Feminism Work, p<.01)
(6) Family Income 16 (Feminism President, p<.01)

Considering first the interaction effect involving subjective class identification which was apparent for feminism politics, it can be seen in table 6.3 that black males are far more traditional than white males, but only among those identifying their class position as "middle class." There is a 27 percent difference for middle-class identifiers compared to only a 9 percent difference for those identifying with the working class. Further, "middle-class" black males are far more traditional than any of the other subgroups, with 69 percent agreeing that women are unsuited emotionally for politics. This pattern of black male traditionalism at middle levels of socioeconomic status is echoed in a number of other SES comparisons, though by the T-test comparisons in table 6.2 they did not reach the .05 level of significance as interaction effects. For example, black males are notably more traditional than white males among managers and sales persons (on the feminist home, president, and politics items), among high school graduates (politics item), and among those perceiving their family income to be average or above average (home and politics items). But at the lower end of the socioeconomic structure differences by ethgender are small. Thus, in their attitudes toward feminism black males who identify themselves as "working class" or who perceive their income to be lower than average, or who are unemployed or in blue-collar jobs, or who have attained less than high school education are usually quite close to white males with these same characteristics. Clearly, this is in opposition to the ghetto-specific masculinity hypothesis, though it is not to say that all differences between white and black males disappear at lower points in the SES structure. In fact, in three of the relationships statistically significant differences in percentages at lower SES levels remain. But the largest contrasts are in the magnitude of 10 to 12 percent differences, not very strong associations compared to those apparent in the middle-level categories. It is true that working- and lower-class black males are very traditional in outlook, but so are lower SES white males; the resulting differences between ethgender groups are comparatively small.

The data in table 6.3 also offer greater detail for the significant interaction effect reported in table 6.2 involving race and mother's employment. For the two dependent variables where interaction occurred (feminism politics and feminism work), black males are far more traditional than white males in households in which the mother was in the labor force. By contrast, when the mother was not employed, ethgender differences in traditional outlook are small or nonexistent. A closer look at the data in table 6.3 reveals that the working mother effect operates differently for black and white males. For white males, the more the mother worked, the more feminist the outlook. But for black males, there is no clear liberalizing effect from a working mother. Indeed, on the feminism politics item a working mother *increases* sex-role traditionalism for black males.

Interaction Effects for Females. Having found little evidence in table 6.1A that black and white women differ in their outlooks, we did not expect to find significant interaction effects when the data for the two groups were analyzed separately. However, the Interaction Summary in Table 6.4 shows a number of effects indicating that black and white women do in fact differ in feminist outlook under certain conditions.[5a]

For three of the feminism variables—home, work, and president—there are significant differences in the slopes for subjective class identification. For black women, the higher the subjective class identification, the more traditional the outlook, whereas for white women no such effect is apparent. Indeed, a percentage analysis for the feminism home measure showed a 15 percent difference between black and white women who identified with the middle class compared to only a 4 percent difference for those who identified with the working class.[6a] This means that black women are more traditional than white women not among the working-class identifiers but among those identified with the middle class, precisely the trend that was visible for black men. Similarly, other interaction effects reflect the fact that black women are more traditional than white women among those who never received government aid and for those whose mothers worked when the respondent was sixteen years-old. All of these findings run counter to our hypothesis in that black women are shown to be *more traditional,* rather than more feminist than white women.

In contrast, however, two interaction effects in table 6.4, both involving education, support the hypothesis of greater black feminism. For the feminism president and politics items, a comparison of slopes indicates that education has a clear positive effect on feminism for white women and virtually no effect on black women. In fact, a closer look at differences by education (not shown) revealed a 12 percent difference between white and black women (blacks more feminist) among those with less than high school education. This difference decreased to 1 percent among the college educated. These are the only findings in the entire analysis that support the hypothesis of greater feminism among black women, and we must conclude that, taking all the data into account, there is little evidence for the thesis of the "already liberated" black female.

One other pattern of interaction effects is evident in table 6.4 that deserves comment. It involves education and work status. Note that on the feminism politics item, white women are liberalized more by education than by labor market experience. For black women labor market experience is clearly more important than education. This finding is of interest because it may mean that white women are more affected by theoretical arguments (that is, education) than by actual work experience. Labor market experience may be less important for them because their work is often supplementary to household work. By contrast, work experience for black women may have a more substantive impact. The job may be more directly related to basic bread and butter support and, therefore, more consequential for shaping attitudes on feminist outlook.

A final word seems in order to place the analysis of interaction effects for females into perspective. When the total black and white female samples are compared, there are no differences in feminist outlook (table 6.1A). Only under categories of some other variable(s) do differences appear and then there is not complete consistency in direction—under conditions of low education, black women are more feminist; under the condition of subjective middle-class identification, black women are more traditional. Moreover, when differences by race do appear among women, their magnitudes are considerably smaller than those observed between black and white men. The largest difference between black and white females (15 percent) occurs for the feminism home measure under the condition of subjective middle-class identification. Otherwise, the differences range from 7 to 12 percent. For males, the magnitudes are in the order of 25 to 41 percent in cases where significant interaction effects were detected. In short, the analysis of interaction effects has added refinements to the findings for females, but it does not dramatically alter or reverse the basic finding that black and white women do not differ very greatly in their feminist (or non-feminist) outlooks.

SUMMARY AND INTERPRETATIONS
Women

The finding that black females are by and large no more feminist in outlook than white females may mean that the black self-sufficiency-independence thesis (Ladner 1971) has been overstated, at least for the period of the 1970s covered by the present data when many white women may have experienced less traditional sex-role training. However, the findings could also mean that black females do have a stronger tradition of autonomy and independence, but that experience does not take them all the way to a feminist outlook as we have characterized it here. Black female autonomy and self-sufficiency may correlate with the particularistic concerns of reliability and trust of men as economic providers or, perhaps, with the need to be able to fend for one's self in the job market by having some occupational skill; but black female autonomy may not carry all the way to a general critique of women's traditional roles. Several findings point to this interpretation.

First, our finding of no significant difference in feminist outlook between black and white women is in basic agreement with other recent studies that deal with broad sex-role outlooks. Significantly, however, one study comparing black and white women on the more particularistic issue of economic reliability and trustworthiness of men (Turner and Turner, 1974) produced clear and significant differences: black women were far more likely than white women to rate men as economically unreliable and untrustworthy.

Another interpretation of our findings is that black women are just as traditional in outlook as white women because of recent labor market experiences. There is some evidence that with more education and legal protection black women are moving out of the "operative" and "service" categories and into the more traditional "clerical" category (Bureau of the Census 1976). But these are occupations that reinforce rather than challenge sex-role beliefs; hence black female autonomy may be offset by current labor market experiences. The interaction findings for females are consistent with this interpretation; labor market participation is a more important predictor of feminism for black women than white women.

The interaction analysis located one instance in which black women were substantially different in sex-role outlook from white women: when they identified their class position as "middle class" they were more traditional than white women. This represents an important point of convergence between black women and black men and we will have more to say about it in the following section.

Men

We have found that black males are substantially more traditional than white males, but only consistently so for the attitude that "women should take care of running their homes and leave running the country to men" and the notion that "most men are better suited for politics than are most women." They are not more traditional than white males on the question of women working. Apparently, then, most black males do not object to their wives working, but they do object to women taking on political positions in the community. This pattern of sex-role traditionalism (work outside the home is acceptable but political leadership is not) matches the Black Power emphasis noted earlier: the assertion that black males need to occupy positions of power and leadership.

When controlling for different variables representing social standing, the higher rate of black male traditionalism continues to be apparent in many, but not all, of the SES categories. It is especially in the large middle area of SES attainment represented by average and above average income at age sixteen, manager/sales occupations, and "middle" subjective class that the differences between black and white males are greatest. In the case of subjective class this produced a statistically significant interaction effect on the politics item when the other SES indicators were controlled. For black males (and, as we have seen, black females as well) the higher the person's social class identification, the greater the traditional outlook. For whites (both males and females), no relationship between subjective class and this measure of feminism is in evidence.

It may be the case that "middle class" has special meaning for black males. Those who call themselves "middle class" may be saying more about their idea of "respectability" and "steady provider" than about their idea of objective standing. Hannerz (1969), for example, found among lower- and stably employed working-class blacks a group he called "mainstreamers," a group who expressed a "super middle-class" life-style (see also Billingsley 1968: 137ff. for a similar argument). They were proud that their families were intact and that they were steady breadwinners and were exerting a dominant role in the household. If this is one meaning of "middle class," then black males who identify themselves with this label may, indeed, be more traditional in sex-role outlook.

In many accounts of Black Nationalism, it is also apparent that the idealized middle-class lifestyle involves a strong patriarchal role for the male of the household. Thus, "middle-class" identification may for some black males be an assertion of black pride. Whatever the exact meaning of middle-class identification in this study, it is clear that it is not lower SES black males with a ghetto-specific adaptation that are most traditional. It is also crucial to keep in mind that black women who consider themselves middle class share this traditionalism.

Another specification of black male traditionalism involves mother's employment. Contrary to what we predicted, black males are far more traditional than white males on the political dimension of feminism if they grew up in households in which the mother worked. For white males on the other hand, a working mother appears to liberalize their outlooks, in support of what we hypothesized. The black respondents' reports of their mothers' labor force participation must frequently have involved employment in service and domestic occupations involving a low degree of autonomy and, indirectly, of feminist expression. To the extent that this was the case, it is perhaps not surprising to find black males growing up in such households expressing a restricted view of women's roles—women are not seen as capably filling political positions.

One final note concerning black male conservatism is in order. The explanations we have considered to this point have emphasized unique race-sex dynamics. These arguments all suggest that the conservatism of black males may be sex-role specific. On issues not related to sex-roles, they may be no more conservative than white males. To test this notion we compared white and black males on five measures of conservatism that appeared to be unrelated to sex-roles: self-classification of political views, attitudes toward court treatment of criminals, legislation concerning marijuana use, effects of pornography, and obedience as a primary value in child rearing. On four of these five measures black males are either more *liberal* or no different from white males in outlook. Only for the last item (obedience as a primary value) are black males slightly more conservative than white males. These findings encourage the interpretation that the black conservatism trend reported in this paper is in fact sex-role specific.

NOTES

1a.   The notion of "ethgender" is somewhat akin to Gordon's "ethclass" (Gordon 1964), but it does not refer as clearly to a bounded social interaction reality. On the other hand, it is more than just a set of statistical aggregates. Black men and women have experienced powerful historical circumstances that affect their gender and racial identities. In particular, black females have increasingly come together in caucuses and special gatherings to define their goals and programs within a minority group context. (Nieto 1974). For our purposes, ethgender lies conceptually somewhere between Gordon's idea of ethclass and a mere statistical category. We therefore prefer the term ethgender to a neutral term such as "race-gender" category.

2a.   We are not hypothesizing that black women will be more sympathetic toward or active in the women's liberation movement. Evidence suggests that they have viewed the women's movement per se with suspicion and as irrelevant to their needs. (King 1975).

3a. The "new" black masculinity of the 1960s and 1970s may be a reaction against the theme of black female domination that has received so much emphasis in the literature, the so-called matriarchy. The matriarchy may be a myth (Staples 1970) and it has certainly been overstated (TenHouten 1970). Nevertheless, it may have a symbolic reality as a stereotype and because of this, black males may feel a greater need to assert a male-in-control ideology.

4a. One problem with the male interaction analysis should be noted. With the variable "spouse's work status" included, unmarried males are automatically excluded from the analysis. Conceptually this was troublesome because we did not wish to restrict the analysis to the married, especially since Hannerz emphasized that single *black* men were especially involved in the adaptation he called ghetto-specific masculinity. Accordingly, work status of the spouse was dropped from the analysis reported in table 6.2. When we repeated the analysis with this variable reinstated, the following changes were worthy of note. First, with the reduced sample many of the relationships for black males (involving education, age, and mother's employment) drop below significance, though the regression coefficients did not change appreciably. Second, despite this, two of the three interaction effects reported in table 6.2 persisted: race and mother's employment and race and subjective class, both of which were apparent on the political dimension of feminism. Finally, work status of the spouse did not interact with race for any of the feminism items. Thus, the removal of this variable did not substantively alter the interaction results discussed in the text.

5a. In this regression analysis for females, occupation was dropped. This was necessary so that the variable "labor force participation" would include the full range from (nonemployed) housewives to full-time employed women. As a result, the regression analysis in table 6.4 is not strictly comparable to that for males in table 6.2.

6a. We examined a complete set of cross-tabular findings for women comparable to that reported for men in table 6.3. Our descriptions of the findings in the text rely to some extent upon these findings which, for reasons of space, are not presented in table form.

References

Billingsley, A. 1968. *Black Families in White America*. Englewood Cliffs, N.J.: Prentice Hall.

Blood, R., and Wolfe, D. 1960. *Husbands and Wives: The Dynamics of Married Living*. New York: Free Press.

Bureau of the Census. 1976. "A Statistical Portrait of Women in the United States." Series P-23, Number 58. Washington, D.C.: U.S. Government Printing Office.

Chafetz, J. 1974. *Masculine/Feminine or Human? An Overview of the Sociology of Sex Roles*. Itasca, IL: Peacock.

Epstein, C. 1973. "Positive Effects of the Multiple Negative: Explaining the Successes of Black Professional Women." *American Journal of Sociology* 78: 912–35.

Essien-Udom, E. 1962. *Black Nationalism.* New York: Dell.

Gordon, M. 1964. *Assimilation in American Life.* New York: Oxford University Press.

Gump, J. 1975. "Comparative Analysis of Black Women's and White Women's Sex-Role Attitudes." *Journal of Consulting and Clinical Psychology* 43: 858–63.

Gurin, P. and Gaylord, C. 1976. "Educational and Occupational Goals of Men and Women at Black Colleges." *Monthly Labor Review* June: 10–16.

Hannerz, U. 1969. *Soulside,* New York: Columbia University Press.

Hershey, M. 1978. "Racial Differences in Sex-Role Identities and Sex Stereotyping: Evidence Against a Common Assumption." *Social Science Quarterly* 58: 583–96.

Jeffries, V. and Ransford, H. 1980. *Social Stratification: A Multiple Hierarchy Approach.* Boston: Allyn & Bacon.

King, M. 1975. "Oppression and Power: the Unique Status of the Black Woman in the American Political System." *Social Science Quarterly* 56: 116–28.

Komarovsky, M. 1962. *Blue Collar Marriage.* New York: Random House.

Ladner, J. 1971. *Tomorrow's Tomorrow: The Black Woman.* Garden City, NY: Doubleday.

Lenski, G. 1966. *Power and Privilege.* New York: McGraw-Hill.

Murray, P. 1975. "The Liberation of Black Women." 351-63 in J. Freeman (ed.), *Women: A Feminist Perspective.* Palo Alto: Mayfield.

Nieto, C. 1974. "The Chicana and the Women's Rights Movement." *Civil Rights Digest* 6 (Spring): 36–42.

Staples, R. 1970. "The Myth of the Black Matriarchy." *The Black Scholar* 1 (January–February): 8–16.

———1973. *The Black Woman in America: Sex, Marriage, and the Family.* Chicago: Nelson Hall.

Stone, P. 1979. "Feminist Consciouness and Black Women." 577–88 in Jo Freeman (ed.), *Women: A Feminist Perspective.* Palo Alto: Mayfield.

TenHouten, W. 1970. "The Black Family: Myth and Reality." *Psychiatry* 2: 147–57.

Turner, B. and Turner, C. 1974. "The Political Implications of Social Stereotyping of Women and Men Among Black and White College Students." *Sociology and Social Research* 58: 155–62.

Vogel, S., Broverman, I., Broverman, D., Clarkson, F. and Rosenkrantz, P. 1970. "Maternal Employment and Perception of Sex Roles Among College Students." *Developmental Psychology* 3: 384–91.

Weitzman, L. 1979. "Sex Role Socialization." 153–216 in J. Freeman (ed.), *Women: A Feminist Perspective.* Palo Alto: Mayfield.

NOTES

1. See Randall Collins, "A Conflict Theory of Sexual Stratification," *Social Problems* 19 (Summer, 1971): 3–21 and R.W. Connell, *Gender and Power* (Stanford, CA: Stanford University Press, 1987).

2. Francine D. Blau and Anne E. Winkler, "Women in the Labor Force: An Overview," in Jo Freeman (ed.), *Women: A Feminist Perspective* (Mountain View, Calif.: Mayfield, 1989), 277.

3. Ibid., 277.

4. Ibid., 277–78.

5. Ibid., 278.

6. Francine Blau, "Discrimination Against Women: Theory and Evidence," in William Darity Jr., (ed.), *Labor Economics: Modern Views* (Boston: Martinus Nijhoff, 1984) and Francine Blau and Marianne Ferber, "Discrimination: Empirical Evidence for the United States," *American Economic Review* 77 (May, 1987): 316–320. See also Donald J. Treiman and Kermit Terrell, "Sex and the Process of Status Attainment," *American Sociological Review* 40 (April, 1975): 174–200.

7. Blau and Winkler, "Women in the Labor Force: An Overview," 279

8. Ibid., 274.

9. Evelyn Nakano Glenn and Roslyn L. Feldberg, "Clerical Work: The Female Occupation," in Jo Freeman (ed.), *Women: A Feminist Perspective* (Mountain View, Calif.: Mayfield, 1989).

10. Collins, "A Conflict Theory of Sexual Stratification."

11. Debra Renee Kaufman, "Professional Women: How Real are the Recent Gains," in Jo Freeman (ed.), *Women: A Feminist Perspective* (Mountain View, Calif.: Mayfield, 1989).

12. Ibid., 332.

13. Ibid., 333.

14. See Sarah Fenstermaker Berk, Richard A. Berk and Catherine White Berheide, "The Non-Division of Household Labor," Paper read at the Annual Pacific Sociological Meetings, San Diego, California, 1976; Sarah F. Berk, "Women's Unpaid Labor: Home and Community," in A. Stromberg and S. Harkness (eds.), *Women Working* (Palo Alto, Calif.: Mayfield, 1987) and Shelley Coverman, "Women's Work is Never Done: The Division of Domestic Labor," in Jo Freeman (ed.), *Women: A Feminist Perspective* (Mountain View, Calif., 1989), 356–368.

15. Berk and Berk, "The Non-Division of Household Labor."

16. Rosabeth Kanter, *Men and Women of the Corporation* (New York: Basic Books, 1977).

17. Jon Miller, Sanford Labovitz and Lincoln Fry, "Inequities in the Organizational Experiences of Women and Men," *Social Forces* 54 (December, 1975): 365–381.

18. Everett Cherrington Hughes, "Dilemmas and Contradictions of Status," in Lewis A. Coser and Bernard Rosenberg (eds.), *Sociological Theory* (New York: Macmillan, 1969), 360.

19. Cynthia Epstein, "Encountering the Male Establishment: Sex Status Limits on Women's Careers in the Professions," *American Journal of Sociology* 75 (May, 1970): 965–982. See also M. White, "Psychological and Social Barriers to Women in Science," *Science* 170 (3956): 413–416.

20. Elizabeth M. Almquist, "The Experiences of Minority Women in the United States: Intersections of Race, Gender, and Class," in Jo Freeman (ed.), *Women: A Feminist Perspective* (Mountain View, Calif.: Mayfield, 1989), 414–445.

21. Pauline Terrelonge, "Feminist Consciousness and Black Women," in Jo Freeman (ed.), *Women: A Feminist Perspective* (Mountain View, Calif.: Mayfield, 1989), 556–566.

22. Patricia Hill Collins, *Black Feminist Thought: Knowledge, Consciousness, and the Politics of Empowerment, Perspectives on Gender, Volume Two* (Boston: Unwin Hyman, 1990).

23. Consuelo Nieto, "The Chicana and the Women's Rights Movement-A Perspective," *Civil Rights Digest* 6 (Spring, 1974). See also Almquist "The Experiences of Minority Women in the United States: Intersections of Race, Gender, and Class," 421–423.

7

Race and Class Interactions
Friendship Choice and Inequality in the Schools

In this chapter, two empirical explorations are presented that are linked to the models covered in chapter 3. The first inquiry has to do with friendship choice, and corresponds to the *open market place* model. Blacks and Latinos who have moved into middle-class occupations are likely to have a high degree of contact with whites. Does socioeconomic similarity overide racial prejudice or social distance such that interracial friendships are common? To what extent do whites, blacks, and Latinos, of the same socioeconomic status, express a willingness to enter into friendship contacts with each other?

The second inquiry has to do with inequality in the educational system. The question posed is whether lower class black and Latino children experience more system linked barriers in educational opportunity than Anglo children? Does the combination of lower socioeconomic status and minority status lead to double jeopardies or combined disadvantage? This inquiry corresponds to the *ethclass* model (chapter 3) in which the joint effects of race and class are studied. There is a vast sociological literature on educational inequality. This discussion is limited to the misuse of IQ tests, bilingual education, tracking, and "effective schools."

RACE VERSUS CLASS IN FRIENDSHIP CHOICE

One of the long held propositions in the study of social stratification is that persons of the same stratum are more likely to interact with each other than with persons of different strata. For example, college graduates in upper white-collar occupations are likely to have in common certain occupational experiences, values, and life problems. Contact, friendship, and marriage are likely to occur within the boundaries of such class worlds.[1] However, one's race or ethnic stratum also has a great deal to do with interaction and friendship. From one's ethnic position comes a sense of peoplehood or shared destiny. The extreme geographical isolation that separates minority and majority group members is often said to breed distrust and awkwardness across race lines such that one can only feel comfortable with a person of the same race. Further, with the ethnic identity movements of the 1960s, many minority persons have expressed a preference for friendship within their own groups and a concomitant feeling that Anglos cannot be trusted, are racist, are overly materialistic, lack soul, etc.

With the many recent publications on the topics of a racially divided nation, ethnic nationalism, and continuing white racism, one might assume that if social class propensity for interaction and race propensity for interaction were put into competition with each other, race would consistently be more important. That is, whites would prefer friendship with whites to friendship with blacks even if the white was of a very different social class and the black was of the same social class.

The question of race versus class as a determinant of friendship choice is more than sociological gymnastics. Stressed throughout this book is the trend of a rising black and Latino skilled and white collar group employed in the dominant occupational structure. This trend suggests that Anglos, Latinos and blacks employed by the same organization in skilled and white-collar jobs have greatly increased opportunities for equalitarian contact, some of which should lead to friendship or at least moderately close personal relations. This is not to suggest that large scale interracial friendship is at hand; for some time to come, close, trusting friendship probably will be most likely to occur within an ethclass—choice of friends will be greatest for persons of the same race and same class. However, we are suggesting that there may be an increased *potential* for some interracial friendship among Anglos, blacks, and Latinos of the same skilled and white-collar positions—that common class worlds may erode racial barriers enough to allow for moderately intimate friendship. What follows is an empirical exploration of this possibility.

In a large survey of attitudes of whites in fifteen cities,[2] a very interesting question was asked: "Who do you think you could more easily become friends with, a Negro with the same education and income as you or a white person with a different education and income than you?" Although there are serious problems with the question—it may be extremely hypothetical for whites who have no contact with blacks at the same socioeconomic level to make such a choice, and friendship can be interpreted in many ways from casual acquaintance at work to more intimate friendship—it is one of the first attempts to put race in competition with class as a determinant of friendship. About half of the white respondents chose the white person with a different education and income, approximately one-fourth chose "Negro same education and income," and the remaining fourth didn't know or felt that it would make no difference. The results of this survey show that race matters more than class in a friendship choice.

I was sufficiently intrigued with the question used in this survey to try it out in slightly modified form with a number of ethnic groups in the Los Angeles area. In the Spring 1973 Los Angeles Metropolitan Area Survey,[3] the same question was asked of whites, blacks, and Spanish-surname persons matched by ethnic interviewers. The following refinements were made in the wording of the question, interviewing procedure, and analysis of results:

1. "Different education and income" was changed to "*very* different education and income." The purpose of the question is to truly put race into competition with class. The original form may have been interpreted by many respondents to mean only a small or moderate difference in education or income (e.g., a college graduate versus one with a postgraduate degree or someone making $25,000 versus someone making $35,000). "Very different" implies that the person is considerably above or below the respondent in socioeconomic level.

2. For black respondents, the question was rephrased: "White person of same education and income" versus "Black person of very different education and income." Similarly, Spanish-surname persons were asked "Anglo same" or "Latino very different."

3. A more systematic interview procedure was used to locate respondents who felt they could become friends with either

(person of the same class, different race or person of different race, same class). Only the race and class alternatives were presented by the interviewer. Persons who felt they could not choose between race or class were probed: "well, in general, which person would you choose?" If the respondents persisted that they could not choose and added that they could become friends with either person, they were coded "both." There are problems with this response. Some may be answering this way because they reject the entire premise that race and class determine friendship. (Similarly, studies have shown that some reject the idea that there are classes in American society.[4]) These respondents are expressing one version of the ideology of American individualism—friends are chosen for their personal qualities, not their income, education, or race. This denial that race and class are important may not carry over into their own behavior. On the other hand, some persons could be responding "both" because they genuinely believe they could become friends with persons of all classes and races. Because of the multiple interpretations for this response, less emphasis will be placed on it in the analysis.

4. Controls for occupation, education, income, and age were introduced for each of the ethnic groups. Holding same level of socioeconomic status constant is an especially important procedure for this question in order to standardize a common reference group. For example, an upper middle-class white who responds "Negro same" is referring to a different reference group than a lower-class white making the same choice (the upper middle-class white is referring to a similarly situated black with high education and income, while the lower-class white is referring to a comparable low income, poorly educated black). Our general expectation is that class similarity will outweigh racial similarity in determining friendship but only at middle and higher SES levels where there is greater occupational proximity, less economic competition, and less of a tradition of prejudice.

Findings for Whites

Table 7.1 presents the white response with controls for occupation, education, and income. Several very interesting patterns stand out in these data. First, it can be seen that whites are most likely to pick "Negro of same education and income" at the higher (objective) levels of the occupation, education and income scales. For example, note that among college graduates and postgraduates, about two-thirds choose the "Negro . . . same " response versus the "white . . . different." The same pattern is apparent for those in professional and technical occupations and those in the highest income categories. Apparently, at the higher ends of the socioeconomic hierarchies class similarity (same education and income) is very important for friendship choice and such class similarity outweighs racial homogeneity for most respondents. (The one exception to this generalization is that managers are somewhat evenly split between the class and race alternatives.) On the other hand, at lower levels of each hierarchy there is a "flipover" point with respondents choosing a white person of a different SES to a black person of the same SES. In the case of education, the flipover point is at high school graduation and lower; in the occupational hierarchy it is among blue-collar operatives, and in the case of income, among those in the $5,000 or less category. In other words, at working and lower socioeconomic levels, white respondents report that they are more likely to choose friends within their own (white) racial group even if the white person is in a very different class position, above or below them. Whites in the middle of the three hierarchies show a stronger class than race preference though generally not as strong as those at the top. For example, 47 percent of the blue-collar craftsmen feel they could more easily become friends with the Negro of the same income and education versus the 29 percent of craftsmen choosing the white of different level.

These findings cannot be taken too far, based as they are on a single question involving, for many, a rather hypothetical situation. Still, the data encourage the interpretation that among whites, socioeconomic equality is far more likely to break down racial barriers to friendship at middle and upper-class levels than at working and lower-class levels.

Table 7.2 shows age is also an important factor in the race-class pattern. Younger whites are more likely to make a class choice (Negro same), older whites a race choice (white different). Among 18–29 year olds a full 60 percent choose the Negro of the same education and income versus the 22 percent responding white different. In contrast, among those over 60, only 24 percent picked Negro same as opposed to 41 percent choosing white different.

Race versus Class: White Response with Occupation, Education, and Income Controlled			
FRIENDSHIP EASIER WITH:			
	NEGRO	WHITE	BOTH	N
CONTROL	SAME SES	DIFFERENT SES		
VARIABLE:	%	%	%	
Education				
Less than High School	26	40	34	(111)
High School Graduate	31	42	26	(205)
Some College	50	25	25	(173)
College Graduate	66	14	20	(74)
Post Graduate	69	15	16	(73)
Occupation				
Professional	58	18	24	(146)
Manager	41	39	19	(73)
Sales	44	32	24	(62)
Clerical	41	32	27	(145)
Crafts	47	29	24	(62)
Operatives	23	44	34	(62)
Income				
Under $5,000	29	33	38	(92)
$5–9,999	42	34	24	(136)
$10–14,999	46	33	21	(156)
$15–24,999	48	27	24	(147)
$25,000 or more	55	24	21	(82)

Table 7.1

Race versus Class: White Response with Age Controlled			
FRIENDSHIP EASIER WITH:			
	NEGRO	WHITE	BOTH	N
	SAME SES	DIFFERENT SES		
AGE:	%	%	%	
18–29	60	22	18	(158)
30–39	49	24	27	(115)
40–49	47	29	25	(126)
50–59	36	39	25	(105)
60+	24	41	35	(123)

Table 7.2

Before leaving the white data there is one other trend involving the response "both" that needs to be pointed out. The proportion saying "both" increases in the *lowest* level of each SES category—among operatives, those earning under $5,000, and those with only a grade school education. This is a surprising finding since these are groups often depicted as the most prejudiced. Apparently, as one moves down the socioeconomic hierarchies, two trends occur:

- there is an increased preference for the racial ingroup; and
- there is an increase in the proportion of persons rejecting both race and class as meaningful criteria for choice of friends.

Again, we are struck with the problem of interpreting the "both" response. Do such persons really mean that they are willing to interact with many persons of different races or classes or are they stating an ideology of American individualism in which race and class *should not* matter?

Findings for Blacks and Latinos

We have found striking differences in the race-class response among whites of different socioeconomic and age groups—notably, young whites and those whites in higher socioeconomic positions report that they could more easily become friends with a black person of the same education/income level than a white person of a very different level. But does this same trend apply to blacks and Latinos? Are younger middle-class blacks more likely to choose a white person of the same SES level or does the "black pride" movement (prevalent especially among young college blacks) produce a preference for black friendship regardless of social class differences?

Before moving to such subgroup comparisons, it is important to note that higher proportions of blacks than whites give the "both" response (41 percent black versus 22 percent white for the total samples). This suggests that blacks, on the average, place less stress on race and class in choice of friends than do whites. Higher proportions of blacks may be saying, "I could become friends with either black or white, rich or poor, well educated or not, and it would depend on the individual person."

Table 7.3 presents the black response with controls for education and age. (The occupation and income control data are not presented as there were no consistent patterns worth noting.) Younger blacks are somewhat more likely than older blacks to feel they could more easily become friends with the *black* person of a very different education and income. There is a moderate trend for some young blacks to prefer race over class. Thus, 29 percent of younger blacks versus only 11 percent of the older blacks respond "black different." However, this is not to say that *most* young blacks feel they can only relate to another black person as a friend since the young black group is almost evenly divided, across the three responses (about one-third each choose "white same," "black different," and "both"). Thus there is a group of blacks who are ethnically exclusive and they are more likely to be young but this is not the majority response for young blacks The other side of the story in table 7.3 is that older blacks overwhelmingly reject both race and class as important criteria for friendship, 61 percent choose "both."

Turning to the education data in table 7.3, we can see that there is an increased preference for black friendship as one moves up the education scale. Thus, only 9 percent of blacks with less than high school choose "black different" while a full 38 percent of those with college experience do. Conversely, black respondents with low degrees of education express the least degree of ethnic insularity with 59 percent responding "both" and 32 percent "white same." A racial in-group preference in friendship is more typical among blacks with college experience, however, this is not the majority response for college blacks since 38 percent of this group chooses "both" and another 25 percent "white same."

One consistent pattern emerges in the Spanish-surname data (table 7.4). Latinos in higher income and education positions (over $10,000, some college) feel friendship would be easier with an Anglo of the same class than a Latino of a different class. Conversely, an ethnic choice (Latino different) increases as one goes lower in the education and income categories. This rather strong preference among middle-class Latinos for friendship with Anglos of the same class may reflect the fact of a more permeable color line and the fact that middle-class Latinos have more opportunities for cross-ethnic friendship (e.g., residential segregation in Los Angeles is far less for Latinos than blacks). Occupation and age controls had no bearing on the Spanish-surname results. Note also that (as with the black sample) the proportion of Latinos choosing "both" is much higher than the case for Anglos.

Race versus Class: Black Response with Education, and Age Controlled

FRIENDSHIP EASIER WITH:

CONTROL VARIABLE:	WHITE SAME SES %	BLACK VERY DIFFERENT SES %	BOTH %	N
Education				
Less than High School	32	9	59	(34)
High School Graduate	34	28	38	(29)
Some College	25	38	38	(24)
Age				
18–29	32	29	38	(28)
30–39	29	29	42	(24)
40–49	35	18	47	(17)
50+	28	11	61	(18)

Table 7.3

Race versus Class: Latino (Spanish Surname) Response with Education, and Income Controlled

FRIENDSHIP EASIER WITH:

CONTROL VARIABLE:	ANGLO SAME SES %	LATINO VERY DIFFERENT SES %	BOTH %	N
Education				
Less than High School	24	28	48	(42)
High School Graduate	50	11	39	(28)
Some College	50	9	41	(22)
Income				
Under $5,000	31	25	44	(16)
$5–9,999	38	13	50	(32)
Over $10,000	51	12	37	(41)

Table 7.4

Summary Statement

In the Los Angeles area we find that different age and socioeconomic subgroups of the Anglo, black, and Latino populations respond very differently to the question of race versus class as a determinant of friendship. Young whites and whites high or medium in the occupation, education, and income hierarchies report that class similarity is more important to them than racial similarity in the choice of friends. Similarly, higher SES Spanish-surname persons show a greater propensity to choose Anglos of the same (high) SES than Latinos of a very different SES. This, of course, does not mean that all of those who express a preference for a person of another race have behaviorally engaged in that kind of interaction. But it does express a readiness to interact across racial lines with persons likely to have similar tastes and life styles (class). However, among blacks, We find a moderate counter trend. It is among the young and college educated blacks that one finds a fairly high proportion choosing race over class. This does not mean that young middle-class whites and young middle-class blacks have no possibility of friendship contact since substantial proportions of young middle-class blacks also choose "both" or "white same." It does indicate, however, that the white response is somewhat out of alignment with the black response and that social class similarity does not in itself sweep over all racial factors.

RACE, CLASS, AND EDUCATIONAL INEQUALITY

Lower-class black and Latino children are far more likely to drop out of school and fall further behind at each grade level in their achievements than middle-class white, middle-class black, and middle-class Latino children. Unfortunately, the most common explanation for failure has been the lower-class minority environment or the "cultural deprivation" or "culture of poverty" explanation. With slightly different variations for blacks and Latinos, this explanation asserts that components of a depressed environment—apathy, low motivation, lack of cognitive interaction between parents and children, and a lack of books and magazines—cause failure. Writing about the education of Mexican-American children, Joan Moore notes "Federal financial assistance has encouraged southwestern educators to develop 'compensatory education' programs to help Mexican-American children compensate for certain inadequacies they display when compared to a 'standard' middle class child. The idea of 'cultural disadvantage' provides a rationale for action to overcome the minority group child's real or assumed deficiencies. It is designed not to change the school but to change the child."[5]

It is only recently that educational institutions themselves, their policies and their programs, have been studied in any critical, systematic way in this regard. In this literature, one finds articles on teacher expectations for failure, abuse in the use of IQ tests in classifying lower-class black and Chicano children, the negative consequences of tracking, and the class-ethnic composition of the student body as the determiner of "cooling out" mechanisms. The study of the patterns of racism and classism in educational institutions is an extremely important area with obvious implications for policy research. The failure to educate lower-class black and Latino children is seen by many as not so much a function of a depressed environment as of an insensitive reaction of educational institutions to children produced from this environment—that is, the mechanical tendency to sort and classify students according to the degree to which they match the middle-class Anglo model. Schools are not so much deliberately attempting to exclude lower-class minority children as they are perpetuating an impersonal "conveyer belt" of failure for them by favoring an unmodified adherence to middle-class Anglo standards. There is often total insensitivity to the background of the lower-class child. For example, Mexican language and culture may often be tied to punishment and failure rather than being creatively integrated into the curriculum of the school.

The Misuse of IQ Tests

A provocative study by Jane R. Mercer[6] titled, "IQ, The Lethal Label," highlights the "overuse" of middle-class Anglo criteria for achievement in school. Mercer states:

> A large number of minority persons who can cope very well with the requirements of their daily lives are being labeled mentally retarded. They acquire these labels, not because they are unable to cope with the world, but because they have not had the opportunity to learn the cognitive skills necessary to pass Anglo-oriented intelligence tests. They do not conform to the typical Anglo, middle-class pattern; thus they appear "retarded" to the white middle-class clinician or teacher. Yet their behavior outside of the test situation belies their test scores.[7]

The research involved field samples of Chicano, black, and Anglo persons of all ages and a sample of 1,513 elementary school-aged children in Riverside, California (N = 598 Chicanos, 339 blacks and 576 Anglos). The study involved two important refinements not often found in race and IQ studies. First, both standardized IQ tests as well as a measure of *adaptive ability* were employed. The "adaptive ability" test was a measure of actual behavioral skill in the environment, the degree to which the person is able to function independently in the environment (e.g., independently shop in a store, choose certain items, and pay for them). The measure consisted of a series of 28 age-graded scales. Second, many studies of IQ differences between the races have been controlled for SES measures such as occupation or income. However, Mercer's study is one of the first attempts to control for both ethnic culture and class factors simultaneously. For example, in comparing the IQ scores of Chicano and Anglo children, both class variables (such as "head of household in skilled occupation," and "mother expects children to have some college") and ethnic variables ("head grew up in U.S. rather than Mexico" and "family speaks English in the home") are controlled.

Similarly, for blacks, class as well as ethnic culture factors (e. g., mother reared in North, nuclear family intact) were controlled.

If it is true that IQ tests are Anglo-centric, then the more Anglicized a non-Anglo child is, the better he/she should do on the IQ test. That is, racial differences in IQ should wash out or be greatly reduced with these variables simultaneously controlled.

There are two findings in Mercer's study that are notably outstanding. First, the standard IQ test was far more predictive of behavioral skills (adaptive ability) for Anglos than for blacks or Chicanos: "Every Anglo who had an IQ below 70 was also in the lowest three percent on the behavior scales. But this was by no means true for minority groups. Fully 91 percent of the blacks and 60 percent of the Chicanos with IQs below 70 had *passed* the behavior test.[8] The implications are clear; a great many more Chicanos and blacks are likely to be mislabeled "retarded" than white children are by the sole reliance on a standard IQ test. In the second part of the article, black and Chicano children in the large elementary school sample were given a score from zero to five, depending on the number of ethnic and class characteristics that their families shared with the "average" Anglo family in Riverside. The mean IQ for each sub-group (e.g., Chicanos having one, two, three, four, and five characteristics) was then compared with the Anglo average IQ. The results (presented in table 7.5) show that children whose families were *least* like the average Anglo family— that is, had none or only one characteristic like the average Anglo family—scored *lowest* in IQ (IQ = 84.5 for Chicanos and 87.7 for blacks). However, with the addition of each Anglo middle-class characteristic the average IQ rose in a stair-step fashion. When all five characteristics were simultaneously controlled—that is, those who matched the Anglo pattern best—the differences between the races disappeared. "In short, when we controlled for the social backgrounds of the children, there were no differences in intelligence between the Anglos and the blacks or between the Anglos and the Chicanos."[9]

Comparisons of Chicano and Black IQ with Anglo IQ as Cultural Factors are Controlled		
Chicano-Anglo Comparisons		
Anglo Average IQ= 100		
IQ= 90.4 N= 598 Chicano Average No Controls	IQ= 84.5 N= 127 0–1 Anglo Charecteristics	IQ=88.1 N= 146 2 Anglo Characteristics
IQ= 89 N=126 3 Anglo Characteristics	IQ= 95 N= 174 4 Anglo Characteristics	IQ=104.4 N= 25 5 Anglo Characteristics
Black-Anglo Comparison		
Anglo Average IQ= 100		
IQ= 90.5 N= 339 Black Average No Controls	IQ= 82.7 N= 47 0–1 Anglo Characteristics	IQ= 87.1 N= 101 2 Anglo Characteristics
IQ= 92.8 N= 106 3 Anglo Characteristics	IQ= 95.5 N= 68 4 Anglo Characteristics	IQ= 99.5 N= 17 5 Anglo Characteristics

Table 7.5

To prevent misclassification of minority children, Mercer calls for a pluralistic assessment of a child's ability based on four types of information. There should be a sociocultural index to classify a child's social and economic milieu. There should be a measure of adaptive ability that would give us information about how the child functions in his home and neighborhood. An IQ test *interpreted against standard norms* could be used to determine whether the child can succeed in a regular public school without additional help. Finally, to determine the child's *potential* for learning, the same IQ could be used but this time interpreted within the child's ethnic norms. "Together these four measures will paint a far more accurate picture of a child's abilities than Anglo-oriented IQ tests can give. For example, if a Chicano child scores far above average for his ethnic group, than his intellectual ability is probably above normal, even if his actual IQ score is 100-average for a group of Anglo middle-class students."

Studies of test bias, such as the one by Mercer, above, influenced changes in test administration and use in some state schools. In the 1970s and 1980s there were court battles over the use of IQ tests to place black students in special education programs. In 1979, U.S. District Judge Robert F. Peckham *ruled unconstitutional* California's use of IQ tests that placed "grossly disproportionate" numbers of blacks into "dead end" classes for the mentally retarded.[10] In 1986, Peckham expanded the ban (at the request of plaintiffs and the State Department of Education) to forbid use of IQ tests for all black students who are candidates for any of a variety of special education or remedial classes. Only those black students being considered for academically gifted programs could be tested.

Peckham's landmark rulings barred California public schools from using standardized IQ tests for determining whether low achieving black students should be placed in special classes. Note that the decision did not affect Latinos or other minorities. California's attempts to avoid misplacement of minority children have been directed at one minority group only. An interesting sideline is that a small number of black families filed suit to overturn the 1986 expanded ruling. These families wanted their children tested for special learning disabilities and felt they were being denied valuable information. In 1991 Peckham issued a preliminary injunction granting the families of two students the right to have their children tested.[11]

Language Problems

In chapter 4, it was noted that the high school drop-out rate for young Latinos is approaching 50 percent in many Southwestern schools. The very high drop-out rate is partly a function of language problems. For example, in California, Latinos make up approximately 30 percent of public school enrollment. One fourth of these students (23 percent) are performing at or near grade level. Another one-third (32 percent) are Spanish speakers and are not performing satisfactorily in English. They are the youngsters most likely to be sent to bilingual programs. The remaining 46 percent—the largest percentage by far—are classified as English speakers, i.e., they speak much more English than Spanish, but their English skills are considerably below grade level.[12] There are actually two categories of children in these statistics who are likely to experience adjustment tensions as they make contact with the schools:

- Spanish speakers who are learning English skills through bilingual programs, and
- below grade level English speakers or those whom some have called the "English dominant Chicano kid."[13] Both groups contribute to the high drop out rate but the policies and reasons for failure are different for the two groups.

Bilingual education and English as a second language (ESL)—the presumed remedies for the dominant Spanish speaker—have had modest success at best. Bilingual education is not a single program, but a cluster of different strategies and programs. For example, depending on the district or school, bilingual education may mean instruction in two languages, English as a second language, immersion in all English classrooms (with bilingual aides), assignment to a Learning Specialist Resource, or a special tutoring program. With so many versions of bilingual programs, it is no wonder that results of studies are conflicting. One version of bilingual education argues that language is intimately tied to a child's self esteem. If a child speaks Spanish fluently, the system should respond to that skill as a resource of strength. Bilingual education by this philosophy means a gradual transition from Spanish to English instruction. Concepts and skills are presented first in Spanish so the child does not fall behind in content areas while learning a new lanuage. English is introduced in small increments. The criticism of this approach is that bilingual children will always be behind because they are required not only to learn new grade level concepts (in math, science, etc.), but also to master a new language. Those children with two languages (their primary home language and English) then are required to learn twice as much in the same time period as English-speaking-only students. Certain schools, however, have claimed success with this approach by very skillfully blending Spanish and English instruction.

Total immersion, by contrast, argues that the child will learn English fastest by complete saturation in the language with no opportunity to speak Spanish in the classroom. The critics of this approach note that a child may feel hopelessly outside mainstream instruction. Unable to comprehend the lessons, children easily fall behind classmates and may feel isolated and unsuccessful. Moreover, there may be a subtle message conveyed that the ability to speak Spanish is a negative factor or something to be hidden rather than a positive ability of which to be proud. Variations in the total immersion approach may involve a bilingual teacher or aide who can ease the child over the first few difficult weeks of adjustment, explaining an assignment or answering questions in Spanish when a child is unable to understand English instruction.

At a broader more ideological level, bilingual education may not be highly successful because it has not been enthusiastically embraced by school districts and the general public. Joan Moore notes that bilingual education irritates many conservatives (even in the Hispanic community) who see fluency in English as the only true language objective of the school. "The fact is that many Americans are extremely reluctant to sanction the use of any language in this country except English. For legislators and many ordinary people, bilingual education seems an expensive dilution of American ideals."[14]

There is a growing concern in California about the plight of the "English dominant Chicano kid"—the 46 percent previously mentioned. These are youngsters whose English skills are below grade level. Typically, they test at or near grade level in the first years of elementary school, but fall further behind each year as the curriculum becomes more demanding in English skills. Quite often, these children are in homes where their classroom English is not reinforced, i.e., a household in which both parents speak primarily in Spanish. The child may slip behind in such small, cumulative increments, that it is only in the upper elementary or junior high school years that the gap becomes glaring. The concern is that many of these children are falling between the cracks in terms of special aid. There is very little research on, and few programs for students who appear to have made the transition in terms of command of the language yet continue to perform in school less well than others.[15]

The joint effects of social class and ethnicity are very much involved in these language adjustment problems. Middle-class Latinos fluent in English experience no problems. It is lower- and working-class socioeconomic status, in combination with ethnicity and language barriers, that produces a system problem. Working- and lower-class children of all ethnic groups often have a more difficult school adjustment experience than middle- and upper middle-class children. There is often a difference between socioeconomic groups in study habits and environments conducive to study, in parental reinforcement, in opportunities for written and oral language instruction, and in educationally enriching experiences. Lower social class in combination with a language problem is likely to produce special demands on the school system.

Even though many children are fairly bilingual in their skills as they enter the school, some functioning as interpreters for their parents or siblings who speak only Spanish, they are viewed as needy, rather than doubly talented. Instead of being valued as a rich resource, the bilingual skills of these children are ignored or treated as a kind of negative handicap. In other countries, bilingualism is one factor necessary for school and societal success. School success stories for bilingual children in the U.S. could be turned around if the U.S. expected fluency in two (or more) languages as most other countries in the world do. Moore notes that bilingualism among Mexican-American children is often assumed to be "detrimental to intellect and thus to the teachability of the child."[16] The child not completely fluent in English has a greater probability of being misclassified by standardized IQ tests. Finally, the school response to differences in language, culture, and socioeconomic motivation, in far too many Southwestern schools, has been to categorize and track children according to presumed ability.

Race, Class and Tracking

It is widely believed that the American educational system is highly congruent with the ideal of an open class industrial society— one in which persons reach positions as a result of hard work, initiative, and ability rather than race, religion, or class. However, Mercer's findings (above discussion) on race and IQ suggest that lower-class black and Chicano children are often mislabeled as "retarded" or "low-normal ability." Unfortunately, such classifications are not neutral. The results of "objective" standardized test scores are used to separate children into high and low "ability" groups. Educators often justify tracking on the grounds that the more academically able college-bound students should not be slowed down in their progress by slower students. Further, there seems to be an assumption that the less bright will be more comfortable and have greater self-esteem in a group of other children with similar abilities. However, the critics of "tracking" note that the system produces failure. Those in a low track receive an inferior education and develop increasingly negative images of themselves and of the school system. More broadly, tracking is likely to be maintaining and solidifying existing social class lines. A diagram of this process might look like figure 7.1.

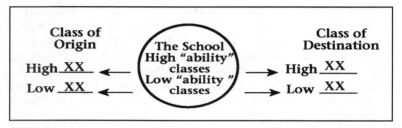

Figure 7.1

Working and lower-class young persons are less likely to be perceived by educators as having the requisite ability and motivation for college success and a challenging white-collar occupation. This results in low track assignment which in turn leads to a lower-class occupation. In short, the American educational institution is increasingly being criticized as maintaining inequality for lower-class segments of racial minorities and lower-class white children rather than facilitating academic growth and achievement. Some changes are being made by "mainstreaming" special education students into regular classes, by requiring that no child be denied access to the core curriculum, and by more heterogenous grouping.

Race and Track

Lower and working class students of all races are more likely to be placed in lower-ability tracks. This likelihood is greater among lower-class black, Latino, and Native-American children.[17] There may remain a backdrop of racial inferiority beliefs to which a minority child can easily be fitted (e.g., "They seem to lack the motivation" or, "Their background has been more deprived"). It probably takes a clearly middle-class, teacher-oriented minority child with actively interested parents to break through these expectations. There has typically been an insensitive reaction to black, Latino, and Native American culture in Anglo institutions in general and in education in particular. Speaking Spanish or Navaho or Black English has been viewed by many teachers as a sign of nonconformity, a learning handicap, resistance or rebellion. Language differences, such as the use of Black English, may work against the child.

Black English, until very recently, was not considered as a legitimate second language. The dialect of black children that many Anglo educators found unintelligible was believed to be a substandard, extremely limited, primitive version of "acceptable" English. Educational researchers have maintained that Black English is so deficient that different tenses cannot be expressed and that abstract-cognitive thinking cannot occur. Susan Houston[18] agrees that much of the language which educators elicit from black children is, indeed, inferior. However, she found that once black children learn that they can trust adults from the educational institutions, their language is far from inadequate. The language that black children use with their peers and adults they can trust is very different from the style, and the "register," that they use in school. Black English is often more creative, imaginative, and elaborate than standard English. There are significant differences between Black English and "White" English, neither of which is superior or more adaptive to their respective communities than the other. Houston reminds us that "An uninformed society has tended to obscure the differences, especially in classrooms that demand competitive and uniform performance irrespective of individual children's inclinations."[19]

Lower-class black, Latino, and Indian parents are least likely to have the bureaucratic expertise and influence to push very hard to be sure that their children are placed in a "high" or college-bound track class. Knowledge of the committees and people necessary to move the system is a resource found more often in middle-class white families.

"Programmed for Social Class"

A number of studies emphasize the importance of race and class on tracking at the high school level. One study, by Schafer et. al., is especially revealing.[20] The authors collected data from school transcripts of the recently graduated classes of two midwestern three-year high schools. One school was located in a middle-class academic community of 70,000 (graduating class that year=753). A second, smaller school had a graduating class of 404 and was located in an industrial city of 20,000. Both schools had a two-track system: college preparatory and "general."

The first finding in the study is that both socioeconomic status and race affected which track a student took "quite apart from either his or her achievement in junior high or his or her ability as measured by IQ scores.[21] With the two schools combined into one total population, 83 percent of the students from white-collar homes were in the college preparatory track as opposed to 48 percent of the students from blue-collar homes. The relationship between race and track assignment was even stronger: 71 percent of the white students were in the college track as opposed to 30 percent of the black. Moreover, once students were placed in the "high" or "low" track at the end of the ninth grade, there was practically no mobility up or down. That is, there was a caste-like rigidity that followed assignment. "Only 7 percent of those who began on the college prep track moved down to the noncollege prep track, while only 7 percent of those assigned to the lower, noncollege track, moved up."[22] Even more important was the finding that track assignment was related to subsequent academic performance: those assigned to the college track made gains while the performance of those assigned to the lower track showed deterioration. This can best be illustrated by figure 7.2.

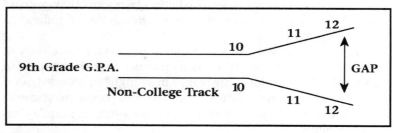

9th Grade G.P.A.

Non-College Track

Figure 7.2

Note that at the ninth grade (before tracking) there was a small difference in mean GPA between the two groups; however, after tracking there was an increased gap with the college group rising and the non-college group falling in academic achievement. By graduation, after three years of tracking, the gap between the groups was very large. Not only was there a deterioration of academic performance in the low track group but less participation in extra-curricular activities, greater tendency to drop out, increased delinquency and more misbehavior in school. In other words, once placed in the lower track, many students showed an increased tendency to disengage from the high school as a source of meaning and self-respect.

These findings strongly suggest that tracking creates a certain amount of failure in the school. That is, tracking is an independent source of demotivation and failure apart from the ability or home environment of the student. However, believers in tracking can still argue that the observed differences between the college and non-college groups are due to individual ability; college preparatory students do better simply because they are brighter than the non-college group. It could further be argued that the less bright non-college group showed a deterioration of achievement because the work in the tenth, eleventh, and twelfth grades was increasingly more difficult. Similarly, the gains made in the college group could be explained on an individual motivation level—college-bound students worked harder and became more grade conscious as they got nearer to college. What is needed is a technique to sort out the deterioration effect of tracking with controls for home background, ability, and past achievement. Fortunately, in this study it was possible to get at the unique effects of tracking. Through the use of a technique known as test factor standardization the researchers were able to assess the effects of tracking on achievement with IQ, academic achievement before tracking (ninth grade GPA), and home environment (father's occupation) simultaneously controlled or ruled out. The argument is that if tracking persists in predicting achievement with the effects of these three factors eliminated, then tracking is a structural effect of the school that cannot be blamed on student ability. With the influence of the three factors eliminated, there was indeed a sizeable remaining relationship. Thirty percent of the college group as opposed to only 4 percent of the non-college group attained the top quarter of the class. At the low achievement end, only 12 percent of the college group were in the lowest quarter as compared with 35 percent of the non-college group. Tracking is carrying its own deleterious effects that are not explained away by the IQ or motivation of the student.

What, precisely, is happening in the low track group to produce a drastic decline in achievement? For one thing, there is likely to be an erosion of self-esteem. The lower track carries with it a strong stigma as illustrated by this interview of an ex-delinquent in Washington, D.C.

> It really don't have to be the tests, but after the tests there shouldn't be no separation in the classes. Because, as I say again, I felt good when I was with my class, but when they went and separated us — that changed us. That changed our ideas, our thinking, the way we thought about each other and turned us to enemies toward each other—because they said I was dumb and they were smart.
>
> *Did you think the other guys were smarter than you?*
> Not at first—I used to think I was just as smart as anybody in the school—I knew I was smart. I knew some people were smarter, and I wanted to go to school, I wanted to get a diploma and go to college and help people and everything. I stepped into there in junior high—I felt like a fool going to school—I really felt like a fool.
>
> *Why?*
> Because I felt like I wasn't a part of that school . . .[23]

Teacher expectations are another major ingredient of the explanation. Teachers with low track classes are likely to underestimate the abilities of students, to define them as losers. Students easily pick up such definitions and perform at a lower level. This is not to say that most teachers in low track sections are *consciously* trying to produce failure. Rather, the teacher, by subtle forms of interaction (tone of voice) unconsciously sets in motion a negative self-fulfilling prophecy.[24]

Schafer, Olexa, and Polk also found evidence of peculiar grading policies in the two tracks. Interviews with teachers and other staff personnel in the schools pointed toward the existence of grade ceilings for the non-college group and grade floors for the college group. In other words, it was extremely difficult for lower track students to get a grade higher than a "C" even if objective performance was equal to a college track "B." Similarly, college track students seldom made a grade lower than a "B." "Several teachers explicitly called our attention to this practice, the rationale being that non-college prep students do not deserve the same objective grade rewards as college prep students, since they "clearly" are less bright and perform less well."[25]

No hard data were presented to assess the frequency with which this "ceilings and floors" policy was practiced. But if widely used in the two schools, it certainly explains why there was so little mobility between the two tracks and why there was a deterioration of performance in the low track. If students perceived that no matter how hard they tried they could not get higher than a grade of "C," demotivation and lowered commitment would logically follow.

The above research piece by Schafer et al. is a classic 1970 study of the negative effects of tracking and teacher expectations. Subsequent research in the 1980s and 1990s has resulted in refinements and updates. Some of the more recent studies find that race, class, and gender have very weak effects in determining assignment to a particular track.[26] Rather, academic performance, relevant course work, and test scores account for the largest part of the explanation of track assignment. The researchers note that it is not race or class per se that affect track assignment, but rather, *class related social-psychological variables* such as a strong desire to go to college and having friends with college aspirations. Having college aspirations, and peer support for those aspirations tends to be more common at middle and upper-middle socioeconomic levels, but such attitudes and peer support are increasingly prevalent in working class levels. The race and class effects on track assignment in the Schafer et al. study seem to overstate the case for the 1990s. Yet, race and class still may be very much involved in track assignment through indirect processes. The conversion of aspirations into appropriate academic program is one such process. Research from a national study of high school students indicates that educational aspirations were significantly more likely to be related to enrollment in the academic track for whites than for blacks and Latinos.[27] It was suggested that especially where student actions and student norms are involved in track placement (more than teacher assignments), whites would be better able to match their educational aspirations with appropriate track enrollment. This greater tendency of whites to convert their aspirations into an academic track may be a function of such factors as access to information and parental involvement. Most studies of tracking have not taken into account parental involvement. Parental involvement in tracking decisions is likely to vary by social class and indirectly by ethnicity. "More educated parents, either through involvement in their children's decision or through direct contact with school staff, are more likely to participate in the decision regarding program enrollment than less educated parents."[28]

In sum, earlier research may have exaggerated the direct effects of race and class on track assignment. However, class and race may still indirectly influence track assignment in terms of college aspirations, peer support for college aspirations, and the conversion of aspirations into academic program placement.

Recent research also indicates that schools vary tremendously in organizational characteristics. These different school climates affect the way race and class play out in tracking assignments. In secondary schools in the United States, the proportion of students in the academic track varies betweeen 10 and 70 percent with an average of 35 percent. Kilgore makes a distinction between exclusive and inclusive tracking patterns.[29] An exclusive pattern exists in schools in which a high proportion of students are below their expected track placement, indicating that standards for entrance into the academic track are higher (more elitist) than expected from national norms. Inclusive tracking patterns occur in schools where a high proportion are in tracks above that predicted from national norms, suggesting standards lower than national norms. Exclusive tracking (higher standards) is more likely to occur in schools of upper middle class student composition where the student demand for an academic program is high. "When student demand for an academic track is high, the organization will experience pressure to establish more exclusive tracking practices to preserve the comprehensive structure of the curriculum."[30] Thus, it may actually be more difficult to get into the high academic track in some upper middle class schools where student demand is high. On the other hand, in schools composed primarily of students of lower or working class background, the organizational response is inclusive—to lower standards to include some minimum degree of enrollment in the academic track. However, in schools where most students have working class backgrounds, there is likely to be more ambiguity regarding qualifications for the academic track. As a result, teachers may use more subjective or arbitrary criteria in tracking decisions (inappropriate matches of student interest and ability with track assignment) than in middle class schools where a large portion of the student body is clearly qualified. Accordingly, some research finds a more meritocratic tracking system in middle class schools and a more arbitrary system operating in working class schools.

Teacher expectations continue to play an important part in the explanation of student performance. In addition to cognitive performance, there are a set of student skills, habits, and styles which are involved in student/teacher interaction and are differentially rewarded by teachers. Teachers' judgements of student habits and styles influence mastery of material and course grades net of cognitive performance, and this, in part, explains the differential success of poverty and ethnic groups. One study finds that teacher judgements of citizenship, study habits, appearance and dress, absenteeism, and disruptive behavior in the classroom are important for student mastery of coursework.[32] Poor students were judged by teachers to have a less pleasing appearance than higher income students. African American students were judged more disruptive, but this was only so when the teacher was African American. Asian students were judged to have less absenteeism, better work habits, less disruptiveness, and better appearance and dress. Thus, teachers can be viewed as gatekeepers to academic success. Teachers' judgements of student work habits was one of the strongest predictors of grades in the study. In particular, Asian students outscore non-Asians both because of their cognitive performance and because they are judged by teacher to have outstanding work habits.

A final update concerns the divergence hypothesis: do current studies confirm the patterns, displayed in figure 7.2, that tracking raises the performance of students placed in high ability groups and lowers the performance of students in the low ability groups. The studies have produced some mixed findings and interpretations. Alexander and Cook, for example, suggest that when a variety of student background factors are controlled (including ability, achievement, and types of courses taken prior to ability grouping) the effects of tracking are almost completely removed.[33] However, many studies continue to find a tracking effect. The pattern of divergence (losses by students placed in low ability groups; gains by students in high ability groups) has been found in both the U.S. and Great Britain.[34] There continues to be much evidence that separation of students into academic, and remedial tracks has an effect on achievment test performance in both reading and mathematics, net of student ability and other background factors. Kerckhoff suggests the following explanations: (a) Students in high ability groups are provided with a different curriculum or program than those in lower track groups. They are provided with the means to gain more in subject matter. (b) Teachers assigned to high ability groups tend to be more motivated to improve the the level of performance of their students. (c) There is likely to be a peer group effect. If a student is surrounded by highly motivated students with college plans he or she is likely to be affected. Conversely, being surrounded by lower track peers is likely to decrease motivation.[35]

Social Class and Ambiguity about Educational Goals

Tracking is a school effect that results in both race and class differentials in achievement. Another explanation for the differences in black-white achievement and Latino-white achievement emphasize the outlooks and orientations that young people hold toward school performance. In an exhaustive review of research dealing with the schooling of Black Americans, Jaynes and Williams note that some black students feel ambivalent about the payoffs of school achievement.[36] For example, Ogbu found that while black parents valued schooling and wanted their children to do well, their own lives, in terms of menial jobs and unemployment, undermined the expectation of school effort.[37] Moreover, young blacks in lower status neighborhoods observed that important persons around them (older siblings, relatives, and other adults) had great difficulty in securing steady employment. "Under these circumstances, black students did not try to maximize their school performance because they did not think they would have equal opportunity to get good jobs when they finished school."[38] A study in the late 1980s suggests that black student peer culture, in some lower class neighborhoods, works against the goal of striving for academic success.[39] Behaviors associated with achievement, such as speaking standard English, studying long hours and striving to get good grades was regarded as "acting white." Students who engaged in such behavior were ostracized from the group. Interviews with some high achieving black students indicated that they had consciously slowed down or put "brakes" on their achievement to gain acceptance and avoid ridicule.[40]

Obviously, there are connections between the school tracking literature described above and these studies about the ambivalence of young minority students toward achievement. If lower class black and Latino students enter the school with different (i.e., non-middle class) orientations and are harshly judged, or led into a "hidden curriculum" (with lower teacher expectations or slow learner track), there is likely to be much more skepticism about the payoffs to achievement and a stronger orientation toward peer culture.

Can a positive school climate cut through some of these structural and attitudinal barriers created by tracking and attitude ambivalence? A number of studies indicate that school environments have little effect on the academic achievement of black youngsters.[41] The thrust of the literature is that school quality (e.g., schools with good equipment and well-trained teachers) has only modest effects in reducing black-white differences in achievement. An interesting exception is the literature on "effective schools."[42] Proponents of this view are critical of the findings that school quality has negligible effects on the achievement of minorities. The study of effective schools began as a search of "outliers" or schools in low income urban minority populations where students were doing extremely well. The research question was simply, what is there about these schools that is producing success? Why are they exceptions? Weber notes that successful schools had some very clear characteristics such as: leadership of a strong principal, high expectations for student performance, a "good social climate," and regular monitoring of student progress.[43] The concept of school climate or school culture is difficult to operationalize. Purkey and Smith set down nine characteristics that make up an effective school culture. Among them are the following:

- instructional leadership on the part of a principal or group of teachers that initiates and sustains a commitment to high achievement;
- parental involvement and support to tighten the home-school link in a way that reinforces high achievement goals;
- maximized learning time so that disruptive behavior and nonteaching bureaucratic activities intrude as little as possible on classroom time;
- district support in maintaining staff stability and initiatives.[44]

Another study indicates that the development of a safe, orderly, disciplined atmosphere is a first essential step toward establishing an effective school climate. "This requires that teachers and administrators demand of students that they become self regulating, disciplined and industrious. If students are not responsive to the authority of teachers and school administrators, if misbehavior, vandalism, violence, absenteeism are rife, progress toward the achievement of even basic competencies will be difficult."[45]

Lightfoot argues that the leadership of the school principal is crucial to the development of an effective school culture. "Effective leadership by a principal requires a mixture of the instrumental qualities of the stereotypical principal and a more expressive, symbiotic, nurturant partnership with the teachers and students at the school."[46]

The effective school research has been criticized on method-ological grounds for small samples, a lack of controls for confounding factors, and an overuse of subjective criteria in designating effective schools. Still, as Jaynes and Williams note, the research is important because a diversity of researchers and methods have produced similar findings, and because of "the common sense power of its principal claims."[47] The effective school literature is one promising policy lead for reducing educational inequality in lower class minority areas.

NOTES

1. See, for example, Dennis Gilbert and Joseph A. Kahl, *The American Class Structure* (Chicago: Dorsey Press, 1987), ch. 5.

2. Angus Campbell, *White Attitudes Toward Black People* (Ann Arbor: University of Michigan, Institute for Social Research, 1971), 8.

3. See note 41, chapter 5 for further details on the LAMAS surveys. This is not a secondary analysis of data. That is, the author paid a fee to have the caste-class question included in the Spring 1973 survey with specifications of exact wording and interview procedure.

4. Kahl, *The American Class Structure*, 167–171.

5. Joan W. Moore, *Mexican Americans* (Englewood, N.J.: Prentice-Hall, 1970), 81.

6. Jane R. Mercer, "IQ: The Lethal Label," *Psychology Today* 6 (September, 1972): 95.

7. Ibid., 44.

8. Ibid., 47.

9. Ibid., 96.

10. *Los Angeles Times*, "Court Ban on IQ Tests for Blacks Sparks Suit by Parents," August 5, 1991, A3.

11. Ibid., 21.

12. *Los Angeles Times*, "Latino Students Advance, Only to Fail," August 1, 1983.

13. Ibid., 14.

14. Joan Moore and Harry Pachon, *Hispanics in the United States*, (Englewood Cliffs, New Jersey: Prentice-Hall, 1985), 154.

15. *Los Angeles Times*, "Latino Students Advance, Only to Fail."

16. Moore and Pachon, *Hispanics in the United States*, 147.

17. See, for example, Ray C. Rist, "Student Social Class and Teacher Expectations: The Self-Fulfilling Prophecy in Ghetto Schools," *Harvard Educational Review* 40 (3, 1970): 411–451.

18. Susan H. Houston, "Black English," *Psychology Today* 7 (March, 1973): 45–48.

19. Ibid., 48.

20. Walter E. Schafer, Carol Olexa, and Kenneth Polk, "Programmed for Social Class: Tracking in High School," *Transaction* 7 (October, 1970): 39–46, 63. See also Jeannie Oakes, "Classroom Social Relationships: Exploring the Bowles Gintis Hypothesis" *Sociology of Education* 55 (4, 1982): 197–212, Jeannie Oakes, "Limiting Opportunity: Student Race and Curricular Differences in Secondary Vocational Education," *American Journal of Education* 91 (3, 1983): 328–355.

21. Schafer, Olexa and Polk "Programmed for Social Class: Tracking in High School," 40.

22. Ibid., 41.

23. Ibid., 43.

24. For a classic study of teacher expectations and the self-fulfilling prophecy, see Robert Rosenthal and Lenore Jacobson, *Pygmalion in the Classroom: Teacher Expectations and Pupils Intellectual Development* (New York: Holt, Rinehart & Winston, 1968).

25. Schafer, Olexa, and Polk, "Programmed for Social Class: Tracking in High School," 44.

26. Karl Alexander and Martha Cook, "Curricula and Coursework: a Surprise Ending to a Familiar Story," *American Sociological Review* 47 (October, 1982): 626–640; Michael D. Wiatrowski, Stephen Hansell, Charles Massey and David L. Wilson, "Curriculum Tracking and Delinquency," *American Sociological Review* 47 (February, 1982): 151–160.

27. Sally B. Kilgore, "The Organizational Context of Tracking in Schools," *American Sociological Review* 56 (April, 1991): 189–203.

28. Ibid., 201.

29. Ibid., 190.

30. Ibid., 192

31. Ibid., 201; James Rosenbaum, *Making Inequality* (New York: John Wiley and Sons, 1976).

32. George Farkas, Robert Grobe, Daniel Sheehan, and Yuan Shuan, "Cultural Resources and School Success," *American Sociological Review* 55 (February, 1990): 12–142.

33. Alexander and Cook, "Curricula and Coursework: A Surprise Ending to A Familiar Story," 633.

34. Alan C. Kerckhoff, "Effects of Ability Grouping in British Secondary Schools," *American Sociological Review* 51 (December, 1986): 842–858.

35. Ibid., 856.

36. Gerald David Jaynes and Robin M. Williams, Jr., *A Common Destiny: Blacks and American Society* (Washington, D.C.: National Academy Press, 1989), ch. 7.

37. John U. Ogbu, *The Next Generation* (New York: Academic Press, 1974)

38. Jaynes and Williams, *A Common Destiny: Blacks and American Society*. 372.

39. Signithia Fordham and John U. Ogbu "Black Students' School Success: Coping With the Burden of 'Acting White'" *Urban Review* 18 (3, 1986): 415–424.

40. Jaynes and Williams, *A Common Destiny: Blacks and American Society*, 372.

41. See, for example, James S. Coleman and Ernest Q. Campbell, *Equality of Educational Opportunity* (Washington, D.C.: U.S. Government Printing Office, 1966); Frederick Mosteller and Daniel P. Moynihan, "A Pathbreaking Report" in Frederick and Daniel P. Moynihan, eds., *On Equality of Educational Opportunity* (New York: Random House, 1972), 3–66. For a more current review see Jaynes and Williams, *A Common Destiny: Blacks and American Society*, 354–364.

42 Jaynes and Williams, *A Common Destiny: Blacks and American Society*.

43. G. Weber, *Inner City Children Can be Taught to Read: Four Successful Schools* (Washington D.C.: Council for Better Education, 1971).

44. Stewart C. Purkey and Marshall S. Smith, "Effective Schools: a Review," *Elementary School Journal* 83 (4, 1983): 427–452.

45. Summary quote from Jaynes and Williams, *A Common Destiny: Blacks and American Society*. 360 from research by Sara Lawrence Lightfoot, *The Good High School: Portraits of Character and Culture* (New York, Basic Books, 1983).

46. Lightfoot, *The Good High School: Portraits of Character and Culture*.

47. Jaynes and Williams, *A Common Destiny: Blacks and American Society*, 361.

8

The White Working Class

Much has been written on the plight of blacks, Chicanos, and Indians in American society. Numerous accounts have made white poverty visible to the average American. However, it is only very recently that the white working-class stratum has been seriously discussed sociologically as a separate group. In the last twenty years, social science literature abounds with articles on the frustrations and grievances of blue-collar workers.[1] The terms "blue-collar" and "working class" are loosely used. They seem to refer most to lower middle, semi-skilled and skilled manual workers. A collective social profile of white working-class persons emerges from a number of studies. They face work situations that stifle initiative and creativity (the extreme of work alienation being an assembly line job); they have made little if any economic advancement when their small wage increases are corrected for inflation and taxes; they perceive a debasement of the American Dream exemplified by blacks and other minorities receiving special privileges and opportunities and college students rejecting the work ethic and burning their draft cards; and they feel a sense of alienation from a distant political system that they cannot affect.[2] One might argue that many other Americans share such outlooks and that this is not a special feature of blue-collar life.

The thesis advanced here is that the protest methods and demands of student and black militants grate especially hard on the values, outlooks, and economic fears of the white working-class person. That is, the white working-class environment is another special combination of race and class that involves unique tensions and constraints. The purpose of this chapter is to make clear the grievances of the white working class and to explore various explanations for blue-collar anger.

Originally, this chapter was written and printed in the 1970s. Twenty years later the main hypotheses and the directions of the findings may still apply. The earlier studies of white working class hostilities that are included here show more resentment than is currently evident but they remain historically valuable for understanding the race-class tensions that exist today. At the end of this chapter, a summary and update appears.

It is interesting to relate the white working class to the paternalistic-competitive trend in race relations discussed in chapter 1. There it was noted that blacks, Chicanos, and American Indians are conquered minorities that have gone through different versions of paternalistic relations and are currently involved (in a competitive industrial society) in building an independent power base, establishing an identity, and competing with members of the majority group for certain resources such as white-collar and skilled jobs, political representation, and a college education for their children. The working class segment of the white majority group may feel similarly engaged in tough competition for these scarce items. In industrialized, multi-racial societies, when the caste-paternalistic lid is lifted, the white working class is most likely to feel threatened by the new stance of racial minorities.

Working-class persons have small, but often hard-earned amounts of power, privilege, and prestige that they are anxious to protect. Studies indicate that it is not so much that white workers are opposed to blacks getting their civil rights[3] (i.e., an equal chance for good housing, jobs, and education); it is rather that they are opposed to black gains that mean heavy losses to them. It is this zero sum problem ("your gain is my loss") that is at the heart of working-class anger. Black militant demands have upset many blue-collar persons and campus activism has also received a cool response, to say the least. Working-class persons are not likely to be sympathetic to student demands for special quotas for minority students, the establishment of black and Chicano studies programs, and more generally increased student power in running universities. Open-ended conversations, found in a study by Sexton and Sexton, clearly express some of these feelings:

> ... Of course, my son's willing to do his duty to his country if he has to. And I feel the same way. But we can't understand how all those rich kids—the kids with the beads from the fancy suburbs—how they get off when my son has to go over there and maybe get his head shot off. They get off scot-free ... and when they see they're going to graduate from college, and maybe get drafted, they raise such a

stink. How come these privileged kids get away with messing up the colleges that we're paying to support? I'd give my right arm to get my son into one of those colleges and all these kids seem to do is parade around and denounce the government. What the hell have they got to complain about? If they don't like it there, let them go out and get a job or get drafted like mine—see how much they like that!

I've lived in this neighborhood all my life, and my father lived here too I worked all my life to buy this house, and now it's almost mine—not much, but the only thing of much value besides my car that I own. I built a lot of what's in it with my own hands. We liked this neighborhood and decided to settle here in the first place because the neighbors were like us. Now the black people have moved in. They've got a right to, I guess, just like anybody else. They want a better life. But they're poor people and they don't keep things up the way we used to. Most of my friends and my brother were afraid when the blacks started moving in—afraid that everything would go to hell and they wouldn't be able to sell their houses—so they moved. Now they're gone. And the schools have gone down. What have I got left? I guess I'll have to move . . . but, damn it, this is my home. It takes a whole lifetime to make good friends, and now they've all moved out. I'll be a stranger wherever I move. If more of the blacks moved out into those fancy suburbs, where all those whites who say they're so hot for civil rights live, then maybe there wouldn't be ghettos in the neighborhoods like this. But the people out in the rich suburbs won't let them in . . . unless, of course, they're from Harvard or Yale.

We're carrying everyone on our backs. The rich don't work. They just clip coupons and order us around. All those people on welfare and those unwed mothers. They won't work. You couldn't *make* them work. They just sit around and collect their checks, and *we* pay for it. Let those women have as many children as they want, each one with a different boyfriend. I don't care. Just don't ask me to pay for bringing them up. I can just barely bring up my own kids.

The hippies and the college kids. They don't work. They just collect on all the things we struggle to pay for. And they all think that we're dopes and drones for doing it.[4]

There are valid points made in these statements. For example, it is not just black demands and advancement that are producing anger, but, in addition, considerable hostility toward the stereotyped white upper middle and upper classes (such as highly visible "privileged kids who escape the draft"). One can also see running through many of the foregoing statements that working class persons are angry because they perceive they are being asked to pay the bulk of the price for justice for blacks and for military service.

There is a certain degree of rationality behind these responses. That is, the anger expressed can be seen as a predictable, understandable response to tangible strains rather than totally as a case of personal bigotry. How typical are these attitudes? If a randomly selected group of blue-collar workers was compared to those higher in the occupational structure, would blue-collar persons stand out as more antagonistic toward students and black protestors than others?

"BLUE COLLAR ANGER,"
A Study of the White Working Class*

In the latter part of 1969 and the first months of 1970, data were gathered by Jeffries and Ransford in a large, white section of Los Angeles (the San Fernando Valley) to test several hypotheses about the white backlash.[5] Not only was this a period of extreme campus unrest nationally but on two campuses in or near the sample area, student demonstrators briefly took control of campus offices. It was also shortly after the bitterly divisive Yorty-Bradley mayoral election. Thomas Bradley, a black candidate, was defeated after being charged by his opponent, Sam Yorty, with being controlled and manipulated by black extremists. Of particular interest to us were the reactions of the blue-collar workers to the black and student power movements.

Is the white working class uniquely antagonistic toward student and black demands? If so, why? Four hundred and seventy-seven Caucasian adults responded to an interview schedule dealing with reactions to student and black protest. The sample involved approximately equal numbers of blue-collar, business white-collar (managerial, sales, and clerical), and professional white-collar persons. Education was used as a second measure of socioeconomic status. Three measures of antagonism toward demonstrators were developed. "Student demonstrator hostility" is a three-item measure (an example of one of the items is "Even if they don't break the law, college students who are involved in demonstrations should be expelled"); "student power" is a one-item index ("Students should be given more say in running the college"); and "black demands unjustified" is a three-item measure (example, "Negroes are asking for special treatment from whites to which they are not entitled"). It is this latter measure dealing with black demands that we are

---

*An Earlier version of this study appeared in *The American Sociological Review* 37 (June, 1972): 333–346.

mainly concerned with here. Note that this is not a measure of civil rights libertarianism but refers rather to the perceived legitimacy of black demands.

There is an important difference between supporting equal opportunity for blacks in acquiring a good job or housing and supporting black demands for quotas or reparations that may result in losses to the white working class. My purpose, then, was to find out if there was a substantial correlation between SES (occupation and education) and the above measures of antagonism toward demonstrators. In addition, I was interested in assessing the importance of three explanations for blue-collar anger. A brief statement of each of these explanations follows:

The "Conformity-Idealization of Authority" Explanation

A number of studies indicate that the blue-collar environment stresses the value of respect for authority. In the socialization of children, for example, one study shows that blue-collar parents are more likely to emphasize external conformity (obedience and neatness) in contrast to middle-class parents who emphasize internal dynamics such as curiosity and self-realization. The stress on conformity and obedience is due in part to occupational environments. Blue-collar persons typically are in occupations which demand repetition, conformity and adherence to rules. Thus Kohn and Schooler[6] find that men's opportunities to exercise occupational self-direction—that is, to use initiative, thought, and independent judgment at work—account for much of the relationship between social class and authoritarian orientations. From this perspective, it follows that working-class persons will be more outraged by campus protest and black demands than those higher in the class structure. Student protest and black protest symbolize a classic flaunting of authority and a down-grading of institutions. The "four-letter words," the styles of dress, and the direct confrontation methods all suggest disrespect for authority.

Belief in the American Dream:
Neglect of the Working Person's Needs

This revised class-conflict model, as opposed to a Marxian model in which the white working class is a revolutionary force for change, sees the blue-collar worker as reaffirming traditional beliefs in the openness of the American system. Hostility is directed toward the black lower class as undeserving of special opportunity as well as toward white liberals in power who seek to remake traditional America at the working person's expense. Working-class people see themselves as having made modest economic gains through union victories and through their own hard work and sacrifices. They are far from economically secure, however. They tend to believe poor people and black people are at the bottom of the class structure because of their own laziness, not because of racism or other institutional barriers.[7]

Given their belief in hard work and in the openness of the American structure, working class persons are hostile toward ghetto rioters and black demands for quotas and preferential job treatment. It is not simply that they feel blacks do not deserve special opportunity. They are angry because it seems to them that they are being asked to pay the biggest price for "social justice."[8] If they yield to demands for special opportunities and super-seniority for black workers, they, not the secure upper middle-class people, face the greatest threat of being laid off.

From the white working person's point of view, far too much attention is being paid to the poor, and especially the black poor. In one survey,[9] 65 percent of white middle-Americans felt that blacks have a better chance than whites to get financial help from the government when they're out of work. Increasingly, white workers perceive that it is easier for an unemployed black to get aid and sympathy than a hard working white. Further, working-class people are angry because they perceive that they are taxed heavily to support welfare budgets for the poor, and they have fewer mechanisms like business expense accounts, to escape taxation. In short, they feel they are paying for the special opportunities given minority persons—compensations they believe to be unnecessary in a free and open society.

Although this second explanation for blue-collar anger (the American Dream and neglect of the working man's needs) is more clearly related to antagonism toward black militance, it also ties in with antagonism toward campus activism. A perception of the American system as open and just is antithetical to the student activist view that the American system is racist, elitist, exploitative, and excessively authoritarian. Further, the quintessence of the American Dream is sending one's children to college so they can advance in the social structure and have a better life. It is only with great sacrifice, however, that the working-class family can send their children to college. The shouting of affluent youth, "On Strike—Shut It Down!" is a multiple outrage to blue-collar people. Activist students are not only attacking American values, but threatening to close an only recently opened channel of mobility for working class children.

The Powerlessness Explanation

From this point of view, a critical dimension of the disaffection of white working-class people is their sense of powerlessness over "radical" changes occurring in the country, and over political decisions directly affecting their lives. Working-class people may perceive that they have few means to affect political change. Their occupational roles do not evoke respect and power in the larger society. Even in their own union the rank and file often have no real voice in making policy.

Recent student and black protest has, no doubt, heightened these feelings of political powerlessness. Workers may perceive that black and student militants have reached power centers and are forcing institutional changes that seem to them a distributive injustice or direct threat (for example, preferential hiring for blacks, relaxed entrance requirements and special aid for minority college students, and plans for increased school and residential integration that may affect them especially as inner city residents living close to the ghetto). Of the "power structure's" various components, blue-collar workers may view the government as especially hard to move and preoccupied with the problems of blacks.

The powerlessness explanation would predict that white working-class people who feel politically powerless, i.e., who expect public officials to be unresponsive to their needs, will be especially antagonistic toward student and black activists. Each gain in power for militant students or blacks may be perceived as a reciprocal loss in power, status, or a way of life for the working-class person.

Note that the concept of powerlessness used in this study denotes a perception of the social system and does not necessarily refer to personal apathy or fatalism. Indeed, the more militant white action responses to black and student protest (such as "hard hat" demonstrations) suggest a high degree of personal confidence and efficacy combined with a low expectancy of being able to move a large impersonal system through normative action.

Independent Variables (Occupation and Education) by Student Demonstrator Hostility, Student Power, and Black Demands Unjustified

	Student Demonstrator Hostility %				Opposition to Student Power %			Black Demands Unjustified %			
OCCUPATION	Low	MED	HIGH	N	Low	HIGH	N	Low	MED	HIGH	N
Blue collar	12	37	50	(163)	34	66	(164)	12	18	70	(164)
Business White Collar*	26	44	30	(159)	52	48	(162)	21	33	46	(155)
Professional White Collar	34	41	25	(137)	50	50	(139)	29	31	40	(131)

Gamma= -.32 Gamma= -.21 Gamma= -.34
p<.001 p<.001   p<.001

EDUCATION											
Less than High School	3	47	50	(60)	27	73	(63)	8	15	77	(60)
High School Graduate	15	40	45	(149)	42	58	(149)	17	24	59	(150)
Some College	35	36	29	(152)	49	51	(153)	22	31	47	(146)
College Grad.	36	46	18	(104)	60	40	(106)	37	32	31	(99)

Gamma= -.37 Gamma= -.30 Gamma= -.37   p<.001 p<.001 p<.001

* Refers to clerical, managerial, and sales
Note: Statistical significance determined by chi square.
Source: H. Edward Ransford, "Blue Collar Anger: Reactions to Student and Black Protest," *American Sociological Review* (June, 1972): 339.

Table 8.1

Findings

Is the working-class person more hostile toward student and black demands than those higher in the socioeconomic structure? Table 8.1 shows that this is indeed the case, with occupation moderately correlated with each dependent variable and education showing a stronger relationship. Seventy percent of the blue-collar workers interviewed scored high on "black demands unjustified" (agreeing with two or all three of the items) versus 40 percent of the white-collar professionals. The relationship is even more striking in the case of education, with a spread from 77 percent (less than high school) to 31 percent (college graduate). Similar results are found for the "student hostility" and "student power" items (though the correlation is noticeably weaker in the case of occupation and student power). People in blue-collar jobs and those with less than a high school education are clearly more antagonistic. But are the theoretical reasons advanced for blue-collar anger valid? To what extent do respect for authority, belief in the American Dream, and belief that worker needs are neglected interpret the relationship between SES and student-black antagonism? The following diagram may help to state the case:

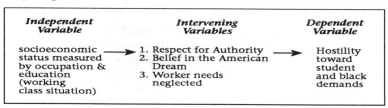

Independent Variable	Intervening Variables	Dependent Variable
socioeconomic status measured by occupation & education (working class situation)	1. Respect for Authority 2. Belief in the American Dream 3. Worker needs neglected	Hostility toward student and black demands

Figure 8.1

Strains inherent in the working-class situation lead to certain outlooks (intervening variables) and these in turn feed into hostility toward student and black demands. Statistical support for this model requires that when the three intervening variables are controlled the size of the correlation between socioeconomic status and student-black antagonism will diminish considerably. That is, by holding the intervening variables constant we should be sapping away much of the effect of SES on antagonism. Table 8.2 shows that the combined effect of the three intervening variables does account for a sizeable fraction of the relationship between the independent and dependent variables. That is, in all instances, the original zero-order correlation drops appreciably when all three variables are controlled. For example, the original Pearson r between education and student demonstrator hostility is a moderate -.31 but drops to -.12 with the three intervening variables simultaneously controlled. Table 8.2 also reveals that control for "respect for authority" reduces the zero order correlation slightly more than the other intervening variables. However, the intervening variables were not standardized: respect for authority had three items in the scale while worker neglect had only one. As a result, one cannot conclude that "respect for authority" is a more important intervening link than "openness of the American system" or "worker needs neglected." One measure could simply be a better index of its respective concept than another. It is also interesting to note that the only surviving relationships are those between education and black antagonism (partial $r = -.16 p < .01$) and occupation and black antagonism (partial $r = -.16$ p<.01). In other words, the three explanations account for about half of the relationship between blue-collar position and antagonism toward blacks. Apparently, there are other reasons for hostility that we have not fully measured, possibly perceived threats from black economic progress, or simple race prejudice.

		(1)	(2)	(3)	
		Respect for	"American	Worker	Simultaneous
Correlation between	Zero	Authority	Dream"	Neglected	Control 1,
Occupation and:	Order	Controlled	Controlled	Controlled	2, and 3
Partial Correlation between Independent Variables (Occupation and Education) and the Dependent Variables with Respect for Authority, Belief in "American Dream," and Neglect of Workingperson, Controlled Singly and Jointly					
Student Demonstrator Hostility	-.20*	-.09	-.17	-.14*	-.07
Opposed to Student Power	-.14*	-.06	-.12*	-.09	-.04*
Black Demands Unjustified	-.25*	-.18*	-.23	-.19*	-.16*
Correlation between Education and:					
Student Demonstrator Hostility	-.31*	-.16*	-.25	-.24*	-.12*
Opposed to Student Power	-.24*	-.12*	-.18*	-.18*	-.09*
Black Demands Unjustified	-.32*	-.20*	-.24*	-.23*	-.16*

*p<.01
Note: Statistical significance determined by students'T (one-tailed test)
Source: H. Edward Ransford, "Blue Collar Anger: Reactions to Student and Black Protest," *American Sociological Review* 37 (June, 1972), 343.

Table 8.2

Specification For Powerlessness

We have predicted that working-class persons who feel politically powerless will be especially antagonistic toward the student and black movements. The data (not shown) indicate definite support for this logic especially in the case of hostility toward student demonstrators. Thus, while 43 percent of the blue-collar workers who score low in political powerlessness are very hostile toward student demonstrators, 60 percent of the blue-collar workers who score high in powerlessness express hostility. Viewing education as the independent variable, the difference between the low and high powerlessness groups is even more striking, ranging from 36 percent to 59 percent. As an overview, it can be said that the blue-collar group and the less-than-high-school group who score high in powerlessness are more antagonistic toward students and blacks than anyone else in the sample.

Summary of "Blue Collar Anger" Study

The "Blue Collar Anger" study shows that white working-class persons are more likely to be antagonistic toward students and blacks demanding massive changes in our society than are those higher in the socioeconomic structure. However, the size of the correlation is a moderate one. That is, although blue-collar workers tend on the average to be more hostile, some blue-collar workers are more supportive of student and black demands than some white-collar workers. Secondly, there was some confirmation for each of the theoretical explanations advanced. "Respect for authority," "the American Dream," "worker needs are neglected," and "political powerlessness" all figure into the explanation for blue-collar anger.

The mass media have tended to stereotype the white working person as a narrow-minded, intolerant bigot. Their angry responses to students and blacks are often viewed as the effect of prejudiced personalities. In contrast, our model shows blue-collar anger to be rooted in the perceived social situation. From this perspective, much of the working person's anger is a rational response to tangible strains, independent of personal bigotry. Lack of decision-making power on the job, the feeling that hard-earned dollars are going for tax programs to aid blacks and other minorities with no comparable programs for working-class whites, a power structure unresponsive to the needs of the working person—these stresses probably affect working-class anger as much as a basic antipathy toward blacks or minorities *per se.*

White working-class people who feel politically powerless are especially antagonistic toward student and black protestors. Research in the black community conducted shortly after the Watts Riot[10] suggests a parallel finding: blacks who scored high in social powerlessness (low expectancy of gaining redress through institutional channels) were more willing to use violence to get their rights. Similarly, a violence commission report[11] notes that militant white reactions to protest (armed citizen's groups) are found especially among those who are angered by excessive concern for minorities and who feel ignored by the polity. Apparently the potential exists for white as well as black militant action when individuals perceive a distributive injustice and, in addition, feel blocked in gaining redress through institutional channels.

WHITE ETHNICITY AND THE BLUE COLLAR SITUATION

The recent assertion of ethnic consciousness among blacks, Chicanos, and American Indians has made more and more untenable the assimilation-melting pot ideology. Pluralism of one sort or another is increasingly voiced as desirable and healthy (and likely) in the coming decades. What is surprising to many is that white ethnics (non-WASPS) are also asserting their cultural distinctiveness Andrew Greeley feels that there is a direct relationship between black militance and the resurgence of ethnic identification among whites. "The new consciousness of ethnicity is in part based on the fact that the blacks have legitimated cultural pluralism as it has perhaps never been legitimated before. Other Americans, observing that now it is all right to be proud of being black, wonder, quite reasonably, why it is not all right to be proud of being Italian or Polish."[12] There are several important qualifications that need to be made concerning this ethnic consciousness. First, a great deal of it is not new at all. Ethnic ties, loyalties, voluntary associations, communities, and bloc voting have always been there but have been often ignored by social scientists. Secondly, certain white ethnic groups are more assimilated than others. Ethnic consciousness is most likely among white groups that were (and continue to be) excluded from WASP society. For example, Michael Novak sarcastically refers to the most-excluded white ethnics as PIGS: Poles, Italians, Greeks, and Slavs. "They were, in a word, 'peasants'—looked down upon not only by the WASPS, who saw them as socially, religiously and, yes, racially inferior, but by intellectuals (of varying backgrounds themselves) who saw them as unwashed, uneducated, and uncouth, as culturally inferior."[13]

Poles, Italians, Greeks, and Slavs are more likely to assert ethnic identity than the more assimilated Germans and Scandinavians (the Irish are, perhaps, midway between the PIGS and the most assimilated). Thirdly, ethnic awareness and identification may vary greatly by the area of the country. For example, in the San Fernando Valley section of Los Angeles (sample area for "Blue Collar Anger" study) one finds a large sprawling suburban region without the white ethnic communities of Newark, Chicago, Wisconsin, or New York. One would expect far more ethnic consciousness among white ethnics who live in or near communities established by first-generation immigrants. That is, common frustrations and interpretations of political events may be more easily identified and more readily shared in such communities.

We can speak legitimately of ethclass effects for white persons as well as for blacks, Chicanos, and Indians. Working-class Italians or Poles may have a unique political stance that is only understood by considering class and ethnicity together. Returning to the "blue collar anger" discussion, it is quite likely that certain ethnic outlooks and blue-collar outlooks reinforce each other.

Not all white ethnics are in blue-collar positions, but many are; when the two statuses occur together one expects an especially well-articulated view toward minority demands. It seems logical that working-class ethnics would especially feel a sense of distributive injustice when the rising minorities (blacks, Chicanos, Native Americans) are given reparations, special opportunities, and quotas. Working-class white ethnics who are close to the immigration experience and have struggled for a piece of the American Dream are not likely to support minority quotas, regardless of the minority group. Greeley writes:

> We must remember that these groups are only a generation or two removed from the old world. To be told that they are responsible or ought to feel guilty for the plight of blacks puzzles them. It was not their ancestors who brought black slaves to this country . . . It was not their ancestors who enacted the Jim Crow Laws . . . Furthermore, the white ethnics are close enough to their own immigrant poverty to realize that reform groups were not particularly concerned about them. No one ever worried about the Polish poor or the Irish poor, and no one seems to worry much now about the residual poverty groups in both these populations.[14]

It should be made clear that we predict that blue-collar ethnics are likely to feel especially high degrees of distributive injustice, not that they are more racist in outlook. There is no particular reason that a working-class Italian should be more racist in outlook than a working class Anglo-saxon. Indeed, Greeley reports from research at the National Opinion Research Center[15] that Italian and Irish blue-collar ethnics are more liberal on matters of race and peace than their Anglo blue-collar counterparts. Even more interesting is the finding that the more involved ethnic persons are in explicitly ethnic behavior (involvement in an ethnic organization, for example) the more liberal are their outlooks on race and peace. That is, high ethnic involvement seems to be inversely related to racism and bigotry.

It should finally be noted, that with increased ethnic pluralism, one no longer has a race relations model in which a uniform white majority group is juxtaposed against visible minorities who are asserting their separate identities. Rather, there is considerable cultural diversity and separate ethnic consciousness within the so-called "white majority" group. To understand such phenomena as political participation and voting blocs, we need to take into account more than social class. Ethnicity and class must be considered conjointly.

A BLUE COLLAR ANGER UPDATE

The anger of the white working class toward black demands and special programs to benefit blacks appears to be less severe in the 1990s than the earlier (1972) study reported in this chapter, yet negative attitudes do remain. Although the strains and tensions of integration are still somewhat disproportionately felt by working class persons, current national surveys of white attitudes indicate that there has been a reduction in the occupational and educational differences in white backlash attitudes.[16] Some research indicates a "remarkable liberal leap" in support of desegregation and equal access to all institutions.[17] Working class persons changed just as much as those higher in the socioeconomic hierarchy in the direction of greater racial tolerance. However, support for racial principles of desegregation and equal access do not necessarily translate into support for policy changes. Whites express considerable opposition to affirmative action and other government programs to benefit blacks.[18]

Coupled with this rejection of governmental intervention is a very strong support for an individualistic, "free will" explanation of black-white differences in socioeconomic status. A majority of whites of all socioeconomic levels perceive that blacks, on average, are in lower occupational and income positions because they have not worked hard enough or shown motivation.[19] The white working class may be especially likely to express this view. I wanted to explore the extent of a class differential in white attitudes over time.

Table 8.3 presents national surveys of white attitudes by occupation and education (taken from General Social Surveys) over four time periods. The first question asked whites if they think blacks have worse jobs and incomes, on average, than whites because blacks lack motivation. In other words the item measures whether whites feel a lack of effort is responsible for black/white inequality. Those agreeing are likely to oppose any special affirmative action efforts. The system is seen as open and non-discriminatory. Success is a matter of individual hard work. The measure ties directly in with the belief in the American Dream discussion covered earlier in this chapter. The data indicate that in the time period, 1972–78, skilled blue-collar workers (i.e., craftsmen) were especially likely to hold this view in contrast to upper and mid-level white-collar workers (78 versus 56 percent). Lower blue-collar workers were between these extremes and similar to clerical workers (69 percent). By contrast, in the 1988–89 period the differences between upper blue-collar and upper white-collar persons are smaller (69 versus 57 percent agreement). By education, however, differences persist over time with less than high school and high school respondents far more likely to support the individual motivation belief than the college group in all three time periods.

Racial Attitudes of Whites by Time Controlling for Occupation and Education

% of Whites "yes" blacks have worse jobs, income, and housing because most blacks don't have motivation or will power to pull themselves out of poverty:

	1972–78	1980–84	1985–87	1988–89
Occupation				
Professional Managerial	56%	X	54%	57%
Clerical	69	X	63	67
Upper Blue Collar	78	X	74	69
Lower Blue Collar	69	X	68	65
Education				
Less than High School	74	X	74	75
High School	66	X	68	65
College	49	X	47	48

% of Whites agreeing "White people have a right to keep blacks out of their neighborhoods":

	1972–78	1980–84	1985–87	1988–89
Occupation				
Professional managerial	15%	7%	7%	4%
Clerical	17	14	10	13
Upper Blue Collar	28	14	11	8
Lower Blue Collar	28	21	14	10
Education				
Less than High School	32	25	20	14
High School	19	12	9	9
College	10	5	4	3

Table 8.3

Another part of the blue collar anger thesis is that workers feel threatened by housing integration that often affects them especially. The GSS surveys had this question: "Whites have a right to keep blacks out of their neighborhoods and black should respect that right." Table 8.3 shows that 28 percent of the two blue-collar groups agreed in 1972–78 versus only 15 percent of the upper white-collar persons. By 1988–89, the differences by occupation had almost washed out with only small percentages of all groups agreeing. The same general pattern of liberalization of all groups is apparent in the case of education.

A final analysis was performed with the GSS data. It has been suggested that white working class persons scoring high in political alienation have been especially antagonistic toward black demands. Are working class persons high in alienation especially likely to oppose housing integration and to give a "lacking motivation" response. One item in the GSS surveys ("Most public officials are not really interested in the problems of the average man"), allowed for a test of the working class-high alienation thesis. The results (not shown) indicate that in 1972–78, politically alienated white working-class persons showed more opposition to housing integration that all other comparison groups. For example, 34 percent of the high alienation-working class group expressed opposition versus 18 percent of the high alienation white-collar (professional/managerial) group. By 1988–89, all subgroups (regardless of occupation or alienation) showed a marked decline in opposition to housing integration. Only 10 percent of alienated craft workers expressed opposition versus 7 percent of alienated white-collar workers. That is, regardless of occupation or felt alienation, whites agree that blacks should have equal access to housing. However, further probing with these data indicate that the "low motivation" explanation is especially held by working-class persons high in alienation. Eighty four percent of such persons agreed racial inequality is due to blacks' lack of effort in 1972–78, compared to 68 percent of blue-collar workers low in alienation. (The corresponding percentages for the professional/ managerial group are 58 and 51 percent.) In 1988–89, the differences were still fairly marked with 78 percent of blue-collar craft, high-alienation workers giving the lack of effort response versus 57 percent of low alienation craft workers. (The corresponding percentages for the managerial/professional white-collar groups high and low in political alienation are 59 and 47 percent.)

To summarize, the racial attitudes of white working class persons have come very close to white-collar professional and managerial groups when it comes to espousing racial principles such as the right to the same housing. However, free-will-lack-of-effort explanations of racial inequality are especially held by white working class persons high in political alienation, and those with less than high-school education, groups likely to feel most threatened by affirmative action programs.

CONCLUSION

Throughout this book I have argued that there needs to be increased attention to the complex interaction of social class, ethnicity, and gender. Three models of race-class interaction— open marketplace of status configurations, minority subcommunity, and ethclass—were presented in the first part of the book. In particular, I have focused on ethclass and ethgender effects as one of the most interesting avenues of inquiry. From the white working class reactions in this chapter to the unique black middle class outlooks noted in chapter 5, to the pileup of educational barriers restricting black and Hispanic youth, to ethgender outlooks on feminism—all emphasize the fact that race, class, and gender intersect to form subsocieties with unique experiences, attitudes, and perceptions of the social system. A focus on ethclass and ethgender leads to the idea that race and gender inequalities do not disappear with class achievement. Race and gender are such important statuses that social class achievement alters, but does not override discrimination barriers. It is hoped that this book will be a stimulus to further considerations of race, class, and gender interactions, an area we are only recently beginning to explore.

NOTES

1. See, for example, Arthur B. Shostak, *Blue-Collar World* (Englewood, N.J. Prentice-Hall, 1964); Irving Howe, *The World of the Blue Collar Worker* (New York: Quadrangle Books, 1972); and Robert E. Lane and Michael Lerner, "Why Hard-Hats Hate Hairs," *Psychology Today* 6 (November, 1970): 45.

2. See Michael M. Schneider, "Middle America," *The Center Magazine* (November/December, 1970), 2–9.

3. Richard F. Hamilton, "Liberal Intelligentsia and White Backlash," in Howe, *The World of the Blue Collar Worker,* 227–238.

4. Patricia Sexton and Brendan Sexton, *Blue Collars and Hard-Hats: The Working Class and the Future of Politics* (New York: Random House, 1971), 51–58.

5. The "white backlash" studies that emerged from these data are Vincent Jeffries and H. Edward Ransford, "Ideology, Social Structure, and the Yorty-Bradley Mayoral Election, "*Social Problems* 19 (Winter, 1972): 358–372; and H. Edward Ransford, "Blue Collar Anger: Reactions to Student and Black Protest," *American Sociological Review:* 37 (June, 1972): 333–346.

6. Melvin Kohn and C. Schooler, "Class, Occupation, and Orientation," *American Sociological Review* 34 (October, 1969): 659–678.

7. Lane and Lerner, "Why Hard-Hats Hate Hairs," 46.

8. Schneider, "Middle America."

9. "The Troubled American: A Special Report on the White Majority," *Newsweek* 71 (October 6, 1969): 28–73.

10. H. Edward Ransford, "Isolation, Powerlessness, and Violence: A Study of Attitudes and Participation in the Watts Riot," *American Journal of Sociology* 73 (March, 1968): 581–591.

11. Jerome H. Skolnick, *The Politics of Protest: Report to the National Commission on the Causes and Prevention of Violence* (New York: Ballantine Books, 1969).

12 Andrew M. Greeley, "The New Ethnicity and Blue Collars," in Howe, *The World of the Blue Collar Worker,* 291.

13. Peter I. Rose, Review Essay of "The Rise of the Unmeltable Ethnics," *Contemporary Sociology: A Journal of Reviews* 2 (January, 1973): 14–15.

14 Andrew M. Greeley, "America's Not So Silent Minority," *Los Angeles Times*, Opinion Section, December 7, 1969, 1–2.

15. Greeley, "The New Ethnicity and Blue Collars," 295.

16. Gerald David Jaynes and Robin M. Williams, Jr., A Common Destiny: *Blacks and American Society* (Washington, D.C.: National Academy Press, 1989), 119–121.

17. D. Garth Taylor, Paul B. Sheatsley, and Andrew M. Greeley, "Attitudes Toward Racial Integration," *Scientific American* 238 (6, June): 42–50.

18. Jaynes and Williams, *A Common Destiny: Blacks and American Society* 124–129.

19. See Howard Schuman, "Free Will and Determinism in Beliefs about Race," in Norman R. Yetman and C. Hoy Steele (eds.), *Majority and Minority* (Boston: Allyn and Bacon, 1971); James R. Kluegel, "Trends in Whites' Explanations of the Black-White Gap in Socioeconomic Status, 1977–1989," *American Sociological Review* 55 (1990): 512–525; and J. R. Kluegel and E. R. Smith, *Beliefs about Equality: American's Views of What is and What Ought to Be* (New York: Aldine de Gruyter, 1986).

Selected Bibliography

Alexander, Karl and Martha Cook. "Curricula and Coursework: A Surprise Ending to a Familiar Story," *American Sociological Review* 47 (October, 1982): 626–640.

Almquist, Elizabeth M. "The Experiences of Minority Women in the United States: Intersections of Race Gender, and Class" in Jo Freeman (ed.), *Women: A Feminist Perspective* Mountain View, Calif.: Mayfield, 1989.

Alvarez, Rodolfo. "The Psycho-Historical and Socioeconomic Development of the Chicano Community in the United States." *Social Science Quarterly* 53 (March, 1973): 920–942.

Berk, Sarah F. "Women's Unpaid Labor: Home and Community," in A. Stromberg and S. Harkness (eds.), *Women Working*. Palo Alto, Calif.: Mayfield, 1987.

Blau, Francine. "Discrimination Against Women: Theory and Evidence," in William Darity Jr., (ed.), *Labor Economics: Modern Views*. Boston: Martinus Nijhoff, 1984.

Blau, Peter M. and Otis Dudley Duncan. *The American Occupational Structure*. New York: Wiley, 1967.

Blauner, Robert. *Racial Oppression in America*. New York: Harper and Row, 1972.

Bonacich, Edna. "A Theory of Middleman Minorities," *American Sociological Review*, 38 (October, 1973): 583–594.

———. "Class Approaches to Ethnicity and Race," in Norman R. Yetman (ed.) *Majority and Minority: The Dynamics of Race and Ethnicity in American Life, 5th edition*. Boston: Allyn and Bacon, 1991.

Brown, Dee. *Bury My Heart at Wounded Knee*. New York: Holt, Rinehart and Winston, 1970.

Blumer, Herbert. *Industrialization and Race Relations. A Symposium.* London and New York: Oxford University Press, 1965.

Cahn, Edgar S. *Our Brother's Keeper.* New York: World Publishing Co., 1969.

Cohen, Elizabeth G. and Susan S. Roper. "Modification of Interracial Interaction Disability: An Application of Status Characteristic Theory," *American Sociological Review* 37 (December, 1972): 643–657.

Collins, Patricia Hill. *Black Feminist Thought: Knowledge, Consciousness, and the Politics of Empowerment.* New York: Routledge, 1990.

Cruse, Harold. *The Crisis of the Negro Intellectual.* New York: William Morrow, 1967.

Cox, Oliver Cromwell. *Caste, Class and Race.* Garden City: Doubleday, 1948.

Davis, Allison, Burleigh R. Gardner and Mary R. Gardner. *Deep South.* Chicago: University of Chicago Press, 1941.

Drake, St. Clair and Horace R. Cayton. *Black Metropolis: A Study of Negro Life in a Northern City.* New York: Harcourt, Brace, 1945.

Edwards, G. Franklin. *The Negro Professional Class.* Glencoe, Illinois: Free Press, 1959.

Edwards, Harry. "The Collegiate Athletic Arms Race: Origins and Inplications of the 'Rule 48' Controversy" *Journal of Sport and Social Issues* 8 (1984); 4–22.

Estrada, Leobardo F., F. Chris Garcia, Reynaldo Flores Macias, Lionel Malsonado. "Chicanos in the United States: A History of Exploitation and Resistance," in Norman R. Yetman (ed.) *Majority and Minority: The Dynamics of Race and Ethnicity in American Life.* Boston: Allyn and Bacon, 1991.

Farkas, Robert Grobe, Daniel Sheehan, and Yuan Shuan, "Cultural Resources and School Success, " *American Sociological Review* 55(February, 1990): 127–142.

Farley, Reynolds. "Trends in Racial Inequalities: Have the Gains in the 1960s Disappeared in the 1970s?" *American Sociological Review* 42 (April, 1977): 189–208.

Feagin, Joe R. "The Continuing Significance of Race: Antiblack Discrimination in Public Places," *American Sociological Review* 56 (February, 1991): 101–116

Frazier, E. Franklin. *Black Bourgeoisie: The Rise of a New Middle Class.* New York: Free Press, 1957.

Freyre, Gilberto. *The Masters and the Slaves.* New York: Alfred A. Knopf, 1964.

Gordon, Milton. *Assimilation in American Life.* New York: Oxford University Press, 1964.

Grebler, Leo, Joan Moore, and Ralph Guzman. *The Mexican American People.* New York: Free Press, 1970.

Greeley, Andrew M. "The New Ethnicity and Blue Collars," in Irving Howe (ed.) *The World of the Blue Collar Worker.* New York: Quadrangle Books, 1972.

Hannerz, Ulf. *Soulside.* New York: Columbia University Press, 1969.

Heer, David and Pini Herman. *A Human Mosaic: An Atlas of Ethnicity in L.A. County, 1980–1986.* Panorma City, CA: Western Economic Research Company, 1990.

Howard, John R. *Awakening Minorities.* Trans-action Books: Aldine Publishing Company, 1970.

Jaynes, Gerald David and Robin M. Williams. *A Common Destiny: Blacks and American Society.* Washington, D.C.: National Academy Press, 1989.

Jeffries, Vincent and H. Edward Ransford. *Social Stratification: A Multiple Hierarchy Approach.* Boston: Allyn and Bacon, 1980.

Jencks, Christopher. *Who Gets Ahead?* New York: Basic Books, 1979. Chapter 7.

Kanter, Rosabeth Moss. *Men and Women of the Corporation.* New York: Basic Books, 1977.

King, Deborah K. "Multiple Jeopardies, Multiple Consciousness: The Context of Black Feminist Ideology." *Signs,* 14(1988): 42–72.

Kluegel, James R. "Causes and Costs of Racial Exclusion from Job Authority," *American Sociological Review* 43 (June, 1978): 285–301.

———. "Trends in Whites' Explanations of the Black-White Gap in Socioeconomic Status, 1977-1989," *American Sociological Review* 55 (1990) 512-525.

Koch, Nadine, and H. Eric Schockman. "Riot, Rebellion, or Civil Unrest? Perspectives of the Korean-American and African-American Business Communities in Los Angeles," Paper delivered at the Fifth Annual Asian Pacific American Community Research Roundtable, California State University, Los Angeles, April 16, 1993.

Ladner, J. *Tomorrow's Tomorrow: The Black Woman.* Garden City, N.Y.: Doubleday, 1971.

Landry, Bart. *The New Black Middle Class.* Berkeley: University of California Press, 1987.

Leggett, John C. *Class, Race and Labor.* London and New York: Oxford University Press, 1968.

Lenski, Gerhard E. *Power and Privilege*. New York: McGraw Hill, 1966.

Lieberson, Stanley. *A Piece of the Pie: Black and White Immigrants since 1880*. Berkeley: University of California Press, 1980.

Light, Ivan and Edna Bonacich. *Immigrant Entrepeneurs: Koreans in Los Angeles, 1965–1982*. University of California Press, 1988.

Los Angeles Times Staff. *Understanding the Riots*, Los Angeles: Times Mirror Company, 1992.

Lurie, Nancy Oesteich. "The American Indian: Historical Background, " in Norman Yetman and C. Hoy Steele (eds.) *Majority and Minority: The Dynamics of Race and Ethnicity in American Life*, 4th edition, Boston: Allyn and Bacon, 1982.

Massey Douglas S., and Nancy A. Denton. "Trends in the Residential Segregation of Blacks, Hispanics and Asians," *American Journal of Sociology* 57 (1987): 802–825.

Massey Douglas S., and Brenda P. Mullan. "Process of Hispanic and Black Spacial Assimilation," In Norman R. Yetman and C. Hoy Steele (eds.) *Majority and Minority: The Dynamics of Race and Ethnicity in American Life*, 4th edition, Boston: Allyn and Bacon, 1982.

Mercer, Jane R. "IQ: The Lethal Label," *Psychology Today* 6 (September, 1972): 44–47 and 95–97.

Miller, Jon; Sanford Labovitz, and Lincoln Fry. "Inequities in the Organizational Experiences of Women and Men.," *Social Forces* 54 (December, 1975): 365–381.

Moore, Joan W. "Colonialism: The Case of the Mexican Americans," *Social Problems* 17 (Spring, 1970): 463-472.

Moore, Joan W. *Mexican Americans*. New Jersey: Prentice-Hall, 1970.

Moore, Joan and Harry Pachon. *Hispanics in the United States*. Englewood Cliffs, New Jersey: Prentice-Hall, 1985.

Moynihan, Daniel P. "The Schism in Black America," *The Public Interest* 27 (Spring, 1972): 3–24.

Noel, Donald. "A Theory of the Origins of Ethnic Stratification," *Social Problems* 16 (Fall, 1968): 157-172.

Olsen, Marvin E. "Power Perspectives on Stratification and Race Relations," in Marvin E. Olsen (ed.) *Power in Societies*. New York: Macmillan, 1970.

Penalosa, Fernando. "The Changing Mexican-American in Southern California," *Sociology and Social Research* 51 (July, 1967): 405–417.

Rainwater, Lee. "Crucible of Identity," *Daedulus* 95 (1966): 172–216.

Ransford, H. Edward. " Isolation, Powerlessness, and Violence: A Study of Attitudes and Participation in the Watts Riot," *American Journal of Sociology* 73 (March 1968): 581–591.

————. "Blue Collar Anger: Reactions to Student and Black Protest," *American Sociological Review* 37 (June, 1972): 333-346.

Ransford, H. Edward Jon Miller. "Race, Sex, and Feminist Outlooks, " *American Sociological Review* 48 (February, 1983): 46–59.

Rex, John and David Mason. *Theories of Race and Ethnic Relations.* N.Y.: Cambridge University Press, 1986

Rosenberg, Paula S. (ed.). *Race, Class, and Gender in the United States.* New York: St. Martin's Press, 1992.

Schafer, Walter E., Carol Olexa and Kenneth Polk. "Programmed for Social Class: Tracking in the High School," *Transaction* 7 (October, 1970): 39-46 and 63.

Schuman, Howard. "Free Will and Determinism in Beliefs about Race." in Norman R. Yetman and C. Hoy Steele (eds.) *Majority and Minority: The Dynamics of Racial and Ethnic Relations.* Boston: Allyn and Bacon, 1971.

Segura, Denise A. "Chicana and Mexican Immigrant Women at Work: The Impact of Class, Race, and Gender on Occupational Mobility," *Gender & Society* 3 (1989): 37–52.

van den Berghe, Pierre L. *Race and Racism.* New York: Wiley, 1978.

Willie, Charles V. "The Inclining Significance of Race," in Norman R. Yetman and C. Hoy Steele (eds.) *Majority and Minority,* 3rd edition. Boston: Allyn and Bacon, 1982.

Willie, Charles V. *Caste and Class Controversy on Race and Poverty: Round Two of the Wilson/Willie Debate.* Dix Hills, NY: General Hall, 1989.

Wilson, William Julius. *The Declining Significance of Race: Blacks and Changing American Institutions.* Chicago: University of Chicago Press, 1978.

————. "The Black Community in the 1980s: Questions of Race, Class, and Public Policy," in Norman R. Yetman (ed.) *Majority and Minority: The Dynamics of Race and Ethnicity in American Life,* 4th edition. Boston: Allyn and Bacon, 1985.

————. *The Truly Disadvantaged.* Chicago: University of Chicago Press, 1987.

Woodward, C. Vann. *The Strange Career of Jim Crow.* New York: Oxford University Press, 1957.

DATE DUE

MAY 0 8 1995	NOV 1 6 1999 FR
JUL. 0 4 1995	FEB 2 4 2000
FEB 1 9 2010	MAR 2 3 2000
OCT 3 1 1996	MAR 1 3 2000
NOV. 2 0	APR 0 6 2002
JAN 0 3 1998	NOV 0 3 2003
	MAR 2 2 2005
OCT 0 7 1997	DEC 0 5 2005
	MAR 0 8 2007
JAN 0 8 1998	
MAR 1 7 1998	
DEC 0 4 1998	
NOV 2 0 1998	
NOV 2 9 1999	

Renewals/ 362-8433

DEMCO 38-297